HELL IN A HANDBAG

Jibz Cameron

With a Foreword by
Dynasty Handbag

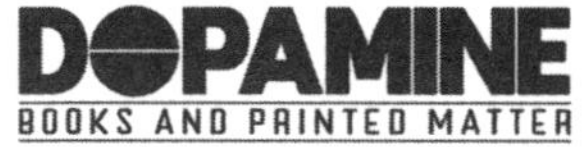

Published by DOPAMINE
P.O. Box 363, Joshua Tree, CA 92252
www.dopaminebooks.org

Covert Art: Jibz Cameron
Layout & Design: Brooke Palmieri
Copyediting: Katie Fricas

ISBN: 978-1-63590-278-5
Distributed by the MIT Press, Cambridge, Mass., and London, England.
Printed in the United States of America

10 9 8 7 6 5 4 3 2 1

Praise for Jibz Cameron

"Pure genius."

—Paul Reubens

"Supremely subversive, obscenely funny."

—*Time Out NY*

"Outrageously smart, grotesque and innovative."

—*The New Yorker*

"The smart absurdity of Dynasty's gestures and facial expressions have an effect akin to Charlie Chaplin's slapstick, mixed with the gorgeous grotesquerie of the late, great Divine —and a nimbleness that is all Cameron's own."

—*Hyperallergic*

"Very funny."

—Eric Idle

"A mimetic performance of a person, a spoiled subjectivity, who is considered a loser, or rubbish . . . and instead insists on her own value as a countercultural heroine."

—José Esteban Muñoz, *Cruising Utopia*

"Hilarious and extraordinarily original."

—*Paper Magazine*

"You're insane."

—Dick Van Dyke

"The world needs Dynasty Handbag—the voice of unreason tying things together in our uncertain times."

—*Artillery Magazine*

"Weirdo Night is the best show in LA."

—Sarah Squirm

"Jibz Cameron is a force of nature."

—Jack Black

CONTENTS

For Buns, Fro, and Dave

FOREWORD

Hello Reador!

Welcome to my bewk. It was written by Jibz Cameron, but it's *my* book. This book is about how I came into being, and how I survived. Without me, she would have no book to write. Without me, she and I would be dead in a dumpster, and maybe better off, but I have forced her to survive because I need an audience. This book is also about my birth, which was not breech exactly, more like it came out sideways, like a loaf of bread. Are there any doctors reading my book who can come help me sew up my vagina? Nevermind, I know there are no doctors reading this. There are a few dancers though for sure, and dancers are always also doulas.

"Content warning." There, I said it, is that good enough for you, you care-queer pansies? If you can't handle hearing about bad 1990s performance art, turn back now. Woe is me who walks through the hidden valley ranch of death beware and abandon all hope who exists light and enters night, etc. That's correct, this is the purgatory page. You're sitting in the waiting room, and you are waiting for something but you don't know what it is, but you are pretty sure it might be bad. You will definitely *feel* bad reading it ("boo hoo, poor little filthy rat child"). But you will also be like, wow, this *writing* is actually bad. Does she think just because she has read a book she can write a book? *Has* she read a book?

Other times you will be like, oh man, this *girl* was bad! A bad girl! And you will say to yourself, what have *I* ever done that was bad? I should go do something bad! And then off you trot to murder your husband, or at the very least practice some non-consensual ball torture. If that is the case, my work here is done. Or you will be like, this girl was *weird*! I wanna do something weird! And then you will go ride a unicycle wearing a dress made out of water bottles and juggle falafels, and I will be like, that's not the kind of weird I am, you have misjudged me, I do not support that kind of weird. But it's ok I guess. Not right, but ok. Like how I feel about Björk or seaweed snacks—I am glad they are there, and people in my community enjoy them, but I find them repulsive. I would rather the weird thing you did was whatever you normally do, but just be more committed to it and try it with an Australian accent. The worse the better.

Sincerely,

Dynamite Bathrobes, CEHoe

This memoir is a truthful recollection of actual events in my life. Some conversations have been recreated and/or supplemented. The names and details of some individuals have been changed to respect their privacy or to keep me from being sued or having to talk to them.

PART I

Can't you see how embarrassing
this is supposed to be for me?
—Jerri Blank

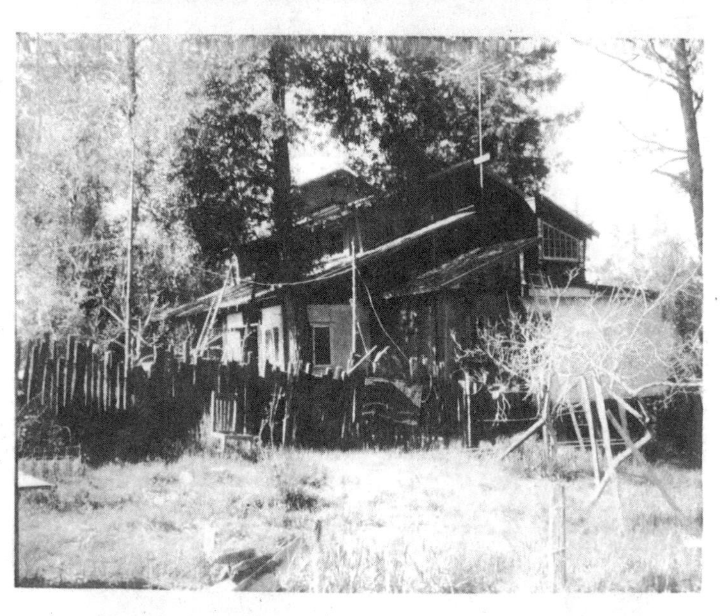

ONE: ANNAPOLIS, CA

I was born at home in 1975 in an area of California where Sonoma County meets Mendocino County. Annapolis, population 130, is roughly six miles inland from the raging drama of the Pacific Ocean and bougie vacation settlement Sea Ranch. I grew up there with my two sisters, J'nai (pronounced Jen-eye), three years my junior, and Jyoti (pronounced Jo-Tee), four years my senior. My brother David (Day-vid) is eight years older and was out of the house by the time he was 13, so I don't remember him much from my early years.

I don't know how my parents found Annapolis. It was devastatingly beautiful and very isolated. Thick redwoods, rivers, low mountain ridges, accessed only by driving curly switchback roads on the famous route US Highway 1. A lot of hippies settled there in the 1970s. I call them hippies, but that conjures more crystal and tie-dye, when these people were mostly idealistic back-to-the-land-ers who raised sheep and listened to PBS: intellectuals, ex-beatniks, artists, musicians, and various criminals. Some people were hiding from the law and growing weed. My father, raised in the aspirational WASP-dom of Pasadena, was somehow handy and knew carpentry.

My dad, James Stewart Cameron, made cameos in the movie of my childhood. He wasn't around much, but when he was, he was charismatic and scary and took up all the energy in the room. He was thin, wiry, and handsome. He drank and smoked constantly. He read all the time and did crossword puzzles. His brain was powerful. My mother, Elaine Lucielle

Grandey (nickname Meaux), was short, sturdy, and crazy. She was raised on a farm in Vermont. She could bake bread, garden, chop wood, compost, and make meals out of virtually nothing. But her mind was fragile.

In 1976, when I was one year old, my dad crashed into a tree and went through the windshield of his truck and broke his back. He spent a year in a body cast. He decided to go to law school while he was laid up. He passed the bar, and suddenly my dad—who drove a dump truck and did odd jobs—was a lawyer. He was more like a *Better Call Saul*-style of attorney, if Saul lived in the Northern California woods and defended small time pot growers and unlicensed dome dwellers. My dad's accident didn't get him sober, though. In the only early childhood memory I have of my parents together, he was drunk.

My older brother was still at home, so I must have been around four. My dad was harassing David by bouncing up and down on his lap, waving a can of Budweiser in one hand and a cigarette in the other. My brother was clearly uncomfortable but unable to do anything about it.

Stop it, James, said my mom.

Oh, come on, I'm just playing! We're playing!

He doesn't like it, get off him!

He likes it, it's fun! It's just a fucking game!

Then my dad stood up, raised his arm, and backhanded my mom across her face. I watched from the bottom of the stairs. My mom fell to the floor with a thud. Her skirt splayed around her. I cried. My older sister came out of the bathroom. She was all wet from the tub and water was pooling around her on the floor. She looked small. She needed a towel.

What's happening? What's going on?

Nothing, go upstairs, go get dressed, now.

My mom threw some clothes in a bag and we took off to her friend Judy, who lived on a sheep farm a couple miles away. I asked my mom what happened to dad. In the dark, in the strange bed, my mom whispered to us:

Your dad is going to have a bad headache tomorrow and he won't remember anything.

How could he not remember anything? That was very scary sounding. But I was relieved that my dad wouldn't have to feel bad about what he had done.

In our rural area there was: a post office in front of a shriveled old lady's house, about a mile or two down the road. She had peacocks. Their sad, noisy calls always depressed me. About ten miles away was the Hollowtree General Store. It had a few trailers scattered around, where people lived. It sold ice, beer, firewood, cigarettes, and some staples like canned goods and hot dogs. You could get popsicles and candy there. It had a wooden screen door with creak and flap slam noises. Trucks, motorcycles, and tricycles dotted the driveway, people socializing and saying, "Hey." Hollowtree was also the place where the welfare food truck stopped. Once a month we would gather around to pluck our rations from the neatly stacked slabs of orange cheese food product and five-gallon peanut butter cans.

The Horicon school was across the street. It was K-12 and we all went there. It had been there since the late 1800s, when the area was mostly apple orchards. Down the road a mile was a church that also functioned as a community center. We didn't attend church, but sometimes potlucks would take place, and a sugary treat could be had at the holidays. There was a small cemetery. Distinctly remembering hearing the phrase "dancing on their grave," I once did a secret tap routine on a dirt pile facing an unremarkable headstone.

In the front yard we had a walnut tree. I liked to pick the new walnuts and feel their gooey insides before they formed into the brown brain-shaped nut that I knew would be food one day. My mother had a big garden with an enormous compost pile. When my father was drunk he held Jyoti over the top of it and threatened to throw her in. She writhed and screamed while he laughed.

My mom had a horse named Sue who had a boyfriend horse that would escape where he lived to come visit. They never consummated their relationship. Sue was bred with a stud named Achilles and we watched the colt get born. He slid out of Sue in a bag of goo, right onto his wobbly little legs. Sue snortled and licked off the placenta. Then he trotted around the small corral.

We also had a bajillion cats, indoor and outdoor. There were always kittens being born somewhere, which was a great thrill for us girls. We had a sweet ancient dog named Rosa, black with patches of fur missing, who ate her own turds, and a goofie hound dog named Ernie. In the summers we would pile into the dumpy station wagon with a bunch of filthy kids and go to the Buckeye swimming hole, which was down an unmarked, rocky road. Ernie would take off up the river while we spent all day at the Buckeye. There were humongous boulders that baked in the sun. We would lay on them after swimming for too long in the chilly water. We made exaggerated “Ahhhhhhhh” sounds as we luxuriated from the warmth rising up to our wet skin.

I was drawn to the corners of the rocks underwater, where the pollywog sacs formed. Gooey, green, bulbous future frogs. Further into the summer, the pollywogs would come and swim around but they had no legs. I was confused—weren’t they just fish? By the end of the summer they grew legs and become adorable frogs.

At the end of the day, we would climb back up the hill to the hot car. Before we left, all the kids would yell at the top of their lungs for Ernie.

EEEEEEERRRRRRRRRRRRRNNIIEEEEEEEE!

Our chorus bounced through the river valley, and eventually Ernie would appear like a superhero and leap into the car, muddy and smelly, and lick all the screeching children.

In front of our house was a sloping hill covered with very fine dirt. It was soft, almost a powder, which I enjoyed eating. I still have an affinity for powdery substances in my mouth, like coffee creamer. When it rained, delightful mud holes would emerge. We would sit in them for hours, covering ourselves with the smooth slop that dried into a gray crust and made us look like mummies.

One day Dad took Jyoti on a motorcycle ride to the post office. They drove off without helmets, Jyoti's golden curls flying in the wind behind her. Instead of coming back to the house down the driveway, my dad plowed down the lumpy hill, and the motorcycle fell over and landed on top of them. I watched it in slow motion. I knew the bike was hot; you were not to go near it if it was turned on, because it could burn you. I knew it was heavy, that only an adult could make it stand upright. I screamed, thinking it surely killed them both. They emerged from under the bike unscathed. My dad laughed it off. My father's attention was all we wanted, but it was dangerous. He could do whatever he wanted.

At the top of this hill was an old school bus that my parents had driven across the country when they were hanging with the Hog Farm commune. It had a big platform bed in the back, covered with various groovy fabrics. I loved to sit in the driver's seat and use the gigantic, unwieldy bus door lever. My dad told me that when I was two years old, our family drove that bus across the country with only one 8-track tape, "The Harder

They Come" by Jimmy Cliff. This, he said, was the reason I liked reggae so much.

There were three old rusting cars on the property. The most luxurious was a black 1950s Studebaker. Me and J'nai would play our favorite game, Taxi, in it. I would be the cabbie and use a "New York accent."

Wheaar to, lady?

J'nai always pretended to be a rich lady because she couldn't quite imagine who else would take a taxi.

Park Avenue, please!

You got it, madame.

Fasten your seatbelt, we'll take Broawhdway.

I loved the musty smell of the car with its hardened leather seats, enormous woody steering wheel, and knobby knobs sticking out all over the dashboard. I put my hands on ten and two and steered us violently nowhere with the pedal to the metal.

Please slow down, sir!

In the living room we played 1950s man and wife. I was the man, naturally, and barreled through the invisible front door, swinging my imaginary briefcase and hollering.

I'M HOME FROM WORK, GO MAKE ME A STEAK! WHERE ARE MY SLIPPERS AND PIPE, WOMAN!

Right away, darling, dinner is in the oven, meatloaf your favorite!

We would also play TV shows. *Star Search*, *Puttin' on the Hits*, and *Solid Gold* were our faves. We also loved *Dance Fever*, a couples' dance competition show.

Please welcome couple number one, Steve and Joyce from Laguna Niguel, California! They enjoy sunset beach walks, French cuisine, and hot air ballooning.

I whisked J'nai onto the floor in our imaginary matching outfits, violently spinning her to and fro, threatening to break her neck with sexy dips, her blonde hair grazing the dusty floor.

We had an old, orange Datsun station wagon, and a big, slow truck for hauling trash and junk. Everyone was always running out of gas, and we were frequently receiving or giving garden hose fuel siphoning. It was almost a way of socializing, my dad and some buddies drinking and observing the two vehicles suddenly dependent on each other. Then, when I was six years old, we suddenly had two brand new cars—a cream-colored Toyota Tercel and a blue Toyota pickup. Not only that, our little two-bedroom house began to get another story. We were *all* going to have our own bedrooms. My father had come into some money. More on that later.

I moved into my room before it was completed. It had two-by-fours on two sides and half a sheetrock wall. Sheetrock is essentially covered in paper, a blank canvas that I scribbled all over. I tried to paint the wall black at one point, but I only had one small tube of paint and managed to get about a 12-inch square filled in. I drew cocknballs and winged hearts, bugs, flowers, turds, dogs, wrote whatever words I knew how to spell. SHIT. LOVE. FART. I also drew a mouth—or, rather, a pink hole—onto which I practiced French kissing, smushing my tongue flat on the wall and wagging it around. Then I would watch the slobber-circle dry up throughout the day. The house stayed a construction zone the entire time we lived there.

I was obsessed with our one radio station, calling frequently to request songs that moved me, like "Cum on Feel the Noize" by Quiet Riot, which I argue might be the best band name in history. I called the radio station while it played, and I asked them to play it again.

But we are playing it right now.

Play it again after it's done!

We can't, we are on a schedule, you have to just keep listening, we will play it again in an hour probably.

OMG, WHAT? AN HOUR!!!???????? I'll be dead by then!

I still listen to music like this, over and over and over on the loudest volume, as though it's the last thing I will ever hear. As an addict, my baseline desire is to be obliterated, and music obliterates but doesn't leave you in pieces. It rearranges you and puts you back together more whole. It makes me think of the line in the Bob Marley song "Trenchtown Rock," "Hit me with music . . . brutalize me with music." You have my consent.

I begged my dad for a boombox for Christmas when I was seven, and he got me one. He loved to spend money. I was so excited. It was silver and shiny. I loved the feeling of pushing the clunky buttons and turning the radio dial until it magically landed on a song that somehow made its way out of pancake sized speakers and into my tiny little ears and hungry soul. I thought about the waves of the songs flying through the air, Duran Duran shot out from the radio tower and landing on my antenna. I didn't want to miss any songs, so I would press record before I went to sleep and then get up in the middle of the night and flip the tape over to record again.

I was a very nervous child. I ground my teeth to square little nubbins. I also had a habit of bucking my flattened top choppers over my bottom teeth and scraping them on my chin, creating unsightly scabs. I had very bad psoriasis on my scalp that my mother would rub rosemary oil into, creating a greasy, menthol-flake salad in the roots of my hair. All us kids had lice what felt like every other day. I also wet the bed. I would piss all over my friends during sleepovers, or have to be picked up in the middle of the night by a parent if I was afraid to go to sleep for fear of pissing all over them. My mom was gentle about the bed wetting, I never got shamed for it, even though I knew it was shameful. I just felt like I was dirty all the time. Even when the sheets were washed, my bed always had a faint peepee smell that I knew wasn't how you were supposed to smell. I also sometimes crapped my pants at school. I did this because I was trying to hold it in. I am not sure why I did that, but it too filled me with self-disgust.

I had a friend named River Forest with whom I formed an organization called the Sassy Girls Club. To join this club, you had to steal a pack of cigarettes from your dad. My dad smoked Camel bullets. Her dad, Bill, smoked not Marlboros, but the ones like Marlboros, only gold. Winstons? No, that can't be right. Too suburban. River and I would nab their cigarettes and go into the woods by her house and hide out in the fort we built out of a plastic tarp around a burned out tree. We would smoke and burn perfectly round holes in the tarp.

The vibe of these men—my dad and his pals—was hippie criminal. They wore blue jeans and T-shirts, had long scraggly hair and work boots. My dad had a beard sometimes. It was sorta hillbilly-esque, which is what most of the people that lived up there were like. Not far off from LA white hipster dads of today, but with real grease in their hair and well-earned holes in their clothing. My dad always put duct tape over the holes in his down jacket. James and Bill also liked to drink and do coke together. We didn't know what cocaine was, but we knew it was special and naughty. They didn't do a great job hiding it, though, because once at Sassy Girls Club we carved up a bar of Ivory soap and made piles of shavings that we then put into sandwich bags. Then we stuck our faces in the bags and pretended to take giant huffs.

I also smoked at my friend Stacy's house. Stacey was one of the more regular households in the area. She wasn't allowed to come to my house, however, because our family was weird and poor. We liked to play Joan Jett Barbies—giving them a wild rock concert with "I Love Rock 'n' Roll" blasting from her stereo, then go have a smoke on the porch. Her mom discovered us one day. I was banished from that house, and my mother was told.

My mom had always hated smoking. Her mother had died of lung cancer in 1977, when I was two. She sat on my bed and gently told me I wasn't allowed to do that.

It's very bad for you. And you are too young.

I sobbed, ashamed at my indiscretion and fearing a forthcoming spanking from my dad.

But I'm not going to tell your father.

What a mercy.

Throughout my teen years my mom would constantly be flushing my cigarettes down the toilet. I'm 51 now and just had a cigarette so that didn't work, sorry mom.

The house remained in construction limbo until my parents finally split, and we moved away. I will never understand how my dad, such a drunk, used heavy machinery without losing limbs or digits. My dad purchased the land we lived on, which was 48 acres of thick forest. I don't know what happened to the land, the house, or anything. The horses must have been sold. The dogs given away. I don't have a single relic from childhood, but here is a butch hippie criminal photo of me at age four.

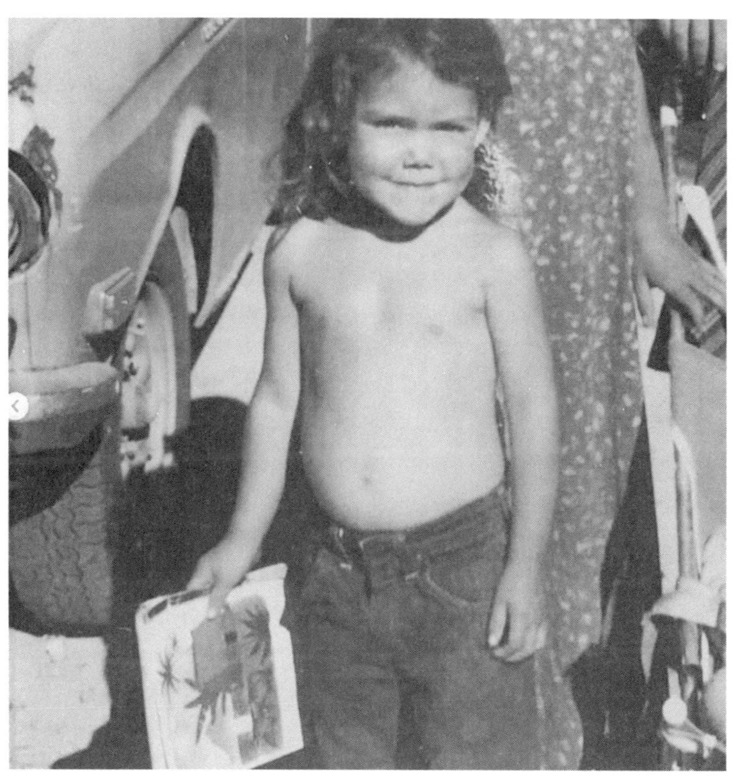

TWO: CONFIDENCE MOM

My mother had bipolar disorder and schizophrenia. She heard voices and she was directed to do things by the voices when she was in a state of psychosis. When I was young, she was either pretty normal and then really crazy, but the older she got, the more she went on and off of her meds, there was less of a veil between the two worlds. Yet she always seemed to have a logic to her weirdness—which I happen to think is true of most weirdness. That's why it scares people. I don't know when she started to become ill. I heard different stories. The most damaging one seemed to blame me.

When did mom start going crazy? I asked my dad. I was probably around 14.

Right around the time you were born. He laughed.

When I asked my mom she sort of corroborated this.

Well, when you were born, he stopped loving me and the other kids, he only loved you. It was around this time.

I grew up believing this. It has caused me a lot of confusion and pain. I always feel like I'm taking up too much space, but I also do take up a lot of space because I am a performer and a hilarious person, but I also don't want to hurt anyone by being that way (as if that is possible). I also know my parents were drama queens and could not be trusted. It was most assuredly not true; I learned, much later in life, that she had been depressed since she was a teenager and began having mental collapses as early as age 25. She was 33 when I was born. The damage of believing that has taken a lifetime to undo. I'm still working on it.

The story of my birth certificate is a good example of the effects of growing up off-grid with my brainsick mom and neglectful father. I didn't get a birth certificate until I was four years old. I am not sure why they bothered, even then. Since I was born at home it is unclear where or when I saw a doctor as an infant. The birth certificate I was finally issued was mostly lies. My name on the birth certificate is Jibra'ila Mary Ann Kalish. The Kalish came from my older brother's biological dad, Barry. My father's name is listed as Mohammad Ashraf, who lives in Afghanistan. I never really needed or cared to see my birth certificate, but when I was 17 my boss wanted to send me to Guatemala, and I needed a passport. I was good friends with her daughter, who was wild and had gone down to Guatemala to "learn Spanish," but my boss knew she was just doing coke with Australian expats and basically wanted me to bring her back to the states. To prepare for this trip I faced a Herculean stack of bureaucratic obstacles caused by the bottomless irresponsibility of my parents.

It turned out my mother had scammed the government (as one should) by receiving welfare for her four kids. You could get more if the dads were gone, so she lied and said she didn't know where mine was. She was a bit of a confidence woman in general, although her schemes did not exactly reach for the stars. Mostly they were little, lopsided grifts, such as going to Starbucks to get an "ice coffee maker" and selling cool beverages to weary shoppers in the Home Depot parking lot.

I don't think you can get an iced coffee making machine FROM Starbucks, mom.

Fine, I will just use a bucket.

Which is not the worst logic. She had great ideas for us, too. She gave David the rock solid advice to invest in cranberries. Why? Everyone likes cranberries.

She told my sister J'nai that she should sell flowers on the medians in Los Angeles. No shame in that job, but not the best idea for a 19-year-old girl.

Everyone loves flowers and would love to buy them from a pretty girl.

I had a good friend my mother knew had rich parents, and she told me we should open a vegan restaurant, which she pronounced *vegg-in*.

She could invest. She's got muhhhhney, hunny. Everyone should be eating veggin food. This world is full of disgusting meat eaters.

She was obsessed with the idea that she had a relative who died in the Revolutionary War, and encouraged me to join the Daughters of the American Revolution. Apparently, there is money somewhere in that k-hole. I just took a quick look at their excruciatingly boring website that showcases objects from their museum, including a little glass, pouchy thing described as a "ladies portable urinal." I take it all back. Where do I sign up?

It sounds nuts that my birth certificate claimed my dad was from Afghanistan, but like I said, my mother's crazy was often semi-rooted in reality, like a "based on real events" mini-series gone on a mid-season acid trip. My dad's brother, my uncle Yusef, married a woman from Afghanistan, my aunt Mambuba, and my father's Sufi name was Ashraf. (My dad got into Sufism in the early 1970s.) These realities jangled around in my mom's brain and came out cockeyed.

When she was 25, my sister J'nai lived near Los Angeles with her friends on a horse ranch. My mom knew vaguely where she was and asked me about it.

How does your sister Shinnn-eye like living with Rachel on the ranch?

I think she likes it ok, there's a lot of cute animals there.

Well, that's good, but I think she should stop cooking meth.

Mom, J'nai is not cooking meth.

Pfffft . . . you don't know!

It's true—besides having fun horse ranches, Agua Dulce does have meth labs all over.

With my falsified birth certificate, I was allowed two affidavits of amendment, as long as I had a witness who'd known me since birth to get it notarized with me. My birth certificate had more than two untruths on it, so the government wanted more evidence that I existed between 1975 and1979. There was quite a lack of information.

The passport fascists were not sympathetic to my plight. To prove I was a person, I had to call all over the place, getting proof that there was no proof, another way for the government to torture people with difficult lives.

I would say, "Look, we didn't have a hospital in my town. There are no records to be had."

They would say, "Give us the negative proof of the non-existent hospital."

I should start a band called Negative Proof.

My elementary school burned down and there are no records from there either.

Fine, show us the documents that say there are no documents.

You guys, there are no census reports, they didn't go up there.

How do you prove that the census didn't go somewhere that the census was supposed to go? This was the early 1990s, so there was no googling to be done on how to solve this labyrinthian, state-administered maze.

I gave up and called my dad. By now we rarely spoke, even though he lived only 15 minutes from me. I told him he had to help me. I think the government challenge excited him. He picked me up in Berkeley, and we went to the passport office in San Francisco. He told the passport agent that my mom was nuts, and that's where the lies came from.

Look, you guys have to account for people who have different lifestyles, you know that is a fact, not everyone in this country plays by the rules. The very fact of the existence of bureaucracy is to keep people like us in line. Which would indicate that there were people not playing by the rules. It's not her fault, she was a baby.

This was the first time a parent took responsibility for something that I had thought was an inherent personality flaw. This strategy didn't work and the agent just repeated it was policy blah blah kill me now. By some miracle, someone I knew had someone they knew who worked in the passport office, and eventually I got one. I have never, ever let it lapse.

THREE: HIPPIE COMMUNE, HIPPIE CAMP

My parents met in 1972 through the Hog Farm commune. The Hog Farm was formed by the famous activist hippie clown Wavy Gravy (Hugh Romney) and his wife Jahanarah Romney (Bonnie Jean Beecher—she was on *Star Trek*!). The Farm had a few early iterations in Taos, New Mexico and Tujunga, California. My mom lived at the New Mexico outpost of the commune with her first child, my older brother David, whom she'd had with a man named Barry Kalish. Barry and my mom met in Detroit. She was getting a degree in child development, and Barry was a social sciences teacher who was also part of the civil rights movement, doing community activist work. He led a student walkout and was arrested. There was a cop there who really had it out for Barry and set him up, reportedly. Barry got discouraged with all of the harassment from the cops and legal system, and when the Hog Farm came to town he and my mom decided to take off with them. They eventually landed in New Mexico. Barry and my mom split up, and Barry left the commune. One day Barry came back and snatched David and took him to Mexico where he was selling stolen office supplies. At the time my mom was pregnant with my older half-sister, Jyoti, by another commune guy, Peter. Alone and pregnant, my mom left New Mexico to find David, who turned out to be in Los Angeles, in the care of some woman Barry knew. My mom showed up at the woman's apartment. The woman's boyfriend was hanging out there, too. His name was James, and he would become my dad. Any questions? I have some.

In all, my mom had four kids with three different men, all related, in some fashion, to the Hog Farm. Subsequently some of those men sired offspring with more women, and those women had more children with yet other commune men. As a result, I grew up with a sprawling clan of half-, quarter-, eighth-, and one-sixteenth siblings. There is a term for this I recently learned. It's called a cross-sibling.

My older half-sister Jyoti has three half-brothers (my cross-brothers)—Willy, Zappo, and Guthrie. Willy's full name is something like RagTime Willy Red White And Wiz Rocket; Zappo was tortured by his name and went by Mike (but is now back to Zappo); and Guthrie, named after Woody Guthrie, got away fairly unscathed. Jyoti's father was called Peter White Rabbit. Peter begat Djuna with Oxygen. Oxygen copulated with Red Dog and begat Moonshadow. Ad infinitum. Peter eventually abandoned the commune and all his children and moved to New York, where he became a rabbi and sired even more children. Henceforth, he was referred to as Peter White Rabbi. My sister Jyoti didn't have a relationship with him, and neither did any of his other kids from the farm.

In my early lesbian 1990s education I read *SCUM Manifesto* and nearly choked on my Odwalla:

> ". . . in the case of the hippie—he's way out, Man!—all the way out to the cow pasture where he can fuck and breed undisturbed and mess around with his beads and flute. Men cannot co-operate to achieve a common end, because each man's end is all the pussy for himself. The commune, therefore, is doomed to failure; each hippie will, in panic, grab the first simpleton who digs him and whisks her off to the suburbs as fast as he can. The male cannot progress socially, but merely swings back and forth from isolation to gang-banging."

If my mom wasn't exactly a simpleton, she was somewhat of an idiot to believe my dad would hold up his end of the family-man bargain. But he was handsome, charming, smart, and ladies loved him. My mom had four-year-old David and was pregnant with my older sister Jyoti, and my dad was into it. She was also vain and competitive, and I imagine she felt proud to have locked him down. My dad wanted kids, he wanted a big family—in order to have a corrective experience, I imagine, and be the dad he never got to have. Oh, well! He wanted to be with my mom, who was about as far away from his mom as you could get. My mother was also idealistic and swoony and loved men in that way that most women do (they hate them, but "men will be men what can ya do?!"). My parents desperately wanted to do things "differently" than the way they were raised. And they succeeded, in more ways than one. However, both of my parents were severely traumatized by their upbringings, so their skills were lacking. If you only have a desire for change but no understanding how the thing you want to change has affected you, therefore propelling you to want to change it, you don't stand a chance.

By the time I was born in 1975, my parents had moved off the commune and were homesteading in Annapolis, but we remained commune-adjacent. It wasn't the suburbs, but my dad was still doing his own type of gang-banging (fucking lots of other women). I sometimes wished it had been the suburbs, but only as a little kid, because it looked fun to have a nice clean house. When I was five, I longed to be called "Lisa," and to call my dad "Sir." I asked him if that was ok. He said, "Absolutely not. I had to call *my* dad Sir." I knew that he thought his dad was a demon, so I gave up on that dream quickly.

At some point the Hog Farm migrated to Northern California where they established a posting in Berkeley, taking up nearly a whole block right off Shattuck Avenue. Later they purchased a gigantic piece of land in Laytonville, California, called Black Oak Ranch. Both are still going strong. Or, at least going, in some fashion.

We stayed close with the Hog Farm. We'd go there for holidays and in the summer before and after camp, which I will get to shortly. The Hog Farm in Laytonville centered around a three-bedroom ranch house where group meals were eaten and a few people lived in the bedrooms. The rest of the property was dotted with various dwellings. There were houses built by resident hippie carpenters, and there were also trailers, barn lofts, domes, shacks, and, most excitingly, gigantic, decommissioned buses. Great behemoth Greyhound-style touring machines that had been gutted and outfitted with a patchwork of quilted bedding, Indian tapestries, papier-mâché flying pigs, musical instruments, stained glass rainbows, Tibetan flags, Christmas lights, and a musty Nag Champa cloud that would follow me like a never-ending fart for the rest of my life.

Some of the buses served as hangouts, and some were people's actual living spaces. These buses carried the Hog Farmer hippie activists across the US in the 1970s, stopping in towns to perform wild political circus performances and get chased out of town by the local pigs. One such tour took place on the "Nobody" bus, home of Wavy's "Nobody For President" campaign. As a kid I was tickled by the complex and truthful puns of their campaign slogans and repeated them in my mind: "Because Nobody Is In Washington Right Now, Working For You;" "Nobody's Perfect;" "Nobody Should Have Too Much Power." There was another bus called "The Asp," its ceilings were covered in extraordinary collages from *National Geographic* magazines, painstakingly pasted together by a bunch of people on acid. Us kids would hang out in the buses when we were allowed. We would drink Cokes or smoke weed while a quarter-brother carefully plucked "Dark Side of the Moon" on his guitar. Flirtations were always extra spicy because of the low-key incest potential.

Commune life had its hierarchies, and certainly its dramas. Like a soap opera starring the cast of *Easy Rider*, and the soap is Dr. Bronner's. The Hog Farm was limping into the 1980s, and everyone had complicated interwoven pasts but were still trying to live as harmoniously as possible. As a dyke who now has what we all call "gay family"—other queers we will know for the rest of our lives, some we actively dislike, have fucked, have fallen out with, then reconciled because after all we will know each other forever and talk endless shit on sometimes but would most likely do anything for—I can relate to the loyalty and chosen family ethos of Hog Farm lifey. I'm 51 now and have known some of these fools for 30 years. Imagine if the dykes I hung out with in my 20s all had children together. WHAT A LIVING GAY HELL.

Many of the commune women were decidedly scary. Cherry was a commune matriarch who was always giving me and J'nai the stink eye. I longed for her to like me because she seemed important. She had a round, pretty face and wore Guatemalan tunics. She was kind to my brother and older sister, though, and I couldn't figure it out. I realized later that my mom had a kid with the guy she had had three kids with: Jyoti fell in the line of ages right after one of Cherry's kids and right before another one. But that didn't really make sense, that she would be mean to me and J'nai. Why not Jyoti? Maybe she and my dad had a fling? Who knows. Jahanara, Wavy's wife, was also a big-timer lady around the commune, and many were frightened of her because she had power and didn't take any shit. But she was always gentle with me and J'nai in particular. Later I learned my dad and her had been hooking up in LA during the time she was an actress and a Playboy Bunny. The women also ruled the food, which was nerve-wracking because kids always wanted snacks and it was a crapshoot who would be running the kitchen that day. If it was a mean one, we snuck in and grabbed stuff; if it was a nice one, they'd make us a PBJ. I always wanted the women to be nice to me, because when we were at the commune or at camp we got to be free of our parents.

After my mother died in 2011, I went to visit Jahanara at the Berkeley house. She told me a time came when she and other women on the commune had had enough of the rampant fuck fest and told their men to get it together or they were out. I imagine many of these women had been made to clean up messes by irresponsible menfolk regularly, leaving them bitter and spiky, toughened by trying to get shit done. And they really got shit done. Dorgie was definitely our favorite. She was 100-feet tall and had a voice not unlike Tom Waits. She was enormously strong and had a tent fabrication company she ran out of the barn called In Tents. Dorgie had built all of the tipis for camp, as well as the canvas sunshades for big, hippie rock festivals. She was one of five people on earth who always called me by my full name. There were also warm, doughy women, like Calico, who had three-mile-long gray braids and wore big glasses. Calico worked for Bill Graham Presents, which the Hog Farm had been employed by for ages. My mom sometimes worked with the Hog Farm as a baby sitter at Dead shows, and she also was on the Hog Farm's security team at Woodstock. They were called the "Please Force" as opposed to "Police Force"—using the tactic, *Please don't do that, please do this instead*. Mostly they made sure people had water and first aid and no one was tripping too hard. My brother can be seen riding around in a diaper on someone's back in the film *Woodstock*.

Sometimes people say, “Weren’t you raised in a cult?” HOW DARE YEE?! As I clutch my amethyst necklace, NO!!! A *COMMUNE*! MUCH DIFFERENT. A cult is much different than a commune, entirely different, their foundational principles are polar opposites. A cult is a dictatorship, and a commune is a communal living situation that makes up its own rules, supposedly by popular vote in democratic process, but that sometimes gets overshadowed by a dominant personality and then becomes cult-like, or people start living together believing they want to share responsibilities and then it turns out women do all the housework and men just spew their jizz everywhere. Sometimes it’s radical, amazing, and harmonious.

Of course, there were actual menacing characters as well. There was a notorious “bad dude” who would drop in and out. He would roar up the dirt road on his Harley and a somber, tense energy would vibrate around the farm. He wore a wife-beater and jeans and smoked a lot. He was one of my one-sixteenth-brother’s dads. He had a nasty coke problem and was a violent asshole. But, like I said, gay family. I also know there was some heinous behavior by some of the older guys, too. I mean, where there are men, there is danger, and at the commune it came in the form of older men preying on teen girls. I wasn’t aware of it at the time, but kids my brother’s age certainly were, and it colored their experience much differently from mine. By the time I was of age to be leched upon by full grown men I was luckily not hanging out at the Hog Farm, so my memories of it are largely positive.

One family at the Hog Farm was bossed by a skeletal, mean matriarch named Dragon and her two beautiful, raven-haired daughters, Indigo and Kalahari. She was German or Eastern European; her accent made her scarier. She had stringy blonde hair and wore a mashup of silken flowery pashminas draped over her bony frame. Her yam-shaped breasts swung freely under threadbare tank tops. She stomped around in flat leather sandals and barked at her children and everyone else's children, too. Apparently, she had arthritis in her entire body, but I didn't know that.

Kalahari was rumored to have a tail. An actual tail. A tail of hair, the cause of great speculation and gossip for us kids. One fateful day, when I was around eight years old, Kalahari and I played by the river, just the two of us.

I have to pee, she said. *I have to pee, too*, I lied.

We crept into some shrubs. She pulled down her cotton underpants. Out tumbled a long blond braid, sprouting from her lower back, just above her butt crack . . . her TAILbone. It was thin and shiny and had a ribbon tied to the end, with bells on it. She noticed my horror.

Oh yeah, that's my tail, my mom won't let me cut it off.

That fucking bitch! I thought. It doesn't matter who you are, parents suck in the same way at every level of society. Kalahari ended up becoming a nurse. Indigo, the boring sister with no tail, got a doctorate from Yale and became a politician.

In the mid 70s, Wavy Gravy and Jahanara, along with other Hog Farmers, founded a performing arts summer camp which I attended from age six to age twelve. It was called Camp Winnarainbow (I know). It is where I learned improv.

Early in the morning, Wavy would blow a giant conch shell, signaling it was time for morning circle, and all campers, counselors, and staff stumbled out of their tipis to gather around the fire pit. It's super cringe to write tipi, as white hippies notoriously appropriate indigenous engineering and everything else. I just looked at the Camp Winnarainbow website, and they now have a tipi acknowledgement statement that expresses gratitude to First Nations peoples and explains why tipis are such an amazing invention—they are portable, stay warm, and since the walls are fabric you can hear if someone in your community is in distress—a baby crying, etc.

At morning circle, we would stretch, warm up our vessels (bodies), and sing goofy, socialist folk songs. There were many bangers. My favorites were the macabre, cartoony ones like "Oh Dunderbeck," about "the sausage meat machine" that made salamis out of dogs, cats, and children; or "Titanic," about rich people drowning. Not to brag, but I knew the counterpoint to "witches are bad" very early in my youth:

Who were the witches
Where did they come from
Maybe your great great great grandma was one
Witches were wise wise women they say
And there's a little witch in every woman today

This is exactly what annoying queers say all the time now. I also enjoyed the enviro-anarchy bop about dirt:

Dirt dirt, top of the mountain
Dirt dirt, bottom of the sea
Dirt dirt, got a bad name
But it became known as proper-ty!
Apples bananas beans and rice
Guacamole with my favorite spice
Milk and meat and cows that moo
Grazed on grasses, grasses that grew from
Dirt dirt . . .

To close morning circle we would do a collective OM before heading off to breakfast. Starving by then, we joked: OMMMMMMM MY GOD I'M HUNGRY. OMMMMMMMMLETTTE PLEEEASE. We'd meander up the forest pathway to the giant outdoor kitchen seating area and line up for food with our trays perched at our bellies, then eat under the oaks on picnic tables. If you were brave enough to get up and face the chilly air before morning circle you could grab a hot cocoa at the communal kitchen, but I rarely could get that together.

Next it was time for the meeting on the stage, where the teachers would announce their classes for the day. A rainbow bridge arched over the stage with stairs going up either side and a curtain that fell behind it to the floor. All sorts of lessons were on offer, two sessions per day: stilt walking, juggling, tightrope, trapeze, belly dancing, unicycle, gymnastics, clowning, face painting, guitar, stick fighting. It was the 80s, so we had topical classes like D+D and breakdancing. The only class I went to was called Space Eat, Wavy Gravy's improv class. I would take Space Eat every single day, sometimes for both sessions. I never learned a single circus art, or anything else for that matter.

On hot days Wavy wore a hat with a rubber fried egg on top. He would appear as different characters throughout the session, such as Al Dente, the Italian restaurant host, who wore a stiff toupee and a tuxedo T-shirt and *talked-a like-a this-a*. Sometimes Wavy would wear a red clown nose. Wavy had no teeth. I remember two different rumors: one was that they fell out from heroin use, one from eating too much candy. At any rate, he had a false set that was rainbow-colored. At night before lights out he would yell, "Brush 'em if you got 'em!" He had a scratchy, hoarse voice, probably from smoking. Wavy had been a beatnik. Before he wore floppy multicolored trousers, he wore black turtlenecks. A true counterculture guy.

During Wavy's Space Eat class we sat in a circle in the woods and played improv games. I loved Machine, where we built a giant, vague mechanism together out of our bodies moving and repetitively making a noise.

I also liked the object changing game. Some kid would start by miming holding a cat in his arms, stroking the soft fur and scratching under its chin. I paid fiercely close attention to the detail, noticing how big the cat was, which end its head was attached to. This kid's cat was actually shaped like a snake if you took their miming literally. In the game, as soon as someone had an idea for another object to mime, that person could go into the scene, play along with the present situation, and then change it to something new.

I crept up to the kid and his invisible tube-shaped kitten. I reached out my arms and picked up the cat, petting it gently for a few moments, then my hands began to cradle it on either side. I was seeing a loaf of bread. I proceeded to mime putting together a sandwich, mayonnaising and mustarding each side, then delicately placing slices of cheese on the bread. I closed it up and brought the gigantic hoagie to my gaping mouth, just as another kid came up and tagged in. She grabbed my sandwich, took a bite, then gave it the shape of binoculars. Raising them to her face, she pretended to look intently through them into the distance.

Improv speaks to the way my brain works: fast and stupid. I love how exciting and imaginative it is. I've never had stage fright or feared looking dumb, which is both a gift and a curse. Even as a kid, I only felt excitement at being in front of an audience. I like the premise of improv because it is about listening and building something that harmonizes with the people around you, something I wasn't getting at home. Much of the craft of improvisation relies on focusing on the moment and making it bigger, bolder, more present, all while affirming the people next to you. Telling them, *I believe your sandwich! I believe you!* The magic and power of believability are in the details, and isn't it incredible that one could actually remember, if one tried, exactly what it felt like in your body to open a jar? The shape of the round lid under your fingers, the resistance at first and then the moment of the top loosening, pop! Removing the top, setting it aside carefully, then putting a butter knife into the jar, feeling the slight weight of mayonnaise against the blade, getting the right amount of blob, and on to the sensation of spreading the mayonnaise. Not too much pressure or you'll scrape into the bread; not too light or it won't spread evenly. If you concentrate hard enough you can do these things and be transmuted into that world and take everyone with you. And it's funny.

Why is it funny to watch someone mime making an invisible sandwich? My guess is that the humor is not in the subject matter per se, but in the audience's surprise and recognition of themselves in this mundane, plebeian task you would otherwise ignore. Taking away the actual materials of this job of sandwich-making—no jar, no knife, no bread—brings awareness to the intimacy of these moments, reminding us of what we know, what is stored in our bodies without even trying, our unconscious brain on display. When we see ourselves reflected this way, we are surprised and delighted and we laugh laugh laugh at the pleasure of that. Also, it's fun to be on the edge of your seat in suspense about what could possibly happen next.

After the two morning class sessions we would all gather at the rainbow stage and kids would present what they'd learned that day, giving each of us a chance to show off and be applauded. Then it was lunch and free time. I spent free time giggling in the tipis or going to the camp store to get "candy"—usually Tiger's Milk bars or some carob monstrosity. The adults put out juice and water or watery juice in the blazing afternoons. Down a long, dusty road a mile away was also Lake Veronica (haha) for swimming. You could walk there or take a shuttle. My mom worked as a lifeguard at the lake, which was insane given her rickety brain and lack of certification, so I mostly avoided swimming there, but telling the kids that my mom worked at camp was a brag. So was being related to the Hog Farm family: that felt great. Like I belonged, I was on the inside. I also wrote a lot of pen pal letters to friends back home, went to the river to fuck around, gossiped, wandered about, and played games with my friends.

My pals at camp included a short girl with frizzball hair named Cecil, who had a very high and scratchy voice. She looked and sounded like a cartoon. We did Space Eat together every day, and she was deeply into putting on plays and doing theater. She is now an adult, the same size, who plays the ukulele and works at camp. I had a hilarious deaf friend named Eddy who once put his tongue through a hole in a tortilla and it made me spit take milk all over the table. There was a kid who was rumored to be missing the part of his brain that told him when he was full, and he would "eat and eat until he exploded." I pictured him forking in a fatal bite of tofu lasagna and blowing up like he had been bombed from the inside, limbs flying everywhere. Fortunately, that never happened. There were also many celebrity hippie kids. One year I hung out a lot with Alex, who was and still is Whoopi Goldberg's daughter. We didn't know at first, but suspected she was fancy because once she told us a story about having dinner with Mick Jagger. And then she kept telling the Mick Jagger story until finally someone asked her if her parents were rich or celebrities. Alex took me to the payphone with her to call her mom once, and I got to say hi to Whoopi. I had never talked to a celebrity before. I can still hear her deep smiling voice, *Hi, Jiiiiiibs, nice to meet ya*. Trixie Garcia, Jerry's youngest daughter, went to camp with me and was in my tipi. We went to college together, too, at San Francisco Art Institute. We were both there when Jerry died. I asked her how it felt to have your dad's death hijacked by millions of hippies who thought they knew him better. She solemnly nodded. *Yup, it's pretty fuckin lame.*

Jerry's stepdaughter, Sunshine, was a camp counselor. She was the biological daughter of Ken Kesey and a woman they called Mountain Girl. Sunshine took us to the muddy river and put glops of it in her thick blond curls and pretended to be Medusa. The son of the drummer for the Dead went to my camp, too, but he was just a little kid so I didn't pay attention to him. To me, the Grateful Dead were boring old-people music. I ended up appreciating them later in life, musically, but I can't look at them—it gives me a mildly grossed out feeling. Mixture of shame, boredom and, like, I am hanging out with dads.

I truly loved everything about camp except for my constant terror of wizzing in my sleep. One time when this happened I masked my accident by spilling a glass of water over my sleeping bag. *Oh no! Gotta get it outta the tipi and dry it out.*

I was told by my mom that if I wet my bed, I was to go see the camp nurse, Hidden Mountain. She was stern but friendly. She wore a neat white nurse's uniform, complete with the weird little hat atop her fraying brown bun. Her outfit made her appear much more official and trustworthy than all the other adults. She was extremely thin and reminded me of Olive Oyl. I had the impression that she was the only adult for miles with an actual job. As in, she would leave camp and go work in a hospital or something. God knows what all those other clowns did the other ten months of the year. She looked me in the eye and said warmly,

Hello Jibria'ila, please sit down and tell me what happened.

Hi, Hidden Mountain, I wet my sleeping bag.

Obviously she knew already, but I appreciated being asked. I clutched it to my chest. It stank, off-gassing from the cheap blue nylon fabric in the blazing sun. It was one of those sleeping bags that is perfectly rectangular and flat with foam inside, not fluffy and round and full of feathers, which would have been even nastier, actually.

Oh, that's no big deal at all, just leave it with me and come pick it up after dinner.

Bless you, Hidden Mountain.

Another frizzy-haired camp counselor I loved was Sharon Share-alike. Sharon wore a costume every single day. Her greatest hit was a flowery old bathrobe, fluffy slippers, and an old lady wig that had rollers in it. The rollers were attached to a tube which was attached to a pump that could make the curlers stand on end like in a 50s cartoon when you squeezed it in your hand. I thought this was the most genius thing imaginable. She went to the grocery store in Berkeley dressed in that costume, shocking the other shoppers. She also donned a bodysuit with the solar system painted all over it and wore it with a hat shaped like Saturn. Sharon was also the president of the Banana Slug Club. If you kissed a banana slug you would get a special pin, of a slug, of course. She picked up a tiny, snot-colored slug about an inch long, and I leaned in and gave it a quick peck. It was more sticky than slimy, but it was so quick I barely noticed. Everyone went EEEEEEEEEEEEW! But we were all delighted. Now, if you *licked* a slug you got *another* prize, but whatever that was, it wasn't valuable enough for me to lick a fucking slug. That just seemed gross.

We had some special guests who would come visit camp every year, like Fred Wahpepah, a Kickapoo tribe elder who hosted a sweat lodge and taught Native American songs to the kids. Fred was even-keeled and calm, which stood out because most camp adults were slightly manic in their enthusiasm. His songs were mostly about animals. One was about how we were all flying high like an eagle, circling the universe. I would picture myself as a big bird, able to see everything below me on earth, stars streaking by me in the chilly sky.

As for the sweat lodge, I had been in a sauna many times. Lots of hippies had saunas, but a sweat lodge was a completely different situation. The adults would circle around the rocks and be mostly naked. Which was gross, of course. There was incense or sage or some intensely rich smell that was so powerful it fried the nostrils. Fred sang and played a drum in the 1,000,000,000 degrees. The rule of the sweat lodge was that you were not supposed to leave. The lodge was a little dome covered in a tarp and many, many heavy blankets. I had to shove my face in the dirt and try to stick my lips out of the dome to gasp for fresh air. I felt pressure to stay in, because it was a real badge of stamina to withstand it. I never lasted more than ten minutes. Maybe five. The adults would straggle out an hour later, slick with sweat and blissed out at their resurgence and healing. There was a stream nearby and they would all plunge in, steam rising from their heads.

Another iconic camp counselor was Reggie. He was tall, Black, extremely fit, handsome, and a martial arts expert. The boys were obsessed with him. Surely not *everybody* was kung fu fighting, but many were at Camp Winnarainbow; wielding nunchucks, being a ninja, practicing karate and Japanese throwing stars, and of course, stick fighting. Reggie was also the camp Dungeon Master, as in D+D, which I knew was important but wasn't sure why. He strode around camp shirtless, his kung fu pants hanging off his hips, an enormous crystal eagle claw on a lanyard on his glistening chest, brandishing a gigantic wooden stick in his hand.

The real, deep, nerd actor kids, such as myself, sometimes put on plays that were not part of regular camp programming. One such play, *Airheads Airlines*, written by resident camp theater dork Joe, was about an airline that was run by drug addicts. I demanded to play the stewardess so I could wear high heels. They were white pumps, and I fell off the stage because I couldn't stand in them. It was worth it. I got to teeter around carrying trays of drugs to the passengers.

Uppers, downers, alllll arounders anyone?

The pilots, who were also children, hallucinated and saw purple elephants in the sky. There was also a Swami on board. Swami Salami? Oh, the 80s.

Airheads Airlines, zoom golly golly zoom golly golly zoom

At the time I thought I was really mature for thinking the drug jokes were funny. In hindsight they were definitely not funny, but children pretending to be on drugs is.

Because the Hog Farm's home base was in Berkeley, lots of kids from the city came on scholarship, many of whom were unaccustomed to nature—and with them came cool shit. I came from super rural Mendocino County where there were probably two Black people in our town, and they were related. I didn't think about it at the time, of course, but so much of the excitement and newness of camp for me was learning about new styles, dances, and music from the city kids. I didn't attribute this to the kids being Black when I was a kid, mostly because in my experience, kids don't think that way. But upon reflection—it was important. I am sure I was super annoying when I went home to my dumb town and showed off my new moves and fashion.

One year, breakdancing took over. The counselors were all annoyed at this, but it was unstoppable. The boys were forgoing stilt-walking and trapeze for parachute pants and fingerless leather gloves, carrying cardboard stacks and linoleum rolls and plugging in their boomboxes with an extension cord that ran through the dusty leaves. I learned to moonwalk and do a slight robot. My moonwalk is still about 30 percent, but I am proud to have been at least a little bit in the conversation.

Camp also introduced me to other city kids, such as *real* punks. A freak counselor named Davey wore a Wham! T-shirt on orientation day when I was ten. I got very excited—that was my favorite band. I had a special savings can with my friend Laurie to pay for flights to England so that she could marry George and I could marry Andrew (blondes = barf).

I LOVE YOUR SHIRT! I LOVE WHAM!

Davey laughed at me. In my *face.*

Then and there, a tiny leak began to form in the bubble of consumerist popular culture I worshipped. I became laser-focused on everything Davey liked and represented. He wore old man pants and weird shoes. One day he wore a shirt repping MDC, the punk band, which I learned either stood for MILLIONS OF DEAD COPS, MILLIONS OF DEAD CHRISTIANS or . . . MILLIONS OF DEAD CHILDREN!!!! WHAT!??? Why do we want to have millions of dead cops!? And what of the millions of dead children?!!! A slightly older city punk chick explained it to me: *Well, we want dead cops because cops are actually a weapon the government uses to terrorize and control people, usually, like, poor people and Black people. The children part is probably about how war kills children. And the Christians are just evil and everyone should hate them.*

Me and my friends whispered into the night about what a freak Davey was.

I heard he woke up in the middle of the night and sat straight up in his sleeping bag and shouted, "TV ROTS YOUR BRAIN SO SHOVE IT UP YOUR ASS!"

TV rots your brain? WHAT? I was very familiar with my dad's rant on the evils of the government and his critique of *Dukes of Hazzard* and *Three's Company*. I can still hear my father's angry review of that show—"Someone says the word 'toilet' and they all fall down laughing." And I heard his endless anti-government viewpoints. I knew that the government was bad, but I didn't really know why and how it was. To me, it was paternal griping and low-key insults to us kids. I recalled my father also saying that advertising was the United States' biggest industry, and that TV was just a tool to sell us things. Davey's anarcho-dots started to connect for me.

I hadn't hit puberty yet, but rage still bubbled under the surface despite the break from my parents I got while at camp. The real splits in reality were on their way—the moments as an adolescent where I discovered "everything is a lie"—and Davey's ironic Wham! T-shirt was the gateway fissure. When they hit me they decimated many parts of me, most importantly the part of me that had so joyously loved Wham! I realized not only would I never marry Andrew Ridgeley, but that Andrew Ridgeley was part of an entire white supremacist capitalist system of popular consumerist cultural mind control meant to keep people ignorant, sedated, and distracted from the horrors of our depraved governments while promoting elitist sportswear. Little did I know I would spend much of my adulthood in recovery trying to reconnect to the stupid joy that I had as a child who loved that idiotic music.

By age 11 I was well on my way to being a punk rocker, but I was still very innocent. I shaved a tiny part of the side of my head, like a quarter of an inch, with my sister's leg razor. My exposed flesh scared me, so I stopped. I looked stupid. My grandmother asked me what I wanted for my birthday and I told her "something punk," and she gave me a novelty shop rock with a bunch of little rocks hot glued on top of it, with eyes, holding a sign that said "rock concert." My dad laughed at my desperation for coolness and my grandmother's shade.

At camp I met Tré Cool, later of Green Day fame. He was already going by that name, which to an 11-year-old was pretty clever. He was 14 and we were "going out." I don't think we did anything beyond hold hands and giggle. He was a drumming prodigy and had already been recruited into the Lookouts by Larry Livermore. He was a jokester with a nasally voice and wore a zebra-print muscle shirt and authentically ripped jeans. He grew up in the sticks near the Hog Farm, which is how he ended up at camp. When city kids would ask him what his parents did he told them (with a wink at me) they "ran an organic tomato farm." I thought this was hilarious, because of course they grew weed and I was pleased to understand something important and criminal like that. After camp that summer we pen-palled a few times. He sent me a newspaper article about the Lookouts that I showed off to my friends. I had a boyfriend! In a band! In the newspaper! But it fizzled out. Tré was already getting famouser and touring so he didn't come back to camp. A couple years later, when I started going to the all-ages punk club Gilman Street, FUCK GREEN DAY was spray painted above the stage. They got too famous. But also that band is truly irritating.

When I was 12, I attended camp for the last time. I had an enormous crush on this beautiful hippie boy. He was from a prominent commune family (lol). Tan and toned, he had long, brown hair with golden streaks. He strode around barefoot in linen pants like Reggie, carrying ancient weaponry (a stick). I lied to him and told him I was 13. He was 17. By the time he found out I was only 12, it was too late. He'd fallen for me. We made out in the dirt next to a tipi, which I can say with perfect clarity was my first psychedelic dopamine trip—my first mainline of the greatest drug on earth. We only did some over-the-bra petting, but that evening my entire being was transformed. We kissed passionately, and my heart hammered nearly right out of my chest. I was transported to another galaxy with desire. Desire for what? For more, that's what. That's all I could think of. I had never felt anything close to this kind of bliss. All my blood rushed to my head, and I was absolutely desperate for more of this feeling. I was a lifelong junkie who had been living for 12 whole years not knowing about junk. Now, I'd gotten an uncut dose straight to my entire system. I looked up at the starry sky, devastated that I had never known this feeling. Where had I been? Doing improv!? What the fuck? It was the feeling that I had captured an unattainable thing. That there was a laser focus on me and my magic. I swore I would hang on to it as long as I could.

We only had one more makeout after that, equally mind-bending. He left camp early and I was in immediate withdrawal. A couple weeks later he wrote me a letter and I was embarrassed at how corny it was. It dawned on me that I didn't really like him, I just liked the feeling I got from him. Now I suspected that he might be dumb. He had written me a generic poem wherein he quoted The Doors, a band I continue to hate, in lavender felt tip marker, and he had drawn pathetic flowers on the envelope. Fuckin hippie.

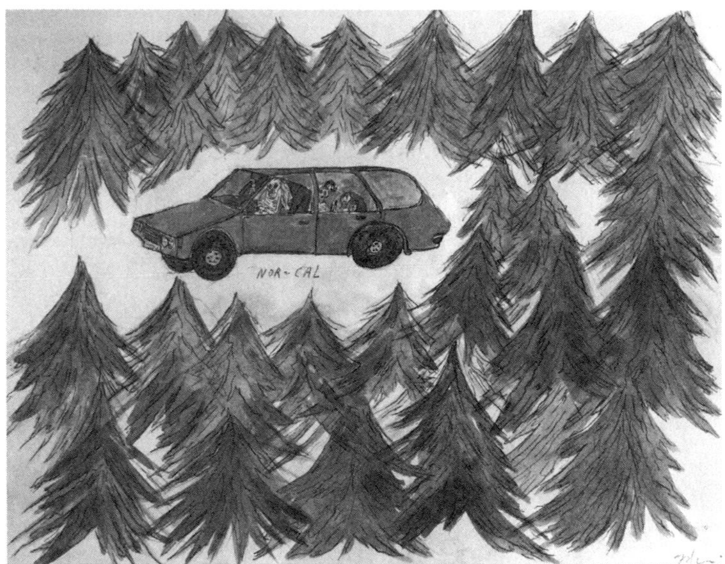

"Nor Cal," watercolor on paper, 2023.

FOUR: YOU DON'T HAVE TO GO HOME BUT YOU CAN'T STAY IN THE PSYCH WARD

When I was eight and J'nai was five my parents finally split up, and J'nai and I briefly lived with my dad in Gualala, a tiny town just north of Annapolis on the coast. He had rented a one-bedroom house in the woods. J'nai and I shared a futon in the corner of the living room. My mother and Jyoti moved to Ukiah (Puke-Kiah), a shithole town roughly an hour inland. They stayed in the garage of a family friend's house. My mom was starting to seriously unravel, her mania triggered by the nasty break-up with my dad, who was never home and had started fucking his hot, younger secretary. Mom had it out for him. In her sickness, she imagined the worst. She came to our house to try to get my dad arrested and take me and J'nai away.

Has he touched you . . . down there?

No mom, please stop asking that.

I mean, No? I don't think so . . . I guess he could have? Did he? My tiny brain would try to picture it. Or look at my dad and try to imagine it. Which was hideous—his stained teeth! His pokey little body! Like when you have a sex dream about your brother or sister and you feel completely fucked up all the next day, guilty and dirty, the memory of the vision creeping in. At that point it's so upsetting it may as well be true. I truly hated my mom in those moments.

She would call the local police and make a report of his abuse. The cops would come check it out. My poor, alcoholic, non-molester dad had to explain, again, that our mom was severely mentally ill, they had just divorced, etc. As is their wont, the cops didn't ask us if this was actually happening. As in, he denied it, so—voila, wife is crazy, the man said no, so it must be true.

Dear readers, you may be thinking . . . hmm, sounds like he probably was molesting them, and this ding-dong is in denial. Through various forms of therapy, EMDR, and many trips up and down the 12 steps I have come to the conclusion that my dad was a creep to be sure, but not that brand of creep. He was an 80s ladies' man; he sexualized women, bragged about conquests, left sheepskin condoms laying around in his car, invited us into his room when he was in bed with a girlfriend, walked around in his boxer shorts, made us massage his feet. I know this is a *type* of incest, which I learned later is called emotional incest. It's inappropriate and nasty and it definitely did its damage, but he didn't sexualize us. He wasn't affectionate at all, let alone touching us inappropriately.

In our old house in Annapolis, even when my parents were still together, my father had seemed like a visitor. Dad's house looked a lot different than the Annapolis house, which was shabby, but more cozy. There was art on the walls and pretty blankets from India. My dad filled his new bachelor pad with ugly used furniture and discounted dinnerware. It was oddly normal-seeming. He had a breadbox, which I had never seen before. The food he made was strange. My mom had done all the cooking when we all lived together—she made stews and porridge and healthy hippie stuff. Dad on his own cooked us greasy fried eggs for breakfast with bacon and toast smothered in butter. This doesn't sound so bad, but the toast was sugary white toast (forbidden by my mother) and the eggs and bacon were slimy with grease. He smoked while eating and held a gigantic newspaper in front of his face. Then he would pick his teeth with the end of a wooden matchstick. He never ate vegetables. It occurred to me later in life that he had probably learned to cook from his mom, or he remembered gross 50s post-war white people dinners he had as a child and made that stuff. Like creamed chipped beef on toast and pork chops with mint jelly, the most heinous pairing from a truly twisted mind. My dad would gobble it down. Who was this guy? We had never spent so much time around him. But it didn't last long. I think we were only there for a couple of months.

One night my mom came for me and J'nai. The house was down a dirt road deep in the woods, which were dark and silent. J'nai and I were asleep in the corner of the living room floor on a twin futon. We woke up startled to a squeaky urgent whisper and mom standing at the foot of our mattress.

Come on girls, get up, it's mama. Time to go.

My mom was generally very easygoing, in the sense that she wasn't rigid in everyday life. But she had this cross-section of Virgo sun with bipolar disorder rising and schizophrenia moon that, in certain moments, made her oddly determined, immovable, and downright terrifying. In a parental landscape where we had no rules, punishment, discipline, or schedule, this tone shift was abrupt and startling, and we knew it meant business. It was as though we were in a mess hall at boot camp throwing food at each other, and the Sarge or whoever comes in. Stand at attention! We rose and put our shoes on quietly in the black night.

I don't know if my dad was asleep and drunk, or awake and drunk, or awake and hungover, but he came into the living room and saw what was happening.

Get the fuck out of here, Meaux!

My mom didn't respond to him, she just kept hurrying us along and gathering up our things. Her eyes were hubcap-wide and she wasn't blinking.

He stomped over to the foot of our bed, where we still lay, frozen in fear. She stood to face him, *I'm taking the girls, James. I'm taking them. We're going now.*

The words came out in a mumbled stream not exactly at him, more like an automaton. Like Robocop. Robomom.

Suddenly my dad backhanded her across the face. She crashed backward into the wall but sprang right back up. Still Robomom. We were frozen on the mattress on the floor while this scene played out above us. Our parents seemed enormous and brightly lit even though it was the middle of the night, like in Citizen Kane where the camera looks up at Orson Welles from below in order to make him appear more menacing. My dad must've given up because he knew there was no stopping her, but he was still pissed and stayed yelling. She managed to hustle us out the door and into the truck, where we rode in terrified silence, hoping she didn't decide to drive us off a cliff.

Shortly after that my father was sent to a rehab for eight months by his mother. My mom, Jyoti, J'nai, and I ended up in a government-subsidized ugly two-bedroom apartment in Ukiah that I loved; it had doors.

In spite of Ukiah being a disgusting shithole and my mom being insane, I enjoyed those couple of years I spent there with just the four of us girls. It was a much bigger town than anywhere I'd lived before. It was a true dump, though. There wasn't the artsy, coastal hippie vibe I was used to. It was full of strip malls and poor whites—primed for the cottage meth industry and opioid crisis that would come sooner than later. It was ugly. The surrounding wilds were still California-beautiful, but the town itself was treeless and crispy from the inland heat. The more affluent neighborhoods looked "normal," like I had seen on TV, with cul-de-sacs and houses that all looked exactly alike. I hadn't ever lived anywhere where people had lawns or dogs on leashes. And in a town this size, there were enough people that you could have a whole subculture to yourself. Where I came from everyone sort of blended into a weird dingy rainbow. I had only been in schools with twelve people in my grade, and everyone was sort of strange simply because of where our parents had chosen to live. The lines were blurred culturally and otherwise. Here, there were goths, which I had never seen before, and jocks who were just jocks, nerds who were just nerds.

I got bullied immediately in school, because I looked crazy. Kids made fun of my boy's haircut and my thrift store clothes. I also chose to wear gigantic neon earrings that I had no business wearing as a nine-year-old. My gender confusion was already showing. The teasing didn't really bother me; I was too young to care yet, plus I was funny and made friends who liked my freaky style.

I was relieved to be with my mom again and away from my drunk dad. Most of the time my mom was pretty normal, although not normal by societal standards: she was broke, dressed in funky clothes, drove a fucked up car, and didn't really have a job. But on the daily she was OK. Weird, but mostly non-threatening.

I wasn't attached to her, neither a mommy's nor a daddy's girl. Because I was always independent, my mom's extremely loose parenting suited me. I liked adventure, and she pretty much let us do whatever we wanted. Somehow, she managed to keep us all in school and fed. We got the free hot lunch at school, which included lukewarm tater tots and gray hot dogs, which I loved because I had never had them at home. Reagan was trying to get ketchup certified as a vegetable, which I was all for. I spent most of my time exploring the town, and I didn't care what she or my sisters were doing.

Mom slept on a futon in the living room of our two-bedroom apartment. Me and J'nai shared a bedroom, and Jyoti, a teenager, got her own room. I didn't care about what our home looked like, and had never really thought about if we were rich or poor, but Jyoti was mortified and never, ever let any of her friends see our house. We literally crossed railroad tracks to get to our side of the town. It was the 80s, and most sitcoms and popular teen movies were about class differences, or racial inequity masked as class disparity. In *Pretty in Pink*, Molly Ringwald desperately explains to a prying Andrew McCarthy why she won't let him drop her off in front of her house (also across the tracks). *I don't want you to see where I live, OK!?* It's a huge moment in the movie. Andrew McCarthy is chill, but it's clear that this might be his first encounter with a POOR.

Diff'rent Strokes, which I loved, was a hugely popular TV show where two orphaned Black brothers live in a penthouse with an ancient white man and his white . . . daughter? The two boys often served as an "equality lesson" plot point, but also showed the world how much better it was to be rich (and white). There was the cartoon simply called *Richie Rich*, which is just a show about a rich white kid who had robots that gave him a bath and got him dressed for school. *Silver Spoons* was also just a show about a rich white kid and all the shit he had, including a bed shaped like a Ferrari and a mini choochoo train that went through the entire house that he rode around in. *The Jeffersons* was about a working-class Black couple who are climbing class ladders through hard work owning a dry cleaning business, as illustrated in the banger theme song—*Movin' on up to a deeeluxe apartment in the sky*—where they no longer have to eat fried fish or burnt beans.

I started to see the inside of our house from the outside, which I reached through the inside of a TV. In the 70s sitcom

Good Times, about a Black family of five who lived in the projects, the brother slept on the couch in the living room, which was apparently a thing that poor people did. I remember thinking, *My mom sleeps on the couch, and so does this guy, and people are looking down on him and his family. Did people look down on us? Should I be ashamed of this? Good Times* also starred a ten-year-old Janet Jackson—my age. I was watching reruns though, and in my time she was already a major recording artist. She was an actress AND a singer AND a dancer. Triple threat. I loved her and wanted to be her.

For the most part, I didn't mind our shitty lifestyle. I had a bicycle. I biked the crap out of that gross town. Every day I biked the three miles to and from school, gagunk gagunk across the tracks both ways. I biked to the pet store and bought goldfish for 15 cents. I kept them in giant mayonnaise jars I pulled from the apartment complex trash. We never had mayonnaise. The fish would die within a couple of days because I used tap water in their jars. Then quickly and without feeling I would flush their sad little corpses down the toilet and go get another one. I biked to the toy store to watch the gigantic model train go around. One day I heard a bitchy girl at school whisper about another student, *I heard she's on food stamps, gross. They buy generic!* But I loved food stamp day. When my mom got her monthly booklet she would tear me out a one dollar coupon, and I would bike to the magical Circle K and buy a Big Hunk and Lik-a-Stix. Heavenly. That bitch didn't know what she was missing!

I biked to the mini-mall to meet up with my friend Francesca. Her mom was young and glamorous and the manager at Payless ShoeSource. She was made more fascinating by somehow being related to Sheila E. Francesca and I would stumble around the store in ladies' pumps and play with the office copy machine. Sometimes her mom gave us money to go to Pizza Hut, where we gobbled a pepperoni pie, sucked down root beers, and shot spitballs through our straws at the ugly lamps. I slept over at Francesca's a lot. She had an older brother who was never home. There was a photo in the house of him wearing a leather jacket and sporting a mohawk. I was wildly intrigued and always hoped for a sighting of him, which I never got. We would play in his bedroom in the basement, where he had posters of punk bands on the wall. One such poster advertised a concert starring the Circle Jerks. Francesca explained to me what a circle jerk was. I pictured her brother sitting criss-cross applesauce in a circle with a bunch of other guys with mohawks, each guy masturbating the one next to him, jizz flying and splattering on the grim brown wall paneling. It gave me a dirty thrill to think about it, which I did often.

I disliked school deeply, it was boring as hell. My mom let me stay home whenever I wanted. I listened to *Purple Rain* on repeat in my bedroom and made up dances. "Darling Nikki" flooded me with sexual curiosity. I imagined myself as Nikki in the "hotel lobby/ masturbating with a magazine": my lobby would be a dark and vampiric gothic parlor with gold banisters that I would vigorously hump while holding the only magazine I could think of at the time—*Teen Beat*. There was more of a story to Prince than to the other stars that I was obsessed with. Looking back, I think I understood that he had created his persona. I knew it was a costume, a fantasy. There was something strange and exciting about making up an entire affect and look that housed the work he was making. The fact that he wore high heels and frilly blouses yet sang about all of his female sexual conquests skewed my perception of masculinity. It was as though he was a man who didn't care what other men thought of him. He cared about what women thought of him. He also directly addressed questions people had about him and his sexuality. In the song "Controversy" he sings, *Am I Black or white, am I straight or Gay?* He knew he was confusing people, he was doing it on purpose. I somehow had the sense, even at age ten, that Prince was a theater project. He was almost like a musical—a story, a vehicle for what really mattered, his music.

When I stayed home from school I also watched hours and hours of TV (as I still do). Our new town had several radio stations, one being a glorious, all-pop radio station. I called in frequently to their contests and trivia games. One day, the trivia question was to name all the actors that starred in *Leave It to Beaver*. No problem. Barbara Billingsley, Hugh Beaumont, Tony Dow, and Jerry Mathers, as the Beaver. I remember it so well because in the credits they say it all out loud and it was always on. It was a boring and stupid show, and all the characters irritated me, but I would watch anything at all on TV. I won a Casey Kasem Top 40 Countdown record set. There were four whole records in there. I also won a Sister Sledge record. Another time I won a free pizza for making up a jingle for a crappy pizza parlor.

Eat at Joe's Pizza
The best pizza around
Joe's Joe's Pizza
In yummy pizza town

I had an important private career as a DJ as well. I sat on the floor of our messy bedroom, plastered in Wham!, Michael Jackson, and Prince posters, with my limp Ogilvie Home Perm topped with a sad Madonna bow. I pressed Record on my boombox and in my smoothest disc jockey man-voice announced:

Welcome to J.I.B.S. radio! And now we have another hit from the most popular band in the UK, it's WHAM! with "Wake Me Up Before you Go-Go!" These lads are great!

Then I'd play the song from a tiny tape deck that belonged to my mom and keep recording. I would listen back to my masterpiece with all of my favorite songs and marvel at my incredible performance.

I had some romance in my life. I had been kissing another ten-year-old girl who lived in another shoddy apartment complex down the street. She was beefy and also had short hair.

Wanna play monster? I asked as soon as we closed my bedroom door.

OK, but I get to be the princess, she replied.

My monster attack was jumping on top of her and immediately squashing my pelvis into hers and grinding it around and around.

She wasn't my first girlfriend. My first was in Annapolis when I was around seven. Her name was Angela. One weekend, her parents took us camping on a lake to fish. We had our own tent. We spent the days catching bluegills and nights rolling around naked in our sleeping bags. We breathed into each other's mouths and touched each other's bodies. I was in love with Angela. These were the halcyon days of my lesbianism. Gay without shame.

Suzy was 13, vaguely sweaty and big breasted. Suzy was a tad rough around the edges, lived a few doors down in our apartment complex and I liked her because she was older than me—a real teenager! Our mutual obsession with Prince was our primary connection, although I suspect it was more that we were both budding alcoholics (*you spot it, you got it* has always been one of my favorite AA slogans). The first time

I got drunk was at her apartment—an event that was also a major flag of what my alcoholism was going to look like down the line. One night, her older sister Audrey bought us a four-pack of Tropical Bliss Sun Country Wine Coolers. I expertly popped off the caps of the glistening bottles, as I had seen my dad do countless times. Ahhhh, I deserve to relax! I knew from watching him and his friends that this was a celebratory moment, and that people change when they drink. I saw myself as a fun-loving young adult; images of poolside giggling co-eds with bulbous and deeply tanned breasts floated through my mind. The brightly colored labels beckoned me with coconuts, beaches, and possibility. They tasted divine, like sparkling maturity.

We got shit-faced drunk immediately, and Suzy passed out on the flat carpet of her identical apartment. Without a moment of hesitation I crawled on top of her and kissed her big, sour, fruity lips. They were damp and not totally functional. Then I moved down to her chest, French-kissing her nipples through her thin white T-shirt. It left wet, round circles. I was 11, and don't know what I thought was happening with Suzy exactly, maybe I thought she was very sleepy. I don't remember thinking, she's passed out so I can violate her, but I knew somehow that she would be more willing to let it happen this way. Plus, I was drunk. This was the first incident of sexual misconduct or sexual-who-knows-what-the-fuck-happened-when-I-was-intoxicated. I never did anything like that again, but as I continued to drink, similar things started happening to me, nearly every time I drank, which was often. It would get much worse.

Days went by after this with no incident—until one afternoon we were in the kidney bean swimming pool in the middle of the apartment complex with some other kids, splashing around and eating popsicles. Suzy turned to me, and with a blazing gaze she shouted:

YOU'RE DISGUSTING!!! YOU'RE A LESBIAN!

Not *not* true. To my astonishment, in the chaos of all the kids' mayhem, no one heard. My face boiled as I backed away and collapsed slowly inside myself, shoving the humiliation away in the tiny little closet right under my small intestine. This was a new level of shame, beyond bed wetting and getting caught smoking. This was sexual shame, gay sexual shame—but of course I didn't connect it to drinking—I was only 11. I was horrified that she was upset, and that I was this awful thing—A LESBIAN! NOOOOOO. I don't remember even having heard the word before. But there it was, and it was definitely not a good thing to be.

That same year, while still living in Ukiah, my mom and sisters and I went to Vermont to meet my mom's dad for the first time, Grandpa Charles. I didn't know anything about my mother's family, except that she had an older brother she didn't talk to, and a sister, Liz, nearly ten years her junior who had come to visit once but wasn't very nice to us. J'nai had given her a feather she found on the beach, and Liz said she didn't want it because it was dirty.

Grandpa Charles lived alone in a little farmhouse, the house my mom grew up in. Her mom had long since died of cancer. My mother began to crack almost as soon as we arrived. She stopped sleeping. I had the shit luck to be the one to share a bed with her, so I saw her insomnia firsthand, how she stayed up all night long, sitting in bed staring nervously into space. I kept waking up every half-hour or so to see that she was still up, just sitting there in the dark as her marbles began rolling away. I knew by this time what the red flags looked like, and it was clear she was past the tipping point. We anxiously waited out the next few days on the farm until we could go home. One evening, Grandpa Charles made us dinner. It was a sludgy beef and onion stew with a layer of grease on top of it.

Jyoti was repulsed and refused to eat it.

You have to eat it, your grandfather made this for you.

She had a few spoonsful then immediately barfed them up onto the table.

The only other memory I have is that my mother got very upset when J'nai sat on Grandpa Charles's lap. That was a big tell, but I was only 11, so I didn't put that together for a while.

On the flight home, my sisters and I did our best to navigate—talking for my mom, making sure the flight attendants didn't catch wind of her insanity. They asked her if she was ok sitting in an exit row, and could she assist if there was an emergency.

NO, I don't wanna do that! she replied indignantly.

I don't wanna HELP people escape the plane! NO!

At least she was honest. They moved us to a different row.

When we landed in San Francisco she wanted to get to the car immediately. We knew that the next step was going to the round thing where the luggage popped out. We had individual suitcases, our little emblems of autonomy. She refused to pick up our bags and marched us directly to the car. We cried out in protest, but she didn't even seem to hear us.

She piled us into the Toyota Tercel and off she drove. We were supposed to be delivered up north, back to my dad's house—about a three-hour drive, but she kept turning around and taking different freeways. Up the 210, back down towards Oakland, then back towards San Francisco, back to Berkeley. She was on one about going to see an old hippie friend named Bonnie Zee. Which was somewhat of a relief, because if we DID get to Bonnie Zee, Bonnie Zee would surely save us. But we never got there. She kept driving and driving the same 50-mile radius, going nowhere for hours as we hollered in protest from the back seat, endlessly. I saw an episode of *The X-Files* once where a man had to keep driving at 90 MPH or something or else she would explode. She cried and sweated as she floored it, zooming down a freeway, eyeing the gas gauge needle going down as she got closer to her destruction.

When night fell, we pulled into a cheap motel on the side of the road, still about an hour from where we were supposed to be. We had been driving in circles all day long. Me and Jyoti pulled rank and forced J'nai to sleep in the bed with mom while we took the other one. Mom wouldn't let us leave the hotel room for the soda machine or to make any calls. We were too scared to call our dad anyway, fearing his wrath. We just sort of gave up. We left in the morning, piled into the car again, and began driving in the right direction—north. She was still completely out of her mind; more so, in fact. We nervously monitored every driving decision she made. Please keep going straight—oh no she turned on the blinker! Is she turning around? Why is she driving so slow? Why is she driving so fast? It was like being kidnapped except . . . actually it was a kidnapping. Like a movie where a woman is gagged and watching her captors' every move as they methodically do weird shit in the basement, wondering when and how they are planning to kill her. There are ropes over there! He's got hedge clippers!? At one point she got off the highway, which was not what we wanted. We headed towards a four-way intersection, which she plowed right through without stopping, and we T-boned a gigantic truck.

It was actually the best thing that could have happened. It was terrifying, but no one was injured, and we were forced to stop. The driver of the giant truck was a horsey, rancher-type ranch-lady who was sympathetic, thank goodness.

The cops came, and I looked up into one of their faces and said, "She's really nice when she's not like this."

Mom got taken to a nearby hospital, we girls went to the police station in Santa Rosa and they figured out what to do with us. The cops gave us highway patrol badges. One of them drove us all the way up to our dad's house, an hour away. He even stopped in Jenner, where there are a million seals on the beach, honking their honks. He bought us deli sandwiches. I will never forget the kindness of this cop. But also, ACAB forever.

After this trip to Vermont, my mom was having episodes, way more than usual, nearly every month. For a while, when this happened, she would check herself into the psychiatric hospital. Jyoti and I would run to a neighbor, who called my mom's friends. They had been fielding calls like this for months, taking us kids in when my mom was in the hospital, dealing with her bullshit. But our time in Ukiah was about to be interrupted, girl. The day came when she could not be convinced to check herself into the psychiatric hospital, and her friends had had enough. These friends got in touch with my dad, who was fresh out of rehab, and told him to come get us. I had just turned 12 and was about to start sixth grade.

FIVE: JR. HIGHS N LOWS N THINGS

My dad didn't have a place to live. He was couch surfing, but with this emergency he needed to put us somewhere, so my sisters, dad, and I piled into the barn of a family he knew. While I understood they were nice enough to let us live there, I was grossed out by them. It was so humiliating to live with this stinky family. The patriarch wore large, ribbed corduroy blazers, smoked a pipe, and sat in a dusty library office. The mom wore floor-length farm lady dresses with patches and she smelled like rotting fruit. Their son was a dumpy nerd whose pants were too short. He was mercilessly bullied at school, and now we *lived* with him. For self-preservation my sisters and I made sure to stand at least ten feet away from him at our bus stop and not speak to him at school or ever. We slept on mattresses on the ground of his parents' sawdust-filled barn. An old boat that was being repaired hung suspended above our makeshift beds, and rusty tools dangled on the walls. It was drafty and cold. We ate meals with the family but also on the mattresses in the barn. We peed outside and had to use the bathroom in the main house to shower or go number two. We avoided shitting and showering as much as we could.

When I started sixth grade, I immediately acquired a bully of my own—a mean girl from central casting, Shelly Holmes. She was an eighth grader with thick arms, feathered black hair, tiny dark eyes outlined in sticky black makeup, and huge breasts. Unbeknownst to Shelly, I knew how to handle a couple of fat titties. Actually, if she had known that, I would probably be dead. I spent most of my time outside of class avoiding her, ducking into the bathroom to eat lunch, and hiding behind buildings at recess. One day on my way to class she ambushed me and slammed me into a locker.

You think you're such hot shit. But you're just a cold turd.[1]

I knew this was a weak insult; it had probably broken her brain to come up with something, but no matter—I was petrified. She began the work of ruining my life daily. I was a tiny person. My hollow bird arms and popsicle-stick legs had zero muscle, I was less than athletic, and I was terrified by any kind of physical violence. I got so scared that I started refusing to go to school. I sat on the barn mattress and sobbed. My dad asked me what was wrong. I remember this clearly as one of the first times he dadded me, which felt amazing. He called up the school and spoke to someone about telling Shelly to cut it out. I couldn't believe it. Someone was speaking up for me! The school refused to do anything, which angered him more than anything, because he was staunchly critical of how terrible the public school was. "Run by fucking dildos," he remarked frequently. He ended up going to the school and demanding to talk to the principal—who already hated me. He had somehow known I was going to be trouble (my hair). My dad told him that he was going to sue the shit out of the school if they didn't make that hillbilly Shelly back off. It kinda worked. She still sneered at me with malice, but she graduated, thank god.

My dad succeeded in getting us a house through some backdoor lawyering. We were all gonna have our own rooms! It was a log cabin-style four bedroom deep in the forest, dark and cold. The woods were thick and let no light or sun in, but I was happy to have my own room, which was on the second floor. I could climb out my window directly onto the roof, where I would smoke cigarettes under the redwood trees,

1 *I Hate This Place,* Video, 2020. See appendix.

puffing into the empty darkness. My bedroom closet was perfect for hiding in. I had a chunky red candle I bought at Pay N Take, the local weekly rummage sale. I would light it and sit in my closet and write bad poetry. The drawback was that my room was up against the wall of my dad's bedroom, so I could hear his and his many girlfriends' suppressed giggling and muffled humping noises.[2]

It was bizarre living with my dad, who was more or less a stranger to us. This was his first time being sober since he was 12 years old. Once I heard him say, "When I got out of rehab I barely knew I had kids," and there he was, all of a sudden taking care of three adolescent girls. Sometimes he would be in a good mood—not exactly kind, but jokey, and would play spelling games with us. When we inevitably fucked up the dreaded VACUUM, he would pinch our arms and say, "Pincher bugs hate bad spellers!" and cackle. My father was a MENSA guy. He had gone to Harvard—only for one year, dropping out to go to Berkeley, mostly so that he could "do drugs and get away from those assholes." He hated the mispronunciation of the words NUCLEAR and JEWELRY, and would pop off into a self-righteous tirade if we didn't get them right. NOO-CLEER, not NOO-KYOU-LER. Two syllables! JOOL-REE! Not JOO-LER-REE. We could say fuck, shit, cocksucker, and his favorite, asshole, which he believed—after Abbie Hoffman—was a perfect, irreplaceable word. But most of the time dad was silent and pensive. He looked like he was constantly solving the world's most complicated and urgent problems. He behaved as though we lived around him, not with him. Asking him for anything was excruciating.

Around this time, I began to realize he was a huge, well, asshole. He would rehearse his arguments or grievances into the mirror in his bedroom next to mine, and I would get woken

2 "I Am The Wolf," Poem, Age 10. See appendix.

up at five or six in the morning by him and his brutal, wordy tirades. They were scary, and also embarrassing, because he was rehearsing being mean. Words randomly penetrated the walls—*You are a total MORON! Do you have ANY idea of the utter DISASTER you have created with your IDIOCY!? I have never met a STUPIDER FUCKING PERSON in my FUCKING LIFE!* When he'd do this, I'd retreat to my closet and furiously journal about my horrible life. Poetry was quickly replaced by, *I wish my dad would die I wish my dad would die.* I had a digital alarm clock that went off at 7:00 AM for school every morning. When I slept over at my friend Harmony's and came home the next day, the alarm was ripped out of the electrical socket. I could practically feel him stomping into my room and tearing it out in a fit of self-righteous rage, instead of simply pressing the "off" button. Then I'd have to reset it, which meant calling the operator to ask what time it was, because we didn't have any other clocks. He never got used to sharing his house with us.

Who ate all my ice cream? he barked while ceremoniously holding up the Dreyer's Special Edition Vanilla Bean carton for us all to see what selfish little children we were.

It's not how much you ate, it's how much you LEFT!

A line he had no doubt rehearsed in the mirror.

You never knew what you were going to get when he came home. His car would fly up the dirt road, he'd slam the door and stomp into the house with his eyebrows furrowed, chain-smoking and mumbling to himself. Everything was in his way. Including us, of course. He barely spoke, and he treated us like maids. We were meant to keep the house spotless: iron his shirts, vacuum, do the dishes, chop wood, carry, and stack it inside. Or at least that is what we thought. He was angry whether or not we cleaned. He also made us massage his bony feet. If these things were not done he would be angry. I thought my actions had a direct cause and effect on my father's mood—that is the trouble with being a child. You have no power at all, but no one tells you that; the parent is your world, and if the world is disturbed, you must have done something to upset it. I began to actively hate him.

Under his unpredictable fascist rule, I began to take my frustrations out on my younger sister J'nai, and to despise my older sister Jyoti. I was charged with taking care of J'nai, so I resented her. I blamed her for dad's terrible moods and awful behavior. Her room was always messy, and my logic at the time was "dad is gonna come home and be angry because your room is filthy so you better clean it up," and she wouldn't. I didn't know that he was angry no matter what happened. My older sister started to cloud over and hide in her room reading fantasy novels. I felt helpless and abandoned by her. It was not her job to take care of me, or the house, either, but this is what happens when children are parentified. Sibling relationships are trashed, and the whole family unit is totally off balance.

I had a refuge in my best friend Harmony, who was the kind of bestie you can only have at that specific age, right before teen years destroy you. When you are brilliant, hilarious, creative, fun, wild, and you bring that out in each other. In front of your peers, adults, or anyone else, you turn into a shy, awkward, defensive loser with no shine.

Harmony and I bonded over our general loathing of everything and everyone. We hated jocks, boys, republicans, hicks, anything girly, cheerleaders, and more than anything we hated school. We were into music and drawing, fart jokes, living in an abundant grotesque fantasy land where we mocked everything around us. These are still my topmost interests in life come to think of it.

When it came to our artistic talents, we mostly drew naked women. We copied the curvy bodies from Archie comics, tracing Betty and Veronica in their skin-tight pants and sweaters, with big, conical boobs. Then we would upgrade their faces, giving them a pig nose or a cyclops eye, or a mouth with blacked-out teeth, or chop their heads off entirely, with gushing blood spurts from the hole in their neck. We slipped a drawing into Shelly's boyfriend Trevor Markus's locker one day. He was a mean redneck whose family owned a dairy ranch. We stood near the lockers and pretended to talk to each other. Trevor opened his locker and found the folded, college ruled paper. You could practically see a cartoon question mark appear over his crew cut.

Oh man oh my god gross, dude, gross! What the fuck?

The drawing was a naked lady with huge boobs eating a turd out of another woman's butthole.

We giggled helplessly.

You two are freaks, fucking freak weirdos!

A few years ago, Harmony sent me a photograph[3] of us from this tween era. In it, she is wearing an ugly 50s house robe, a gray-haired wig, and pearls. I am wearing boxers with a sock poking out of the dickhole, holding a newspaper and a beer and pretending to beat her. She's laughing hysterically while I mug angry-drunk-husband.

Harmony had enormous freedom, so I stayed at her house at least half of the week. I despised being at home, and my dad didn't care where I was. Her parents were divorced and her dad lived in the woods in a corny, orientalist-style compound he designed. She called her parents by their first names, Sam and Laura, which gave them critical distance and made it easier to make fun of them. Her "room" at Fred's was a standalone cabin with a porch, fireplace, and an outhouse. You had to wipe with the pages from an expired phone book, then cover it with hay and dirt from a bucket on the floor. She had pet rats and built a

3 See appendix.

housing complex for them out of an old dresser. She also built tunnels for them that ran across her bedroom walls. Her room stank of the piss of 10,000,000,000 rats, but it was the best.

At her mom's place, on a farm about ten miles north, Harmony's room was in a barn, up a private ladder-entrance to a totally independent space above the goat pen. The goats were loud and smelly.

Shut UP! We hollered at them in vain.

BAAAAAAAAAA

Harmony hated the goats. I thought they were cute but a bit scary. They were so desperate, hooves clattering on the wooden fence below, thumping through the night. When they bleated, their mean little teeth were exposed and their wild eyes locked in on you. Give me something! Anything! Their milk was delicious, sometimes we would get to drink it fresh and still warm. Harmony's mom made yogurt from it. Harmony always had food at both Fred and Laura's houses. Bagels and fluffy organic cream cheese with avocado or sandwiches on squishy brown bread with sprouts. Fred always tried to get us to eat his repulsive homemade kimchi. I don't know if it was especially bad because he made it, or I just didn't like it. I know it's sacrilegious to be a queer who doesn't like kimchi, but I still don't.

Laura lived on the farm with a married couple, Victoria and Michael. Michael was Laura's boyfriend. They were in a throuple or a polycule or something. Victoria was very stern, with long, straight black hair. I got the sense she was not enjoying her situation. I had never heard of such an arrangement, but it didn't strike me as weird, just gross, because all adults were gross. They all grew weed.

Laura started a business on the farm, a dog kennel called Bed and Bone, which drove us mad with how perverted it sounded.

Darling, let's take the dog to BED! AND BONE!!!!!

Laura would frown at us in despair and go back to walking 70 dogs a day. She had a pedometer.

Harmony had an old, steady horse named Murphy. I was not the most confident horsewoman, so I rode Murphy and Harmony rode Laura's horse, roaming bareback around the fields.

Victoria and Michael had two girls. The older one, Rowan, was a few years younger than us. Rowan dressed like a boy, had a boy's haircut, and played sports. At age ten, Rowan wanted only one pierced ear! LIKE A BOY! On a road trip to the Monterey Bay Aquarium, Harmony and I were making fun of Rowan. Laura told us that some people were born with more Y chromosomes, that Rowan simply had more boy material in her body. This may or may not have been true for Rowan, but for me the concept was mind-blowing and introduced "born this way" into my consciousness. I am grateful to Laura for breaking it down for me so clearly. I just looked Rowan up, and they are currently an emergency services firefighter. God bless. The younger sister, Julia, was a sweet blond femme child that we liked having around.

On the farm was a lawn mower tractor. Michael let me drive it around sometimes. One day I got on it to drive it, and Rowan and Julia sat on the hood of the tractor with their legs dangling down. The mower had an electrical problem and required an adult to turn it off. We rode blissfully around the field until we hit a bump, and Julia fell off right in front of the mower. I tried to stop this giant dangerous machine, but the electrical problem wouldn't let me. The mower ran her over, slicing cutlet-sized chunks from her leg. She screamed in agony. It was so fast. Michael sprinted over and fiddled with the wires to turn it off, as only he could, but not before severe damage was done to this poor kid.

I steered clear of the farm for a few weeks. Julia went to the hospital and got a skin graft, which I had never heard of and the sound of it horrified me. When I returned to the farm, I was scared to see her. I felt so guilty. When I walked into the living room she cried, "Jibz tried to kill me!" I was so ashamed she thought I would try and hurt her on purpose. The adults in the room didn't respond and just let that hang there. My god, these stoned idiots. I carried the guilt around for so long, likening myself to a hatchet murderer, or perhaps a Jeffrey Dahmer pre-teen—would I soon start killing small animals? I never told anyone this story until I was doing my fourth step in AA. I wrote it in my amends list of people I hurt, still thinking I owed this kid an apology. My sponsor was like, "This is nuts. Erase this. The parents owe you an amends for letting you drive that death trap with their kids barely hanging off it. I know you, and you would never hurt a child on purpose." This was a huge relief.

A few years later, when I was a professional teen drunk, I went to the farm in the middle of the night with some out of control punk dudes. I was there to destroy things because I was angry at Harmony for betraying me to Ali, our other friend. She had told Ali a secret I asked her not to tell anyone. And, upon reflection, I had probably turned my guilt about the mower incident into rage. In a drunken whoop, I got these punks to drive to her farm, wake up every person and every animal to harass them, cause a major ruckus, and destroy property. Danny stumbled into the horse paddock, singing Hank Williams songs at the top of his lungs to Murphy, the horse. I passed out having sex with one of these miscreants—pretty sure it was Danny the crooner—in some random shack on the property. One of these dudes, Brendan, crawled into Harmony's bed and she hooked up with him, even though he was a belligerent vandal wrecking her house. At some point I fucked that guy, too.

We left in the foggy dawn and drove back up the coast to where I lived. To Harmony these were dumb teen hijinks, but to me this was the entree into serious teen alcoholism. Later that same night I found myself on their dirt road, the same dirt road where Laura walked all those dogs, where we had blissfully roamed on horseback, on my hands and knees, puking so hard I fell over. Dry heaving in the dust and having a moment of lucid thought: how am I still barfing? Nothing is coming out, but it feels so good.

Between these drunken ruckuses, which were increasing in frequency, I was still living at home with my dad, in what J'nai and I now affectionately call "the murder house." I hid in my room mostly and drew pictures or made mix tapes and collages. I bought an old photo album at a yard sale, the kind with black paper pages you glue pictures into. I remember one collage that I thought was particularly sophisticated, which had a cut-out of Michael Jackson in a suit with rhinestones all over it, doing a high kick with a strained expression. His crotch was prominently displayed. Then, from a fitness magazine ad I cut out a man's muscly arm and fist. I glued it on Michael's crotch so it looked like Michael had a fierce punching dick-arm. I showed my dad, who giggled. My father talked frequently about advertising being the most important industry in the United States, the absolute most manipulative, corrupt bullshit that was only there to uphold capitalism. There was no truth in it, he said. So, I knew that they were trying to sell me Michael's dick, and I wanted to let the world know I was in on its dirty secret. The way to my dad's heart was to make him laugh. Despite wanting him dead, I still wanted him to like me. He loved movies, especially comedy. We watched Mel Brooks, Monty Python, and *SNL*. I was obsessed with Gilda Radner. She was adorable, and her characters were so silly. I watched

Roseanne Roseannadanna over and over again, particularly the episode where she talks about violins on TV. The wordplay thrilled me, and I thought about it over and over. I watched the sketch in my mind when I wasn't watching it on video tape. You could make an entire scene out of one wordplay joke? So much better than just a regular joke! The suspense in the discomfort of her being so stupid was revolutionary to me.

The first time I saw *All of Me* I decided that I knew what I wanted to do with my life—I wanted to be Lily Tomlin as a bedridden awful rich lady. One could argue I made that dream come true in a way. I love Steve Martin as well and listened to his records repeatedly. But the women comedians of my youth truly mesmerized me. For one thing, a lot of them were not traditionally pretty—like Carol Burnett. I adored *The Carol Burnett Show*. I loved that her show was just on a big stage, without realistic sets—it looked like a play. Most of the time she came out and did her own little monologues directly to the audience, bringing them into the experience. It was fascinating to see a woman in control of that kind of environment. I found the men on her show so irritating. They had no subtlety and yelled all their jokes.

For some reason, the Paul Bartel film *Lust in the Dust*, starring Divine, was on TV a lot in the 80s. I'd never seen nor heard of Divine. I couldn't believe that this big, sweaty woman was actually a man in drag. I'd never seen a cowboy spoof, and I thought it was genius. I hated cowboy shows, and they were always on. It was so tiresome that the women were always either whores or standing by an oven waiting for some mean guy who's out on the range to come home. *Lust in the Dust* helped me understand how you could say everything about how dumb a genre was through parody. Then I saw *The Kentucky Fried Movie* and *Amazon Women on the Moon*. Both films are made up of sketches and were hugely influential to me. The content was more raunchy and offensive than *SNL*. I will never forget the commercial for a beer called "Willer," where a bunch of Hare Krishna are dancing on the sidewalk with a VO saying:

After a long day jumping around in your robe, it's time to kick off your sandals and have a Willer.

Sadly, a great portion of these movies do not hold up. They are brutal in that special racist, fatphobic, homophobic, sexist, rape-forward way that movies from the 1980s so often are. Alas.

The first John Waters movie I saw was *Pink Flamingos*. I was probably around 16. Of course, the dogshit scene was what everyone talked about, which I thought was the punkest thing I'd ever seen in my life, but the celebration of criminals and dirtbags was the outstanding content for me. I thought, *This person stands for everything I stand for, this person has articulated everything that I think is stupid in the world*. My sister and I watched *Hairspray* on repeat. I am 50 now and she is 47, and we still send each other text messages with quotes from it. "Mashed potatoes? Faster!" "I happen to have a blemish!" "Let's get naked and smoke." It is a perfect film, and it really showed me how comedy can be such a powerful platform for radical messages.

Hairspray may be the best film about race that a white person has ever made. At least for me it is. From what I've read, Waters was writing about his experience as a teenager, growing up in Baltimore, being obsessed with music and dance TV shows and repulsed by segregation. He not only celebrates Black music in the film, he also uses humor and camp to directly address white supremacy. But it's not without gravity. More than anything, the film shows the stupidity of white supremacy by presenting the white racists in the movie as ghoulish idiots who are dangerous because they are running things—the public school, the TV station, the amusement park the kids want to all go to. And kids just wanna be free! It celebrates the ferocity of teen spirit that is so beautiful even though it's ridiculous. It celebrates Tracy, but Tracy is imperfect. Through Tracy, the film mocks the clumsy imperfect way white people come into consciousness about race and usually act self-righteous and annoying about it. I like the way Waters is speaking from his experience as a teen, which is different from the generally heavy-handed and congratulatory lens of an adult coming into consciousness. I had yet to understand that dance music in America was rooted in Black music, or that moving your body has basically been outlawed by white Christian fuckheads repeatedly for hundreds of years in all kinds of ways.

Another big movie for me at this time was *Dirty Dancing*. By contrast, while *Dirty Dancing* spoke to the prohibition of moving the pelvis; it certainly did not celebrate or even really recognize the Black music that drove the whole story. I absolutely loved this movie as a 12-year-old. I loved it for the dancing, though, the story never grabbed me because Baby was so annoying and the whole thing seemed fake. But I still wanted to live at that sweaty staff dance party. I had the soundtrack on tape, which was 50% excellent. It had all the jams from the dance parties, including "These Arms of Mine" by Otis Redding, which crushed me with longing as a 12-year-old, but it was interspersed with songs from the 80s?! Like, "I Had the Time of My Life." This made me furious, I felt duped. You could TELL it wasn't for the right era! I still hate modern flourishes in period pieces. I like my Jane Austen stiff and stuffy and if the characters talk with modern slang, I am out. How are you supposed to get the tension of the repressed horniness if someone is like, "Spill the tea, bitch?" APPALLING!

I had another saving grace besides Harmony during this time, which was a family who more or less semi-adopted all the weirdo kids in the area. Herb Kohl, a writer and educator, had started the alternative elementary school, Acorn. J'nai went to Acorn, but I was too old to attend. Herb was a short, Jewish man originally from Brooklyn who had also lived for a long while in London, gracing him with a thick New Yorky/Britishy accent that made him seem altogether more worldly—New York and London in one guy?! Herb offered an afterschool poetry class to kids of any age at his artsy compound. Us kids sat around a large oak table in Herb's library outbuilding. We read and wrote poetry at Herb's class in his artsy compound in the woods.

One day Herb brought a real live British Punk Rocker to talk to us. Lizzy looked like she'd stepped out of a frame from my favorite movie at the time, *Sid and Nancy*. She was in her early 20s and dressed in a leather miniskirt, shredded T-shirt, safety pin through the nose, Docs, plaid tights, *Fabulous Stains* eye makeup and a two-foot spiked mohawk. She was magnificent. Herb briefly explained the poverty and fascism of London Town under Thatcher, then asked Lizzy how she and her friends were coping.

Well, most of us are on the dole . . .

. . . *on welfare*, Herb translated.

. . . *we've been squattin'.*

. . . *Living in a building, usually deserted*, Herb explained, *and not paying rent.*

We spot an old biling that looks abandoned, wiff the windows shot out or whateva, and we goy in, drop ah gear, then we piss off for a while and. . .

Explain to us what "piss off" is? Herb asked. *To Americans it means get mad.*

Piss off means we go and fuck off somewhere else for a while, in case someone saw us go in—they would see us come out, you know sose they wouldn't call the filth.

. . . *The police*, interjected Herb.

I went home and immediately shredded up my tights. It was hard to be a punk in the sticks, though. Getting a hold of the accessories needed was nearly impossible. I did chop all my hair off and bleach it. Which my dad was not pleased about.

What the fuck! You should have asked me if you could do that.

Why? You wouldn't have cared.

Yes, but you could have at least asked.

This made zero sense, as he cared about zero things I did. I didn't get it. I had had short hair before, and even bleached my bangs. There was a whole drama about it with the PTA demanding my father stop me from dying my hair, because now all the normal kids wanted to do it. And my dad told them to basically go fuck yourselves. Something about this was different, though.

You don't like it?

No, not fuckin really!

Well Cody's mom likes it, I saw her at Coast Mart.

Well of course Cody's mom liked it! He hollered at me and stomped off.

I was flummoxed for a second at his barking sarcasm, then I remembered that Cody's mom was one of the town lesbians. Although my household was staunchly liberal, we never spoke about gay rights. My dad never said anything disparaging about gays and spoke openly about the importance of not being a racist prick (any Asian accent was fair game, however?); he had reverence for the Civil Rights Movement and for general disruptors, but specific people, such as the town gays, were not discussed. As in, he was a basic white liberal Democrat man in the 1980s. I had already been called a queer, a faggot, a freak, and suffered many a "are you a boy or a girl" holler from redneck pickup trucks, but getting this from my dad was particularly shameful. Could he see my suppressed gayness coming through? I had kinda forgotten about it. Dad's *do whatever you want, be whoever you are, I don't care* attitude had a limit, and it was being a dyke.

Meanwhile, I was still busy being a tiresome sixth grader. Harmony and I got in so much trouble at school that eventually her parents removed her, and she was home schooled. We were especially despised by Mr. Shimon, our nasally, mean math teacher who had webbed arms from a Vietnam injury. He also taught P.E.—the scourge of every child freak. When forced to jog around the baseball field, Harmony and I would walk slowly and drag our feet and make grunting noises at the jocks. Frustrated, Mr. Shimon separated us, making us run the opposite direction from each other, so we wound up running towards each other in a romantic, slo-mo, arms-wide-open moment. Then we were punished further.

My father, always up for a battle with authorities, miraculously convinced my school that the reason that I was so terrible was because I was too smart, and therefore bored. They let me skip seventh grade. The school just wanted me out.

After Harmony left for home school, I had to make some friends. A new girl showed up at school, Melanie. She lived with her single mom, Nancy, who ran a garden store and wasn't home much. Nancy smoked Winstons, which we stole and smoked.

One day we ditched school and, bored, walked around Melanie's neighborhood, with its unremarkable streets and houses along the road—unlike my rural dirt road. You would have to be an avid hiker to rob my "street." There was no one around. We went up to the window of one house and peered in. We tried the front door, which was unlocked. Without fanfare, we walked right in, wandering around like we owned the place. I was excited to be doing crime, but mostly I was curious what other people's houses looked like. I didn't want to rob the place; I just wanted to find something extraordinary. We weren't thieves, we were seekers. That would definitely hold up in court.

I wanted something interesting to happen to me, like discovering a safe in the wall full of stacks of unmarked cash that needed to be ferried out of the US. Or a secret cache of weaponry, or pornography—regular or child, anything would do! But there was nothing untoward or dangerous or interesting in our only breaking and entering spree. I grabbed three quarters from a heart-shaped bowl on the coffee table on the way out.

Nearly dead from ennui one afternoon at Melanie's house, we scoured the place for something resembling a thrill and found a bottle of brandy and a bag of shake weed. Melanie didn't really drink yet, unlike me. So, I showed her how it was done. We went to the park nearby and sat in the middle of the empty basketball court with our supplies on the ground in front of us. My genius plan consisted of first eating the entire bag of shake, then drinking as much brandy as we could manage. Next thing, I was vomiting blood at a picnic table. Apparently, in a blackout moment I had drunkenly chased a jogger down the road. This unfortunately foreshadowed my brand of blackouts which often included chasing people.

I guess someone must have called Nancy, but she was at work and couldn't come get us, so she sent her friend Steven, a tan, blonde, gay man. One of the first gay people I ever knew. When he came to retrieve us, he picked me up and carried me back to Melanie's house in his arms, saying soothing, gay things to me on the way back to her house.

Oh honey, we'll get you home. Oh girl, you really did it.

The town was ablaze with gossip over our debauchery, the news trickling up to the ears of our wretched principal. I was punished once again. The injustice of it all! I wasn't even at school when this happened. I despised this fucking hick town fascist junior high school. I was mandated to see a counselor who tried to get me to talk about my life.

Jibs, what is going on at home that makes you want to drink?

Nothing.

Do you think you have to drink to be cool?

No.

Is there anything you want to tell me?

No.

Of course, everything at home made me want to drink, and, yes, I absolutely thought that drinking was the coolest thing in the world, and that I was most certainly the coolest person at school now that everyone knew I drank like a sailor, and there was no way I was going to tell this dork anything at all about myself.

When I was alone in the detention room, I did my best to imitate bad teens from cool movies. I leaned back in my chair and tried lighting my pen on fire. I would get really scared I was going to start a real fire, and scramble to put it out before anyone caught me. My Bob Marley T-shirt got me sent to the principal more than once.

You cannot wear that shirt to school Jibs, it has marijuana leaves on it. Marijuana is an illegal substance.

Well, it shouldn't be! And besides, Trevor Markus wears a Spuds Mackenzie T-shirt almost every day. That's a BEER shirt, and BEER is way worse than pot! Drunk people kill people in car crashes like every day! People that are stoned don't do anything!

Despite my fact-based weed vs. alcohol crusade, I began to bring vodka to school in a travel-sized Scope bottle and sip it during math class. I lifted up the wooden desktop and peeked at it periodically, as though I were hiding a tiny pet frog or a mouse.

Hiyeee . . . just making sure you are still there and doing ok!

Then I got my 18-year-old boyfriend. I was 12 when we started dating. Yes, you heard that correctly. He had already graduated high school. He and some other juvenile delinquents had been recently arrested for playing mailbox baseball, which had been reported in the local paper, so he was basically famous. He was a punk rocker—most assuredly not the coolest one—perhaps that's why he was dating a 12-year-old—but old enough to hang out with them. He gave me my first mixtape: 7 Seconds, The Cramps, Black Flag, Dead Kennedys, Bad Brains, all still on rotation for me except 7 Seconds, who were shouty—the straightedge bands were always so shouty and self-righteous. Snore. When I told my dad about him, he said it was ok he was 18, that he would rather have me dating this guy than a hillbilly who was age appropriate. I guess he would also rather have me dating an adult man than be a lesbian.

Me and my boyfriend and I genuinely liked each other. This could be Stockholm Syndrome-level delusional thinking, but I do think I was mature for my age, just not sexually. I was quick-witted with a big imagination, like many young girls, and had many adult level responsibilities. I was privy to adult situations, language, and problems. And girls mature quicker than boys, as everyone knows. I actually feel like this boyfriend and I were "friends"—we laughed at the same jokes and liked similar movies and music—but obviously I was far too young to hang out with this guy, and way too young to have sex. Many things are true here, which is what makes this type of crime so complicated and pervasive. Too many girls go through this—insanely bored, under-stimulated, intelligent and capable, with nothing to do, or no encouragement to do anything, maturing physically before they mature emotionally. And in my case desperate for attention—specifically, the male variety, which girls are conditioned to feel gives us value. My boyfriend was an artist, he skateboarded, he was funny, he knew about stuff. I was thrilled to be close to him, but I don't think the thrill was sexual. The attraction was more energetic. Something was *happening*.

I didn't really know anything at all about sex. I knew he had sex; he was "experienced" because he had been dating a high school girl, and I had heard rumors that she gave him a blow job. She knew things. I would have to know things, too.

I asked Harmony while we rode her horses through the brambles one day.

Why isn't it called a suck job!?

I KNOW! What if you didn't know and you went down there and started blowing on someone's dick!

HAHAHAHAH

I was over the moon to have an older boyfriend. Even Shelly blessed me with a nod of approval on the bus one day, which utterly confused me until I realized that she was honoring my accomplishment of statutory rape.

Blow Job Day arrived. We met behind the natural food store, "The Natch," as we called it. We found a spot in the back of the brick building to make out. We kissed for a while, then he lay back on the grassy mound and unzipped his black Ben Davises and pulled out his penis. I glanced at it. I knew it wanted attention because it was moving around and getting slightly longer. Terrified, I crouched on my knees next to him and lowered my head over his groin. It had a fragrance that was musty and claustrophobic. As it turns out, everything about sucking dick is suffocating. As I moved closer to his freakish appendage I felt the warmth of his crotch on my face and inhaled the stuffy, freshly-baked-balls aroma. I took the penis in my little hand and put the top of the penis in my mouth and began to lick it cautiously with the tip of my tongue. It felt soft on my tongue but the little hole in the top startled me. Pee came out of there. Then I remembered I was supposed to suck on it. I put the bulbous knob in my mouth and timidly began to suck. One of his hands went to the shaft, and he guided my head gently up and down with the other. I was startled at how unpleasant it was. How could this be a sexual act? Isn't sex supposed to feel . . . sexy? Or like, good? This felt like a tedious, uncomfortable personal body chore like flossing or combing your hair for lice but you were choking at the same time.

He started to pant rapidly and he said he was gonna come, he was gonna come and then he said I'm coming I'm coming and then he sounded like he was choking for a second, and then something warm and slimy spooged weakly into my mouth. I was not prepared for this. I knew what an orgasm was, sort of. I knew what coming was, so I thought. But I didn't know that they happened at the same time. The stuff that got deposited in my mouth was sweet and gummy. I gagged and looked around helplessly, holding the blob on my tongue with my mouth closed. Eventually I spit it out on the ground. It was white but kinda see-through, like milky snot. It shimmered and glooped in the weeds. He zipped up his pants and murmured, "Oh baby that was amazing." I had always hated that health food store. The 18-year-old waited like a gentleman for me to turn 13 so he could deflower me, which he did in my bed when my dad was out of town. It hurt terribly and I bled. I did not like it. But I very much needed the world to know I was no longer a virgin. I was proud, and made allusions to how much I loved sex to anyone who would listen. I made a big deal at school, acting like I was so sore from gettin' some last night to impress Melanie and whoever else would pay attention to me.

And I drank.

Now that I had given a blow job and was no longer a virgin, the drinking amplified my sexual acting out by a 1000%. I low-key began hating this boyfriend, I thought he was annoying, and I probably knew deep down he was a loser for fucking a 13-year-old. I wanted to hurt him, and I wanted him to know I had sexual power. I got drunk at a party at Herb's house and, in the same room where we had the poetry class and I met the punk rocker from England, sucked my boyfriend's friend's dick. I wasn't coerced this time. I was on my knees at the foot of the bed blowing another 18-year-old with what I thought was professional expertise. My boyfriend caught us exiting the little cabin together. He immediately began yelling in my face, *You're such a fuckin slut*! I slapped him and he pushed me to the ground. I laid in the dirt and looked up at the stars. *This is fucking awesome,* I thought. *I am causing sexy drama, I am a wild party queen, and all the boys want my blow jobs. I am alive, motherfuckers!* I thought I had agency in this. I thought I was at the center of an event. I didn't think I was being assaulted, abused, and exploited. In hindsight, the fact that this asshole called me a slut makes me so furious—god I hate men. Of course I was a "slut," you idiot, you literally taught me how to suck dick.

During this time, my dad spent more and more time away, working the entire week in Santa Rosa, two hours south of our home. We largely had to fend for ourselves. He set up a charge account at the local market so we could buy food. It was four miles away, down treacherous Highway 1, which we would trudge, nearly getting run down by cars whizzing by around the blind corners. We ate a lot of quesadillas. When it got real desperate, we ate tortillas with butter. Which are actually delicious. Sometimes my dad would appear, after being gone for a week, with a car full of groceries. He would say he'd done a "big shop." It felt like Christmas, and he basked in the glory of his responsible, excellent parenting. Then it would go right back to tense silence as the food ran out.

The one good thing my 18-year-old boyfriend gave me was driving lessons. Occasionally my mom would come to take care of us. One day she arrived well on her way to a manic episode. She was pacing and rubbing her fingers together. The first night she was there she didn't sleep, and in the morning we asked her if she needed to go to the hospital. "No, no. I'm fine. Stop worrying."

She didn't sleep the second night either.

The next day she was over the threshold. The other voice, her demon, had taken over and was pulling the strings. She was no longer connected to anything real. She talked about imaginary men coming to get us. She mentioned the next town over, and said it was hundreds of miles away. She talked about people from her past we didn't know as if they were in the room.

I had a green and gold cigarette case from the 1960s I got at the flea market, where I kept my babysitting money. I grabbed it in case we needed gas. We coaxed mom into the passenger seat of her Toyota Tercel, and my two sisters got in the back. Jyoti was 16 but couldn't drive yet. Lucky for me, my 18-year-old boyfriend had taught me how to drive in his mom's white Datsun with a stick shift. So, at 13, I drove us to the hospital two hours away, up the treacherous, foggy coastline, then inland, east over winding narrow mountain roads flanked by towering old growth trees, dark as a cave except a few stars and the headlights on our little car puffing up the hills.

When we got to the hospital the staff wouldn't admit her. They told three terrified adolescent girls who had just driven their mom to their stupid hospital two hours from home that she wasn't sick enough to be admitted. We argued lamely and begged them to let her stay, but they sent us away. Then I drove us all the way back home.

The next morning, our mom was sitting on the couch, having not slept, her eyes wide red with meltdown. We begged her to go back to the hospital. We couldn't tell our dad. He would lose all sight of the situation and just rage at her. How incredibly stressful it must have been to have an ex-wife who was always trying to get you thrown in jail for being a child molester, kidnapping your kids, and otherwise putting everyone in danger. He was fresh out of rehab, and if what they say about alcoholics is true—that we stop maturing at the age we start drinking—he would have had the emotional maturity of a 12-year-old. He took my mom's mental illness personally. I don't blame him. Everyone felt sorry for her and thought of him as the villain because he was such an obvious asshole.

What a difference it would have made to my little psyche if someone—her, my dad, some other adult—had just sat us down and told us what was happening. That we hadn't done anything wrong, and that it was not our job to care for her. Within my family there was a thick silence around all information regarding her sickness. Occasionally, mom would mention her mental illness, which she pronounced "mennal illnuss," and I would feel a pang of shame, as though her acknowledgment was somehow a secret she was betraying. When mom was having a breakdown, we referred to it as an "episode," but never, ever used the terms Manic Depression or Schizophrenia. My father didn't speak of it, either. We had no instructions from anyone on how to handle her meltdowns, even though they kept happening. It was as if she were a time bomb everyone knew was going to go off, yet no one ever thought to train us in disarming it, or to simply stop inviting the bomb to babysit us.

Of course, we had no context for what was happening within the health care system either; we just focused on mom, trying to get her help. In the late 1960s and 1970s, the films *Titicut Follies* and *One Flew Over the Cuckoo's Nest* were released, and Geraldo Rivera won a Peabody for investigating the ghoulish conditions of Willowbrook State School, an institution that housed kids with intellectual disabilities. In 1980, Jimmy Carter signed a bill to fund longer term care of treatment for people with SMH (Severe Mental Health) issues. But a year later Reagan squashed it, and thousands and thousands of people with mental illness were let out on the streets with nowhere to go and no treatment plans to support them. The US—and California, specifically—are still suffering terribly for this.

The 18-year-old eventually went off to college and left me in my horrible little town. I started High School. Which was even worse than the pits of Junior High. I continued to spiral, drink, and cut class. I got in less trouble—because there were more kids to worry about, I suppose, but the general vibe was terror and torture. On the first day of school someone graffitied the hallway with a huge note that read:

Stephanie Richardson's Pussy Smells Like Tuna Fish

I must avoid Stephanie and her pussy, I thought, and I must remember to wash mine. I also had my boyfriend away at college to worry about. We were writing letters while he was away, and I had to maintain that situation so I appeared cool with a boyfriend in college. But it didn't last long. Partying became my life. I found a way to bring the two sides of the aisle together at my school—the freaks and the jock rednecks—

and that was drinking. I had massive parties when my dad was gone. I would demand J'nai go stay at her friend's house. She would cry and say she didn't want to, but I wasn't having it. Teens would fuck in her bunk bed and leave cigarette butts and beer cans amongst her Barbies and special stuff. And I had sex with all of my boyfriend's friends. *ALL* of them. And all when I was drunk. I don't think I had any sober sex after my first boyfriend until I was well into my teens. Many of these guys were older—older than my boyfriend, even. Some by a lot. I wrote a tally, running down the underside of the shelf above my bed, all the boys (and men) I had fucked. The list made me feel like I had control over what was happening to me. Like a checklist of responsibilities or accomplishments.

One of these sleazebags was a 22-year-old gentleman who had been dating my older sister, Jyoti. He was a drummer in the super cool local reggae band. One night after his band played at the community center, he took me to his weed shack in the woods. I was in a blackout. All I remember is crawling around the side of the cabin and retching violently into the ferns. Then he had sex with me, which is beyond comprehension, really. This guy was a handsome surfer, and he married one of my sister's friends. I even went to their wedding. Oh look, there he is on Facebook, living his best life, still in that stupid town. Here's a cool pic of him in a funky hat DJing a local reggaetón night.

In the early morning hours, we left the weed/rape shack and he drove me home in his lecherous, brown Ford Econovan, which had a lionhead airbrushed on the side of it. He dropped me at the foot of our long dirt road so that my older sister wouldn't see us pull up. She found out anyway, of course, and was enraged. Another reason to hate me. They really added up. Many mornings I arrived home like that: destroyed and unable to remember anything at all.

I drank to be accepted. I drank to be obliterated.

At a party that included a pig roasting in a hole in the ground I got punched in the face by a mean girl in our friend group who was a bit older than me. She saw her 25-year-old boyfriend leading me down the road to where his van was parked (another van!). She opened the sliding door and saw us sitting side by side on the back seat. She took a drunken swing at my face, which grazed my chin, then she stomped off. I ran after her. In front of everyone at the party I cried and begged her forgiveness, but also lied and said I wasn't doing anything. Which of course I wasn't, because I was a child. But I couldn't really square what had happened in my mind. I didn't want to fuck her boyfriend, but I was excited that he was paying attention to me. And I was drunk. I did want something, but what? I began to believe that I was a bad person. Her evil best friend cackled in my face. Jyoti was there, too, watching this all go down. Suddenly Jyoti looked at this girl and said, *You're a bitch*. I was startled that someone had stuck up for me, especially my sister, who had every reason to want me punched in the face. There I was, her wild little sister who was creeping into her friend group and fucking her boyfriends. I never took her feelings into consideration, and thought I was more mature than she was. But deep down I wanted her attention just as badly as I wanted everyone else's.

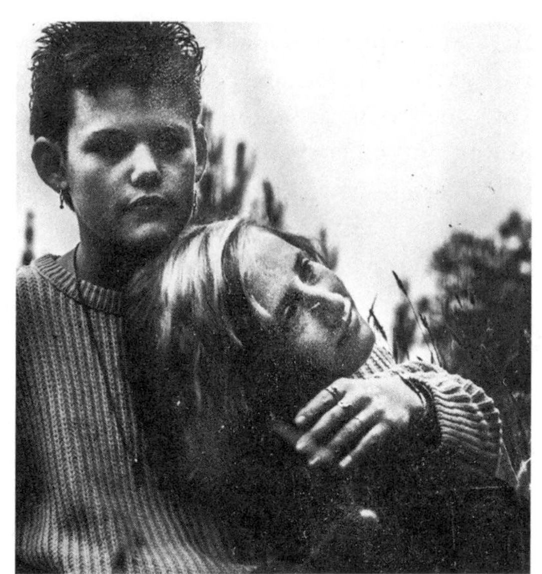

Me and Harmony - 6th grade, 1987.

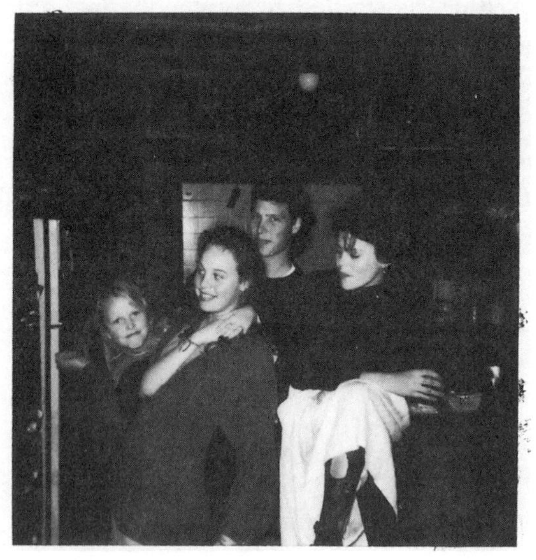

1988 with the siblings.

SIX: SHE WENT TO BOARDING SCHOOL

A miracle occurred in my so-called life. At 14, I was sent to the Athenian School, in Danville, California, just east of Berkeley. Herb, our aforementioned poetry teacher, had heard about blow-job-gate at his compound and convinced my dad to send me away to school. In fact, he said, *You need to get Jibs out of here or she will die.* My father respected Herb. I will be forever grateful to this man and to my dad for listening to him.

I had to start over again as a freshman, which was fine because I had skipped a grade. It was somewhat like being at camp again. A large majority of the kids were weirdos. There were kids who didn't fit in elsewhere, and a lot of rich kids from the nearby affluent area; it was the only private school around. And there were many foreign exchange students from China and Japan.

The campus sat in the rolling foothills of Mount Diablo, dotted with stately oak trees. My brother, David, had also gone to Athenian. When he was there, the area was mostly farmland. By the time I went in 1989, it was surrounded by a wealthy suburb. It was a liberal arts school founded in 1965 and at the time was one of the first co-ed boarding schools, and one of the first integrated schools in the US. The academics were challenging, and they had a service bent that was very serious. There was an Outward Bound program and mandatory volunteer work. I joined the student Amnesty International group. I felt safe there and taken care of. I knew where to go and what was expected of me. And I always ate. There were three meals served a day and there were always snacks available. They had sugary cereals like Froot Loops and Trix, which I had never eaten before, and I could get them any time of the day or night. What had happened to my life?! It was a miracle! My dorm matron was an older woman named Betty who lived in an apartment attached to the dorm. On Sundays we were all invited over to her place to eat junk food and watch TV. We scarfed nachos, soda, and candy while watching Arsenio Hall.

There were roughly eight dorm buildings, built in the 1960s, each housing around fifteen students or so. The girls dorms were up on a hill, the boys on the other side of the campus. There was a large main building where we had meals and held assemblies. We also had our own little mailbox cubbies, which was thrilling whenever someone would leave you a note. Classrooms were scattered around campus and in the library. A lot of students lived in the Bay Area and were day students. I made friends with kids who lived in Berkeley and Oakland, and we'd spend our weekends exploring the city.

Being around these city kids in a place where education was valued showed me that another world was possible. My friends were all artsy music nerds. Everyone was listening to Laurie Anderson's masterpiece, *Big Science,* which was a huge influence on me. I heard Sonic Youth, Negativland, and Parliament Funkadelic for the first time at Athenian, along with countless other bands, and saw films that changed my life. The sounds I was hearing were more complex, nuanced, and brainy than what I had known. On the weekends my friends and I would go see art films at the Elmwood Theater in Berkeley which played the infamous "No Smoking PSA" with John Waters smoking a cigarette before each movie. It was at Athenian that I decided to start spelling my name with a Z instead of an S. I became Jibz. I thought it sounded much cooler.

Another incredible part of going to this school was that at Athenian, every quarter I got to be in a play. I also choreographed two dance performances, for the winter and spring recital. One was a sexy duet with my friend Julie, to Prince's "Alphabet St." We wore fishnets, jean shorts, white button-down shirts, black bowties and bowler hats, and we had canes. This is not unlike a Dynasty Handbag look, come to think of it (minus the shorts). We were especially proud of our mime-driving during the lyrics:

I'm gonna drive my daddy's Thunderbird
A white rad ride, '66 ('67) so glam it's absurd

The second dance, which involved me and three other girls, was more involved, had aspiring political influence, and it made use of my "DJ skills." We recorded a dedication that kicked off the performance. We each had a line:

This dance is dedicated to freedom
Freedom for all people
Freedom for all races
Freedom for the world

Public Enemy's "Fight the Power" kicked in, and we walked solemnly onto the stage in our matching outfits: Hammer pants, black turtlenecks, and monkey boots.

In the end we each picked up an 8.5 x 11 sheet of paper with a letter on it and held them over our heads to spell F R E E. I am pretty sure the Cabbage Patch, the Wop, the Running Man, and the Roger Rabbit were all featured in this performance.

One of my closest friends at boarding school, named James, was a genius-level mixtape maker. He was sort of a mod—he rode a scooter and wore white T-shirts, pegged slacks, Docs, and a parka. He was painfully shy, skinny, and had bad skin. He was silly and fun and incredibly smart. He had rich, neglectful parents who lived in the Oakland hills. He used to take his dad's Porsche out and we would drive crazy all over San Francisco, mostly going to former beatnik cafes and City Lights Bookstore; since we were not even 18 there wasn't much else to do. We drank insanely strong coffee and smoked lung-slashing Gauloises cigarettes at Caffè Trieste in North Beach, had lattes and wrote poetry at the commie hangout Cafe Macondo in the Mission, which was wheat-pasted over with Che Guevara posters and always had a nearby table of activists plotting a failed revolution. James had an incredible music collection, was desperately in love with me, and made me exquisite mix tapes. The tapes went all over the place, into every corner of his massive collection: freaky jazz, James Brown, Albert Ayler, old school ska and rocksteady, blues, early country, obscure punk bands, romantic old Black crooners, British Invasion outcasts, Pérez Prado, Yma Sumac, flute music from the Andes, Gregorian chanting. He would intercut the music with audio recordings from vintage commercials, instructional records, communist propaganda tapes and all kinds of novelty recordings. Sometimes he would call into Christian radio stations with an actual problem and record himself praying to be saved with the on-air pastor. It was masterful.

I still drank at boarding school. For a minute I had a delicate, intellectual boyfriend who dumped me because I returned to school from the weekend "green in the face." Me and my roommate Pilar—who was from Berkeley and introduced me to Gilman Street and Ashkenaz, along with drugs—had a tiny fridge with a PARTY TILL YOU PUKE sticker in our dorm room, where we hid beer. Was there another way to party? Pilar and I would crash UC Berkeley frat parties and steal their stuff or take acid and drive around the Oakland hills all night. One time we saw Eek-A-Mouse, the rail thin, 6'3" reggae singer who wore all leather. We were so blasted on LSD that his arms and legs turned into snakes.

Pilar and I even had a little pop-up acid business for a second. We would buy sheets on Telegraph Ave, go back to the boarding school, and sell them to the rich kids at a 500% markup. This was nothing like being a wasted teenager in the horrifically dark and boring wilds of northern California, but it was still not great. I loved acid. If I could have, I would have been on it 24/7.

Summer break came and I had to figure out where I was going to go. I couldn't live with my dad, who was now in a tiny apartment in the Central Valley's stankest armpit, Stockton. My mother hadn't had stable housing in years but was now situated in Mendocino County in a two-bedroom house she rented for $500. She lived on Social Security and welfare, sometimes cleaning hotel rooms. I didn't have much of a choice, so I went to my mom's.

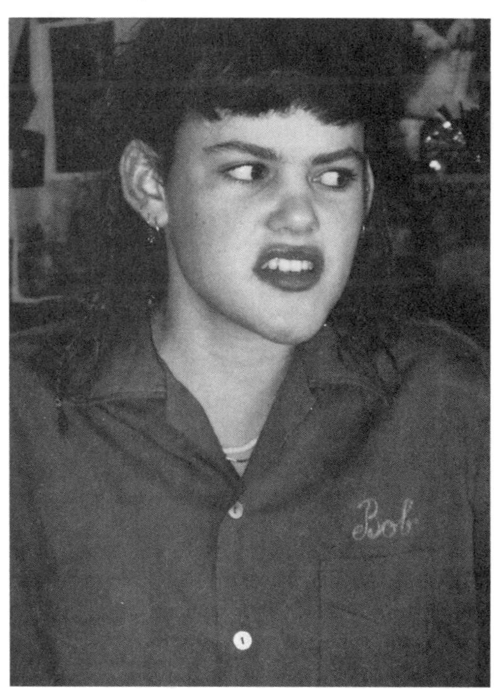

In my chaotic dorm room, 1989.

SEVEN: WHAT MONSTER

This was the last time I would live with a parent. Mom's house was up a narrow paved road, through the redwoods that wound into the mountain. An ancient cemetery sat at the foot of the road on a cliff above the raging, icy Pacific Ocean. I was afraid to stay with her, but she seemed relatively steady, and I wanted it to work out. I was also kind of proud that my mom finally had a real house after so much bouncing around—living in a trailer on the Hog Farm and staying in people's garages. Her friends had built it and rented it to her for cheap. It was a funky house, and in my memory it was spacious, but J'nai recently visited that area and said the house was actually tiny. It had a living room and kitchen area with high ceilings. Like most of the houses out there, it had a loft and a wood burning stove. There were two small bedrooms and a bathroom with a bathtub. A porch, where my mom would sunbathe in the nude, jutted from the side of the house towards the woods. The postman would come, and she'd scramble for her tie-dye wrap to cover up while we watched in horror. She had a lumpy compost pile in the back that wafted rot into my bedroom window. I was alone with her. J'nai was living with my dad, and Jyoti was already away at college. My mom had lucid, even happy days when she would garden, sunbathe, cook, chop wood. Sometimes she would make bread and black bean soup, or sugary donut holes or buckwheat pancakes that we ate with maple syrup and sour yogurt. If she was cooking and accidentally got a blob of olive oil or avocado on her hands, she would immediately start rubbing it into her skin. She regularly made us a special smoothie made of orange juice, bananas, and nutritional yeast. Which is surprisingly delicious. I have never seen or heard of this drink since. For a real treat she rented a VCR from the local hardware store, and we watched movies all weekend. Her favorite film was *Black Narcissus*. She also loved *Stranger than Paradise*. She had excellent taste in music; I still have the records she gave me: Janis Joplin, Bessie Smith, Otis Redding, Sly and the Family Stone. She loved Brian Eno, a favorite of mine, too. Sometimes she would sing while making us snacks:

I'm making a salad for my Jibsy
Here is some cucumbers for my Jibsy
I hope she eats all of the salad
Oh my Jibsyyyyyyy

But this chill nurturer was unreliable. An impending manic episode or a bout of extreme depression was perpetually lurking in the corners of my life. She would spend days in bed, sleeping all day or reading novels in her flannel nightgown and not speaking to me, the house freezing, the stove dead, no food cooking or groceries in the fridge. This would sometimes magically resolve itself, and she would crawl out of her room and back to momming for a spell.

That summer my friend Rose came to live with us. Her family was moving from California back to her father's native Ireland, and we wanted to have some fun before she left the country. Rose had had the world's greatest boyfriend; the kind of guy that sort of floated above all the other ne'er-do-wells, with a cool, bohemian family that was safe and cozy. He had graduated high school and left for Boston to study music, where he fell in love with a concert pianist and broke up with Rose.

Stinging from being dumped, Rose picked the worst guy in our orbit to date. His name was Jesse, a classic, menacing moniker. He looked like a hawk. He had a long, pointy nose, a shaved head, and big nervous eyes that shot around looking for vulnerability. He always wore a leather jacket and had no other interests like skateboarding or playing music or drawing. Actually, he did have a hobby, which was small town crime, like robbing old people. Like all small-town losers, he was tolerated and hard to escape. The kind of person who you're always mildly on edge around, relieved when they don't show up at the party. Everyone was flummoxed by Rose's decision. WHY? Jesse? EEEW! But she wanted this bad boy. Perhaps she loved alcoholics, too. I have been surrounded by drunks and people who love drunks my whole life, so that tracks.

I had a boyfriend, too. Johnny, 23 to my 15, a full-blown alcoholic disaster. One morning my mom and I pulled out of the driveway, and he was lying in the ditch by the side of the road. He had been trying to find our place but passed out before he made it.

Good day, mother! He gurgled. *I am the gentleman caller, here to woo your lovely daughter.*

My mom giggled childishly and brought him inside. She fed him pancakes and we all hung out on the porch. She loved a charming alcoholic, too.

Oh Chonny, yer so funnehhhh!

When we weren't partying and looking for mischief, Rose and I would listen to music and have dance parties in the living room. We were obsessed with The Specials, The Sex Pistols, The Pogues, The Clash, Bad Brains, Toots and the Maytals, The Selecter, Boogie Down Productions, the Dead Kennedys, and especially Sinéad O'Connor. We screamed out the lyrics to "The Emperor's New Clothes" and pledged to shave our heads. Which we both did eventually but just not at that time or together. My mom liked Rose. She was pretty and delicate and had good manners because she was shy.

Rose, yer so nice and so prettehhhh, I wish Jibsy would wear a pretty skirt like that. Jibsy why don't you wanna look pretteh like Rose?

Thank you, Elaine, ha ha, I wish I had legs like Jibs. I'm like a little spider.

PFFFT, no you're like a fairy. Jibsy is wild! She's a wild one.

She didn't say this in a mean way, but she didn't say it in a nice way, either. She generally had a layer of shade atop her commentary. Which was confusing, since my mom sounded like a baby.

Rose provided a spongy buffer between my mom and me. During this time my mom appeared relatively steady; there were some days she would disappear, but I was so preoccupied with our criminal boyfriends and making up dances with Rose, I barely noticed my mom at all.

One day Rose and I went to the river. We arrived at a sandy spot by the water, twisting open 40s and munching mushrooms. Jesse approached me, crouched down, and whispered in my ear.

You know you're the one I really want. His breath was damp and sour. A cigarette hung limply from his claw.

Oh, no. Oh no, no, no. I froze for a moment then shot up from my raggedy towel, bound down the beach and into the water. I splashed around nervously, laughing too hard and too loud. Rose had a deadly jealous streak. We'd already fought over one guy, Sean, another loser who was once my boyfriend and then dated her. While they were together, Sean and I talked at a party at her house. She saw us and got so mad she kicked a hole in the living room wall. A scrawny five feet tall, she loomed large and menacing. She hadn't noticed this interaction with Jesse, to my great relief. But it left me on edge and slightly paranoid all the time that she would find out and suddenly be angry at me and leave.

At my mom's, Rose and I shared a bed. Once, when she was at Jesse's, I woke up in the middle of the night to a shape lying next to me. I was fuzzy drunk and thought it was Rose, then remembered she was gone. I turned away and faced the wall, but I could feel the shape vibrating. The intense confusion brought on terror. My body became rigid with fear. I slammed my eyes shut and eventually passed out and forgot about it. It was probably a dream.

Jesse would always find a way to corner me, no matter how much I tried to stay out of his eye-line. He lurked around after me at Reggae on the River, a big music festival that everyone within 200 miles of nothing to do went to. I watched the bands for hours, until I was so drunk I couldn't stand up. Everyone camped out and got completely shit-faced. I was still hanging out with 23-year-old Johnny, but I was on guard for Jesse for the entire festival weekend.

Rose and I had scored a case of Hamm's and a bag of shake weed. We sat on a log in our jean shorts and bikini tops and immediately ate all of the shake and pounded three beers each. Then we decided to go for a dip. I waded into the sparkling water and immediately vomited up the beer, which floated downstream and ran into some white hippies washing their dreadlocks.

One night me and Johnny were sleeping outside on the rocks. A guy was stumbling around and almost tripped on us.

You and your bitch should watch the fuck out.

Johnny made an attempt to protect my honor.

Fuggg off, assshole.

The guy socked Johnny in the mouth. He sprouted the fattest fat lip I have ever seen, and a blueberry-sized puss bump bloomed on his nose. Always prepared, Johnny had brought a green terrycloth bathrobe with him and spent the rest of the weekend walking around in it while rattling a can for money because he was "deformed."

Jesse spent the sweltering weekend on the shore, roasting in his leather jacket and black jeans, smoking cigarettes and drinking. He came up to me on the riverside the next morning and told me he wished it was me he was there with.

Johnny is a fuckin loser, I would have fuckin murdered that guy for you.

I was terrified Rose and/or Johnny would find out. Johnny was a surfer and could happily beat the shit out of Jesse—if he was ever sober enough to do so—but Jesse was scary and carried a knife and probably had a gun somewhere in his eagle's nest.

Rose moved to Ireland at the end of the summer. Johnny left for Santa Cruz to surf and smoke crack. He would eventually get brain damage when a surfboard crashed into his skull. We remained in touch until he died of an overdose in 1997.

With Rose gone, I could drop the hypervigilance around the Jesse situation, tremendously relieved to know he wouldn't be creeping around as much now that she had left. But he lived up the road from my mom and still came by just as much as when Rose was there. In fact, with Johnny gone as well, Jesse's visits increased. I tolerated it for fear of angering him. I didn't say anything to my mom, who didn't seem to care. My mom—who would go into a full, bipolar meltdown convinced a predator was coming to rape us—didn't mind when an actual predator was in her kitchen, drinking beers, shooting the shit, and stalking her underage child. (Or, in the case of Johnny, having sex with her.)

Then something else started coming to the house. A presence, the one I had felt in my bed weeks before. My eyes would fly open in the dead of night. I would be facing the wall. Ink black darkness. My chest would seize up. Something lay next to me. I was usually bleary with alcohol and thought to myself, *I am in bed with someone, and I don't know who.* As I came more and more out of sleep I would realize I was in my own bed, and that there was no guy there. No Johnny or Jesse or anyone else. Just that shape, a vibrating mass of dark energy. I turned around slowly, my heart pounding violently in my ears. There was nothing.

I had a window in my small bedroom that faced the woods. One night I woke up in the pitch black and saw the shape of a man's head, but bigger and more lumpy, with no discernible features in the frame. It was moving, like TV static. A shuddering and gauzy gray mass. The physical sensation of being frightened by the unknown is very specific, and different from worldly terror. I was frozen. I felt immovable. I felt pressed into the bed. I couldn't speak. I also couldn't tell what was real, if I was awake or dreaming, if I was high or sober.

Jesse kept coming around. One night we went to a party on a farm in Albion. He came home with me after. I remember being on the bed, with him on top of me. His lips were small and cold. I had a red bra on, which I vaguely remember him removing. I was so drunk that I can't remember anything else, but I knew the next day we had had sex. I was sore and I woke up naked, which made my shame and guilt unbearable. I couldn't get rid of him, and I was mortified that people would find out. I stayed home and out of sight for a few days. Home didn't feel safe either. The presence was now visiting me nightly. I got so scared to sleep in my bedroom that I dragged my futon into the center of the living room and slept with all of the lights on. When I woke up in the morning there was a blob of clear goo on the outside of my long johns. It was sticky and see-through. About the same amount as a load of jizz, but it was definitely *not* jizz. There was nothing to indicate where it had come from. The cat had been outside all night. It didn't come from me, because it was on the outside of my pajamas—on my leg, no less. I stretched it between my fingers: it was really sticky. I marveled at its alien nature but also tried to forget about it immediately and washed it off my hands in the bathroom sink.

I told no one. Who would I tell? It was dangerous to tell my mom anything. She was mentally delicate on the one hand, and on the other, she could be nasty. I had to monitor everything I said, for fear she would use it against me, or it would send her into a paranoid meltdown. I was not about to inform her of a possible phantasm in my bed that had been flying around the living room squirting me with goo.

Jesse went to jail for a couple of days for stealing a purse from an old lady. I had a small break and tried not to think about him. Then the day came he got out and called me from town. He told me to meet him on the headlands in an hour. The headlands was an area on the cliffs above the ocean, with paths cutting through the long grass leading down to the beach. He had a liter of Crystal Palace vodka and a jug of orange juice and wanted to celebrate getting out of jail. It was around five in the afternoon. We walked out into the grassy, windy headlands. It was half-sunny California, half-foggy Northern California. We found a log to sit on and started drinking.

I woke the next morning in my mother's futon. I had hospital bracelets on my wrists, and my face and knee were bandaged up. My stomach twisted and throbbed. I had a colossal headache. I was wearing a thin hospital gown. My mom told me gently that I had been in the hospital last night, and that I had gotten my stomach pumped. I didn't remember a single thing past sitting on the log with the vodka and messy Jesse.

My friend Phoebe, who was a cool older girl, called me later that morning and told me what happened. She was running an errand in town and saw Jesse dragging me down the sidewalk. I was unconscious, and he was trying to throw me in a truck to take me to a party with some scary hillbillies. She forced him to relinquish me and guided me into her car. She said I kept telling her I had something to confess, but I could barely talk.

We drove around town, with me trying to say something and not able to. At one point we were parked on a cliff. A big truck pulled up next to us. I looked over at them and one of them said, "What the fuck are you looking at?" I got out of the car before Phoebe could stop me, and started to say, "Lisssen, you redneck piece of schit," etc., but instead fell forward flat on my face, onto the gravel, and cracked my eyebrow open. I still have a thin purple scar there.

Phoebe took me back to her house, where her husband Paco immediately saw that I needed to be hospitalized. They were about to put me in their car when Jesse showed up at the door, demanding I be handed back to him. Paco punched him. Then they took me to the hospital and the doctors pumped my stomach and called my mom. The nurses didn't believe Phoebe that I had only been drinking. I was so fucked up, they thought I was on heroin. My mom and I didn't talk about what had happened. For a couple of days, she nursed me as though I had a bad cold. Internally I was in turmoil. I didn't understand what was happening to me. I thought I must have somehow wanted this, that I was just rotten, not worth caring for or protecting.

Jesse came by one evening while I was still recuperating. I didn't have the strength to tell him to go away. My mom of course let him in. She and I were watching a movie. He sat down on the couch next to me. Suddenly a thin blue haze, like a giant puffy spiderweb began floating through air in the center of the room. It wasn't smoke—it wasn't anything I had ever seen before. I was afraid my mom would see it and it would scare her, but she didn't notice, just kept watching the movie. I looked at Jesse. His eyes were bugging out of his head, staring directly at it. It floated closer to us. We both subtly tried to blow on it, wave it away, but it didn't move at all, just stayed the same shape. He leapt up from the couch.

I'm goin for a smoke.

I followed him. He stood on the porch staring at his feet and sucking on a Marlboro.

You saw that? I asked

Yeah man I fuckin did. What the fuck?

I think this house is haunted.

No fuckin shit. This whole road is haunted. I got chased down my driveway once by a fucking demon. It's the cemetery. I'm out.

And then he left, and he never came back.

EIGHT: GAY AREA

Rose found out, somehow, about my "sleeping" with Jesse. I didn't know it was date rape. I didn't know it was statutory rape. She wrote me scathing, brutal letters from Ireland. Pages and pages of typed rants about what a whore and a terrible friend I was. How people talked about me and what a hoe I was, and that she had always defended me, but she wasn't going to anymore! I really believed I was a terrible, deeply flawed and deeply sketchy person. Every time I got drunk I fucked someone, or, rather, someone fucked me. I didn't tell anyone this was happening, of course. I felt too much shame. It was unbearable.

Finally, I couldn't take it anymore. I quit drinking on my own at age 16. I didn't know I was an alcoholic, though it seems pretty fuckin obvious. My dad was an alcoholic, not me. I had been to AA meetings with him, and I definitely didn't belong there. I also didn't see being sober in AA as some kind of great life—my dad still sucked. I would later learn that it wasn't AA's fault. Turns out there are lots of sober assholes, but better a sober asshole than a drunk one!

All I wanted was to get back to school and continue my new life at Athenian, where I was safe from my mom, these heinous country trolls, and my unstoppable drinking and its consequences (or so I thought). My dad called us one day about a month before I was supposed to return to school. He had failed to fill out the financial aid forms for my sophomore year. I wouldn't be going back. I was utterly crushed. I felt I would die if I had to stay in this shit town, which I probably would. I hid the disappointment, pretended I didn't care and didn't talk about it with anyone.

There was something inside of me that knew this was not enough for me. That I had more to do, that this couldn't possibly be where it stayed. I had seen things. I had seen Divine in *Lust in the Dust*. I had seen Roseanne Roseannadanna. I had heard Richard Pryor records. I had met kids who were smart and interesting, who loved theater and weird jazz. I knew there was more for me beyond my mom's haunted mind and the rapist dirtbags in this big ol' trash pile of a world. So, to prevent further humiliations, and to get the fuck out of that town, I quit drinking and went to live with my friend Saara, who I had met at Athenian. We had been keeping in touch as pen pals.

Saara was a couple years older than me and was on her summer break after graduating from Athenian. She invited me up to her mom's house in southern Oregon. Saara was (and still is) a bubbly, short girl who was tough and bossy. We complemented each other well. She had a small boozy teen crowd in her hometown of Ashland, Oregon; like me, she sorta fit into it, but also like me, had gotten a taste of living in a city and knew she wanted more. We both were weirdos who loved to party. Even though I wasn't drinking anymore, we still did psychedelics. She loved music in the same obsessive, ear-splitting, head-banging way I did, and loved to dance to old soul and hip hop. And like me, she was thrilled with big city culture but not afraid of nature or wilderness. That summer we went on adventures, camping on riversides in Oregon and Northern California. She had a lot of energy and loved fun.

Saara's mom Marta had a long history of taking in strays, as it turned out. Marta was a super intelligent stoner hippie and a consummate fag hag and freak-lover. She had long, brown, fuzzy brushed hair and wore colorful, woven muumuus, but if she was at home she was usually butt naked. It is not lost on me how many fuzzy-haired women are featured in this book. Marta was gorgeous. She looked like a white, Jewish Diana Ross. She had a lush garden and a house crammed with art and wacky old shit from yard sales. She was constantly shuffling around, making jam and digging up weeds in her garden. She had a great love of puns and crosswords, like my dad. She had a big record collection, and at Saara's that summer I heard the two Nina's who would change me forever—Hagen and Simone. She also loved Bette Midler and *The Rocky Horror Picture Show*. She was sort of a glam hippie. She was the first adult friend I had, or at least the first adult I actively trusted. At the Oregon house they had an above ground swimming pool, lots of food, a VCR, art supplies and books all over the place, and Marta had her very own costume room, which we would raid often to make stupid videos dressed up in her musty collection. I was awkward about receiving her care and probably didn't show my appreciation well, but I adored her to the moon. I could feel that she saw me, that she appreciated me, that she thought I was special. Once she left me a message on my answering machine that said:

Yer a bitch Im a witch
Yer a witch Im a bitch

Saara and I bonded because we were both from tiny rural towns with weird hippie parents who sent us away to boarding school so that we didn't end up pregnant with a redneck baby. Marta generously gave us jobs at the organic flower farm she owned. We were terrible employees. At 6:00 AM we would take the truck to the farm and find our way to the blueberry patch and start picking. It was painful and tedious work, and we sang "Waiting Room" and "Raspberry Beret" to keep ourselves entertained. By 11:00 we were exhausted, sweaty, and bored. Then we would sit in the shade and wait until around 2:00 when we could reasonably leave the job. Marta of course knew what we were up to, as our daily hauls were pathetic.

After that summer, me and Saara lived in Santa Cruz for a couple of months, which was awful. Saara had been an excellent student. She was in advanced calculus and had gotten straight A's in high school. She had a clear plan to go to the junior college in Santa Cruz, then transfer to UCSC for marine biology, as it was the 90s and everyone did that. I don't think I realized that was the plan, however. In hindsight I wish I had tried supporting her more on her endeavors, but I didn't get it. My future was very one day at a time. I tried going to the junior college but couldn't afford it and didn't really know why I was there except to copy what Saara was doing. I had asked my dad to help me out with tuition, and he said he would, but he didn't. He couldn't. Or wouldn't? Who knows, but I was disappointed, and jealous of my friend getting to learn stuff while I worked in a movie theater downtown and was forced to wear a polyester uniform that gave me a yeast infection.

When Saara wasn't studying, we took a lot of psychedelics and ate candy and listened to pre-sellout Nirvana in Saara's bed and felt depressed. We ate $1 bean and cheese burritos from Taco Bell, which we called Doo Doo Bell. One time we pledged to only eat orange food. We ate cheese, oranges, Cheetos, Cheez-Its, and nutritional yeast on toast for a whole week. Saara and I didn't exactly know how to take care of ourselves, but it was sort of fun trying. Thank god once again for Marta, who sent us gift boxes full of jams and bread.

We had a studio apartment near the depressing boardwalk. There was a tiny kitchen with a linoleum nook, a bedroom, and a bathroom. I didn't have any stuff, so my "room" was the little nook kitchen. I had milk crate shelves and a foam mattress. I painted a lot on the floor of my kitchen-room. Much of the best art I have ever made was made on the floor.

Santa Cruz sucked and still sucks and will probably suck forever. It was lousy with white baby boomer burnouts and obnoxious gutter punks. There's a hyper masculine surfer vibe as well, along with a thin layer of druggy scuzz on everything. It's also got a long history of poverty and racial violence—white supremacists skirting the town—and a legacy of cops harassing Latinos and Black people and suppressing social justice movements. One night we were on our way to a party, and we stopped at a friend's place so he could grab something. I was watching him from the passenger seat walking into his house, and a girl walked by and said, "What are you looking at?" I answered, "Oh, my friend." She started walking away then stopped, turned back and said, "What the fuck did you say?" and began punching me in the face. Our other friend in the back seat yelled "DRIVE SAARA JUST DRIVE!" We screeched away in the car leaving our friend at his house, with the girl shouting after us, "My boyfriend is going to kill all of you!"

A few months into our stay in Santa Cruz we were eating French fries at a diner when we had a miraculously honest moment for a couple of teenagers.

I hate it here.

I hate it here, too.

That settled it.

We moved up to Oakland where most of our friends from the punk scene and from Athenian days were living.

Saara gave up on going to UCSC, and she and I moved into a one-bedroom apartment in Oakland on 50th and Telegraph near MacArthur BART. It had two proper rooms in it, with French doors dividing them. I had a room! Our neighbors were a couple of leather dykes who were always trying to peer into our apartment and figure out if we were lezzies. We would often hear their chains clunk around and them whipping the living shit out of each other. Which we thought was hilarious and intriguing.

I was dating a guy from a famous Berkeley punk band. I met him at Gilman; he was nine years my senior, 25 to my 16. He had a tender baby face and was quirky. He lived with this other older punk dude Saara describes now as a "jock pig," ha ha, I will call him John. Saara had these heinous dreadlocks Jeff Ott from Crimpshrine gave her (he somehow managed to dread her hair in one evening), and she cut them off and glued them onto John's head. His head started to smoke because there was a reaction with the superglue. I, too, had very embarrassing dirty punk dreads for a hot minute that I made with superglue. Mine didn't start smoking, though. I cut them off with a Swiss Army knife at Reggae on the River. God what a couple of sentences. Kill me.

My boyfriend was plotting a new band he was determined to become famous with. We collectively rolled our eyes at this. It was as though he had a business plan. No one did that! They were trying to come up with a band name. There were many good ones around at that time: Anal Floss, the Wynona Ryders, Frightwig, Trashwomen. One day he told us their choice. WHAT A STUPID NAME! NO! Joke's on us—they laughed all the way to the bank on rotten piles of money. I really want to write the band name here, but I am afraid to get sued. What if I Stormy Daniels'ed that turd? I just did some research on this guy, and he dated, then married, someone who was 16 when he was 30. Puke.

I blew up our cute romance—for the best, considering that I was literally a child. We were at a show together and he ignored me, or so I thought. He was punk famous, being the man on the scene and talking to people and girls, being generally adorable and charming. I wrote him a scathing, unhinged letter about how he was a hypocrite and didn't care about humanity or equality—which was meant to sting because he had "Equality" in Old English font tattooed on his forearm. I guess maybe he thought we were equal in age?

That wasn't the first time an unsuspecting young adult man would feel the wrath of my daddy issues. Later, when I was about 19, I penned a similar letter to Daniel Clowes, my comic artist hero, after he politely declined my invitation to visit the school I was attending. I also wrote a letter to the guy in the band Chumbawamba, because they sang about hunger issues, claiming there was "not enough food" or something to that effect. I thought they should know, IT'S NOT ABOUT QUANTITY OF RESOURCES, IT'S ABOUT DISTRIBUTION! I was unwell, but I was right.

I hung out with my arty friends from boarding school and my Bay Area punk friends, but I never felt punk enough. I had been going to Gilman Street since I was 13, which was a blast, and I loved the bands and bouncing around, but I was afraid of a lot of the boys and the pit was scary. I longed to be tough like Linda Manz, or the women in the Yeastie Girlz, a trio of rapping dirty dykes I saw play there once.

We're the Yeastie Girlz and we got yeast power
We don't shave our armpits and we don't shower

I was still scrawny and weak and scared of confrontation. I always had many infected safety pin ear piercings. One of them came out after getting caught in a ratty knitted blanket. I lied and told everyone it got ripped from my ear in the pit. Many of our friends dumpster-dived for food, and I decidedly did not want to do that. Partially because I didn't want to eat garbage, but also, I was not a suburban kid trying to get away from middle class oppression. I was the child of irresponsible poor hippies who'd never had any food in the house besides government cheese and dried up tortillas.

I think it was Aaron Cometbus who had the grift of putting shards of glass into peanut butter jars and sending them back to Jif HQ. Jif would then send an entire pallet of safe and creamy peanut butter to compensate, and he would live on that peanut butter. Once my friends dumpster-dove behind a chocolatier, and they brought back gigantic slabs of milk chocolate that were perfectly edible but had hay stuck to them. Why hay? I ate it anyway, to be cool. But I really didn't want to live on free peanut butter or eat cold French fries off people's leftover plates in restaurants, and I felt very Reagan Youth for not being tough enough to crawl into a trash bin and find a burrito stump. I also liked showering and being clean, which really set me apart.

I got a job at Amoeba Records on Telegraph when I was 17. I worked behind the counter as a salesperson, which I was decidedly terrible at. I lost people's money and credit card receipts, and I couldn't work the machines or keep track of anything. I soon got fired for not being "professional enough." I sobbed in the boss's office. He was a white, middle-aged, conscious hip hop lover. He stared at me with a clear "not my problem and thank god for that" look on his face.

Saara decided to apply to Hampshire College on the east coast, and she got in. I was going to be on my own again. I was scared and sad, what would I do? I got lucky, though, and moved into a house in Oakland near Ashby BART with some friends of friends, all in college or somewhere in that age. They became my new family. They were all musicians and artists. Patrick wore dresses at the house because "he liked how they felt." He also wore giant wooden Dutch clogs to the liquor store, where all winos on the curb would laugh at him. Eli was a musician and worked for a natural foods warehouse delivery service. Every day he would back the truck up to our front door and unload boxes and boxes of almond butter and Eden Soy. Ross was into Asian cooking and there were always tiny dried fish on the kitchen floor that hurt my bare feet. He told everyone how he ate a girl's butt and there was a dingleberry. I decided to never have my butt eaten. Joan played me *Hounds of Love* at this house for the first time. She also told me that I could take Advil for cramps, and drink coffee to feel more energized during my wretched period. Two of the most important and consistently soothing gifts of my life. Kate Bush and ibuprofen. I was still drawing all the time, mostly on the floor of my bedroom next to my record player, which was also on the floor. My bed was on the floor and my books were on the floor, too, come to think of it. I wonder if my art would get better if I decided to be a person with no shelving again. I had a comic zine called *Glax'O*[4] that was full of morbid cartoons and illustrations to songs I liked.

I got hired by the mom of my friend Pilar (former LSD sales business partner and roommate at boarding school). Pilar's mom, Jessica, was a professor of animation at San Francisco State and was making a film. She lived right off Telegraph Ave. I had spent many weekend nights when I was at Athenian hanging out at Jessica's house and barfing in her bushes. It was odd and a tad humiliating being back in that house as her employee—a staunch reminder that, even though I was still high school-age, "those days were over." But Jessica was a godsend. She knew I needed help—*You just got fired, you're 17, you need work, I like you, you like art, why don't you paint my film?*

I worked from 10:00 to 7:00 every weekday and painted hundreds and hundreds of cels. The movie was an animated version of the Aztec creation story, *The Five Suns*.

---

4 See appendix.

The animation was backlit—meaning, when it was being filmed there was light coming from the underside of the shooting table, and through the cel, as well as light from the top. It gave the film a gorgeous, luminous effect, but it was incredibly hard and annoying to paint in this way. Generally, cel animation has an opaque background of some kind, with opaque cel characters over it—essentially you are only animating the characters, and the background stays the same, flat and with no light coming through the back, like *Bugs Bunny*. With the technique I was doing, you couldn't have a single mistake or bubble or piece of hair or lint or dirt or brush stroke showing because the backlighting would reveal it. It was a forensic hell but satisfying. I became an expert at this skill I would never use again. I stared into the light board and pushed the paint around day in and day out, for two years. I got paid $7 an hour.

I became friends with Linda, Jessica's lead animator on the job. She was a bit older than me. She read mystery novels and rode her bike everywhere. She wore clothing that was new and not full of holes. I didn't quite understand this kind of person, because at the same time she was living more radically than any of the punks I knew by being gay. Jessica also had two other lesbians working on the movie. I guess she liked dykes, probably thought I was one, too. The camerawoman was a lez and there was an Indigenous woman named Connie who I think was a consultant or writer for the film. One day Connie came to work, and I asked her a question, I don't remember what it was, but her reply was, *No, because I am a lesbian*. This was startling as I had never heard anyone simply say that out loud, so frankly and without shame, like, *No, I am a Capricorn*.

Linda was Cuban American, and her crew were mostly Latinx dykes from San Francisco. These were women who had nothing at all to do with men. They didn't talk to men, didn't talk about men, didn't care *about* men, didn't patronize men's businesses if they could help it. I thought men were idiotic, but I had so many of them as friends. What was I missing?

These advanced humans would take me on what they called "a journey" over the weekends. We went to clubs in San Francisco, got wasted (I was drinking again), went to dyke softball games, and drove around crazy. We frequented a club called Colors, which had a POC dyke dance night. Linda was definitely guiding me out, although I didn't totally get it at the time. She knew before I did that I was a big dyke. Straight women simply do not hang out with lezzies all the time unless they want some pussy, even if they are in utter denial. But as they say, if you hang out in the barber shop, you're gonna get a haircut. One night at Colors, Linda asked me who I thought was attractive. I saw a beefy woman, butch, with long black hair parted down the middle. A hot as hell LHB (Long Haired Butch).

I think she's hot, I said.

HER???

Linda's reaction confused me. I wasn't sure what I was supposed to like. I also had a crush on Linda, but knew I was nowhere near femme enough. Her girlfriend at the time was a frightening, buxom lady with saloned hair, a heavily made-up face and adult-lady clothing. I never hooked up with Linda, but I did end up hooking up with one of her friends. This came about through a sordid girlfriend swap.

It was my first time with a real adult butch lesbian. Linda had a crush on a good friend of hers named Rosemary, a blonde femme who was in a relationship with a hot butch carpenter with an undercut named Dev. Rosemary also had an unrequited crush on Linda. Linda asked me one day if I thought Dev was hot. I said definitely. It was arranged that Rosemary would be allowed to hook up with Linda, and in exchange, Dev would be allowed to hook up with me. We went out a few times and we fucked, but I was too scared to really go for it and keep seeing her. I couldn't quite see myself living a fully lezzy life like these women. While there was such a sweet safeness to it that I loved, there were cultural things I felt didn't fit me. I thought the fashion was bad and corny, lesbian music was bad, too earnest, and in fact the whole thing felt too earnest. Too vulnerable. I ended it, and over the next ten years living in SF I kept seeing Dev around. They became a marathon runner and just kept getting hotter and hotter. Linda and Rosemary have been together ever since. They are married and have a kid. I am an idiot. I should have wifed hot Dev! But then I would probably still be in San Francisco lookin corny.

I think Linda considered me to be a baby butch, or at least heading in that direction. I experimented with dressing like her. This particular 1993 dyke look consisted of khakis, white T-shirts, and big flannels, and this other detail, which was to wear Calvin Klein men's boxer briefs with the elastic band showing. You tucked your T-shirt into the underpants band. I tried it. It felt good on my body, and I felt attractive, or something, but I didn't feel like it told my whole story. This was back in the days when how you looked most definitely meant something about you, unlike now where those old signifiers don't mean shit. Hair, piercing, tattoos, clothing, style spoke to your politics, your social scenes, the music you liked, those things helped you figure out who you were aligned with. This was both cool, because you could easily identify a group of people who you'd probably get along with, but also a lot of pressure to pick one thing. And I have never been good with labels. I was extremely confused, because I had another life where I was an art punk, where I still was dressing like a man, but an old man with cigarette burn holes in his cardigan. Even before that, I had worn men's clothing. Very common for teen girls of every era, in fact. For me, as for many of us, it was my hideous developing body that needed hiding. My boobs, in particular. I did not want men looking at me. I was ashamed, and also thought femme presentation was tacky and uncomfortable, which is true. I have gone through many ins and outs, so to speak, with femme presentations. In the early 2000s I had a hot girl phase, where I wore the tightest pants I could possibly find and the dumbest, smallest T-shirts—usually meant for six-year-old boys—paired with a gigantic chunky white belt. I thought it was so hot. Might have never looked stupider. Talk about corny.

When I was around boys, men, what have you, what I wanted was to absorb their freedom. I loved how funny they were allowed to be, at least the ones I was around. Their dynamic was about cutting up and being as harsh and witty as possible. It was exciting, the way you had to be so quick and mean, like being in the middle of a "sports game." I didn't know any cunty fags yet—or, like my close friends now, cunty lesbians. The lack of vulnerability seemed so easeful. Just making jokes and talking about facts. Facts of music, facts of movies, facts of skateboarding, facts of cars, facts of what makes a guitar sound so specifically special on one record as opposed to another record. What a relief to only think about facts, and then be admired for knowing them.

I thought I longed for the obsessions of boys. But really, I longed for the freedom to care about something and be encouraged to do it. As a young adult I realized men's "inherent" freedom to be more comfortable, confident, easeful, encouraged, physically brave, and self-possessed was the entire basis of our patriarchal societal structure. Even if they were abused and unhappy, they were still allowed to dress comfortably, walk around in relative safety, be taken at their word, and pursue niche interests. Not even niche, just interests in general. Naturally, I wanted what they possessed, and the way I knew how to get it was to get them to be obsessed with me, too. Then I could be really, really close to it, and sponge it up. Given my history with my dad—wanting his attention and absorbing his misogyny—I absolutely felt like the attention and admiration I got from men was feeding something, a need in me I couldn't quite imagine getting from a woman. Because in reality, you can't get it from a woman; it's a dynamic that is inherent to hetero relationships. One could certainly argue the contrary, and I have been in butch-femme dynamics that came close, but it is just not the same.

For me, to be with a woman was way too vulnerable. Men and boys were absolute simpletons. I had an almost innate knowledge of how to get what I wanted—I think this is also attributed to early sex and love addiction. Addicts are monstrously manipulative.

This is not psychological rocket science over here. But it has taken me years of therapy and recovery to untangle why this deeply lesbian person that I am had sex with so many men and was in so many relationships with men. In order to do so, I have had to spend time with my hideous feelings of admiration for them and also contend with my addictions. Turns out what is theirs is not *theirs*. Women, queers, nonbinary, trans people, everyone else—we have all of it, too, but they don't tell you that when you are 12, or really ever. The world does not tell you that. If we were told that, this whole shitshow would collapse.

When one of those hicks yelled at me as a teenager,

Are you a boy or a girl?!

what they were really yelling was,

Excuse me, what is a boy and what is, in fact, a girl? Are either of them real? And, if not, then who am I? What do I like? What is football for? What do you know that I don't? Wait, why won't you talk to me, hello? Forget I said that, now I have to kill you.

I tried going to school again, at San Francisco Community College. I took a drama class, which I told no one about because I was embarrassed. But it was too hard to get there with the hours I worked. I was feeling behind, and envious of my friends going off to fancy colleges around the country. I felt like I had missed out. I didn't realize at the time this was not a personality flaw but in many ways a class issue, and alas, decided to give myself an education in the classics. I read the books you are supposed to read in high school on my own: Dostoevsky, Steinbeck, Nabokov, Joseph Heller, J.D. Salinger, Edgar Allen Poe. All white men or women who pretended to be men—I even read *Middlemarch*. What a beast.

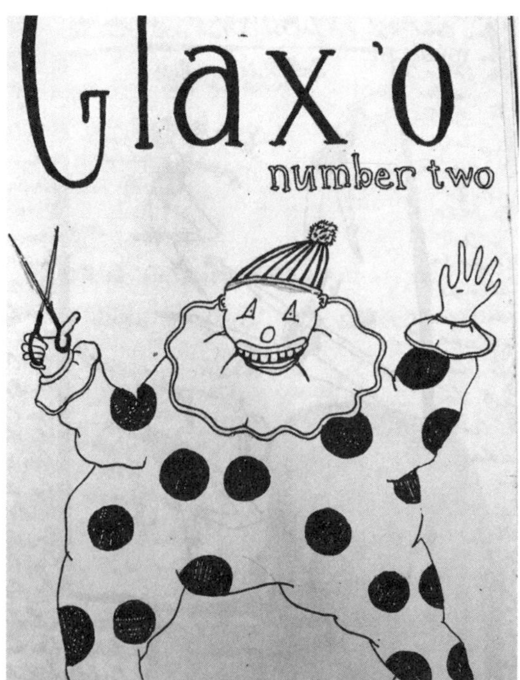

My sad zine, *Glax'O*, 1992.

Crime and Punishment scared me so bad I had waking nightmares about my spine being chopped in half with an axe while I was sitting waiting for the BART. I wrote a diss rap with a Dostoevsky line that I am still equally ashamed and proud of:

Yer more like a sack of flour than a daring cavalier

My friend Oran was going to the San Francisco Art Institute and told me I could get in with my drawings, which I thought was preposterous. But it sounded intriguing; I had never thought about going to art school. You just made art to make it—what could they possibly teach you? I thought it was probably corny (it's pretty evident that being corny was my biggest fear, which is corny in itself). But I was secretly excited to be part of something, and thought maybe my life wouldn't just be working to survive then dropping dead in a pile of sad drawings and bad poetry.

He was right, and I got in. The school wanted my parents' tax information in order for me to qualify for student loans and grants. Marta came to my rescue again and wrote them a letter saying I was an independent woman already on my own for three years. I took out massive amounts of student loans, which I knew was free money. I would just hide or change my name if they came for me. Or just simply ignore debt entirely, like my daddy did.

I moved to the city, into a scuzzy Victorian floor-through apartment on 24th and Shotwell in the San Francisco Mission with three older, working women. One of them drank milk straight from a gallon jug every day after she went jogging. This was the first in at least 15 apartments I lived in with other people during my decade in San Francisco. Most of them were in the Mission, and all of them were either gross or uncomfortable in some way. Or both.

My time at the Art Institute started out shitty. I was depressed and lonely. Always "mature" for my age, I didn't like being a freshman. To combat this despair, I thought myself superior to all the other kids in my year, since I had been a working man and they were all straight out of high school. I was insecure and already world-weary. One of my first humiliating assignments was to make a piece of public art. I drew pictures of women on leashes and in cages and wheatpasted them to the wall of a strip club in North Beach. Little did I know everyone in San Francisco was a stripper and a hooker and they would become my friends. I had a lot of feminist theory to get to, which is something that happens to you when you live in San Francisco whether you like it or not.

When I started going to art school I was mostly interested in printmaking and formal drawing techniques. We had nude models who took breaks every 20 minutes to stretch; usually, they'd put a robe on and go outside for a breath of fresh air. One day an older lady model just put on a T-shirt and walked around looking at everyone's drawings with her gigantic bush hanging out. Which no one seemed to notice.

The Art Institute was an accredited school, which meant they had decent academics. I was hungry for knowledge. I can say that I got a very good college education there. They had a mandatory class called Methodologies of Modernism which led me through the roots of Modernist thinking and being—much of it was about race and explored the ways that American culture was essentially Black culture—thanks to the iconic lecturer Ray Mondini. At one point I thought I was done being an artist and wanted to maybe be an academic. I tried transferring to Rhode Island School of Design so that I could take classes at Brown University, but RISD didn't offer me any financial aid. I guess I will always be California smart.

All through college I worked at least two or three jobs at a time. I was a tutor, and I worked in the cafe where I was really mean to customers, and in the library where I was nice.

I checked out slides, mostly for professors building their lectures. The slides went into carousels. I can't be bothered to explain what that is. Ask Jeeves.

The library was my favorite place on campus. It was beautiful with big windows overlooking the San Francisco Bay, hardwood floors, high ceilings, and stacks and stacks of literature, art books, poetry, zines. They also had an incredible rare books collection. The iconic head librarian, Jeff Gunderson, was an American History nerd and knew about everything that had ever happened, ever. I was in there all the time before I worked there, reading, but mostly napping on the brown leather couches in the quiet corners.

Another job I had, which was off campus, was working as a barback at The Lexington Club, a famous dive dyke bar, often referred to as "the Lex," in the Mission. I was 22 and it was 1997. I had a huge crush on the manager, who shall remain anonymous but would be easy to figure out. We had the hots for each other, and they would schedule me to work their bartending shifts. The Lex was started by Lila Thirkield, who was frustrated with how many gay bars for men there were and how few (none) there were for queer women. Particularly in the Mission, which was lousy with dykes at that time. I had a very good time working there. Too good, some might say. A lot of it is a bit hazy, but I met so many amazing people through that job. I also had the honor of doing a "closing time poem" every night I worked. These poems were not unlike the pizza jingles of my youth. At 1:45 AM I would ceremoniously stand on the bar and shout,

Lesbians, dykes, and freaks that are queer
You don't have to go home but ya can't stay here!

Or something corny to that effect.

One year they held a Halloween costume contest. I came as JonBenét Ramsey. I wore a little girl cowgirl outfit, complete with frilly skirt, blonde wig, white cowboy boots, and white tights with fake blood all over the crotch. Despite it being intensely offensive, I won. Who says lesbians have no sense of humor?! My prize was a Hitachi Magic Wand that is still going strong almost 30 years later. I often had my weirdo friends from art school visit me on the job, which may have been annoying for actual lesbians in the place because many of them were straight dudes. I don't know, I was clueless.

Eventually I was promoted from barback to bartender, starting out doing the day shift, which was one of the saddest jobs I've ever had. The night shifts were full of hot butches and wild femmes, lesbians from other towns, countries, from all over, coming to experience queer nightlife. Joan Jett came in one time, with a lavender crop dangling from her belt loop. There was a great jukebox—people danced, made out, laughed, did drugs, partied, played pool, socialized, gossiped, intrigued, fought, it was the best. But in the daytime, it was practically deserted, with only a scant handful of day-drinking alcoholic lesbians, hunched over the bar in the muted dusty daylight. They seemed lonely as hell. One woman would order four, FOUR cranberry and vodkas minutes before happy hour was over. I always gave them to her, even though it wasn't allowed. It was just too sad not to. Besides not making very good money, the day shift depressed me. I don't ever want to see a sad lesbian. The Lexington Club tragically closed for good in 2015, thus creating more sad lesbians.

Back at school, it was only a matter of time until I got back into performing. There was a big performance and video contingent at the Art Institute. At the time, the department was called New Genres and consisted of a few studio classrooms and a video editing suite. It was all analog when I started there, but soon they added an AVID video editing system. And there was a room with a green screen. A lot of students were making performance art; Karen Finley and Paul McCarthy had gone to SFAI. There was an undercurrent of competition to make the most shocking, or at least the weirdest, work. I thought a lot of the work was too self-serious, sometimes because it was, sometimes because I didn't understand it or was scared of it.

Much of the performance work I saw at SFAI would get the school shut down today. Almost every semester, a dude would make an inverse 16mm film of themselves masturbating, so that their spooge would be black when it came out and their pubic hair white. I can't count how many installations I saw that were made out of doll parts. Dismembered dolls, dolls hanging from nooses, dolls being raped by other dolls, dolls glued onto other dolls to create a long centipede doll.

A serious, Eastern European girl with a severe bowl haircut did a performance in which she smashed the pavement of the faculty parking lot with a sledgehammer until her hands bled. A friend of mine once went to the painting department and slashed dozens of student work while he was tweaking, ruining young artists' bad paintings and lives forever. That wasn't a formal performance, but it might as well have been. A good one, in my opinion. My friend Jennifer Locke did an S/M demo wherein she electrocuted some guy's balls and then made him jack off. It took him a long time to ejaculate—like, an uncomfortable amount of time. That was in Tony Labat's class, of course. You probably can't even say *balls* in a classroom anymore, let alone electrocute them. A student led a Simon Says-style performance with several students following him along on the school's mezzanine (upper deck). Simon Says stand on one leg, Simon says stick out your tongue. Simon Says jump off the roof. Simon did. No one followed him thank goodness, I think he got away fairly unscathed, maybe with a broken leg. There was one performance that went too far, even for SFAI, and made it into the newspaper. For an in-class presentation, a student had stood up and walked over to another kid in the class and slapped him in the face. Non-consensually, of course. Consent wasn't a word yet in 1998.

At SFAI, I took a class with Kathy Acker, who was guest teaching for a semester. We sat in a circle in a cold little studio room. She wore all leathers and had purple hair. She seemed much bigger than everyone else, although I think she was actually smaller. She was mean. Everyone wanted her to like them, but she didn't like anyone, especially me. I wrote a long story about a campy romance between an obsessive mod DJ and a slutty bisexual French girl. She hated it, and announced to the class that it was pedestrian, silly, and boring. I wish I had stood up and said, *YOUR WORK IS FUCKING BORING, KATHY!* That would have been a good performance.

A performance I still think about is when my friends lived in the Diego Rivera Gallery for one week. They had beds, food, a hotplate, and tents. They wore early-VR headset-goggles connected to a camera on the ceiling that had a bird's-eye view of them. Every day, all day, that is what they were looking at the entire week in the gallery. They could only see themselves, from a wide shot 20 feet above. Students could go visit them whenever, or just visit the gallery and watch them like zoo animals. I sat with Jason while he tried to eat oatmeal. He was like a baby shoving it in his face and smearing it on his cheek. He said most things were easier to do if you just closed your eyes instead. I think it broke their brains a little. When the week was over they looked like they had been shipwrecked, and their pupils bounced all around, unable to focus, with big, goggle-shaped indents around their eyes. Not unlike what we are all doing with our phones all day long nowadays.

I finally got up the courage to start making videos. The first one I made has been lost to the analog un-compost pile, unfortunately, but the premise was that it took place in the Methodologies of Modernism class, opening on Ray Mondini talking about Jacques Lacan. There's a flirtation happening between a hot and dumb girl student (me) and a hunky art boy (the excellent and flaming Martiniano López Crozet, who, along with Milena Muzquiz, lead the fabulous punk mariachi band Los Super Elegantes). Soon we stand up and start singing "I Sing the Body Electric" from the soundtrack to the movie Fame. Then the whole class gets up and starts dancing, like they do in *Fame*, but it's art school so it's unhinged. Everyone is a terrible dancer, doing weird stuff, crude Butoh moves, or just staring at their hands.

The other video I made at SFAI was a musical called *Take the Art Bart to Station Broken Heart.*[5] A cornfed idiot girl named Judy moves to San Francisco to meet other artists, but she finds everyone to be bitter and competitive, sex-crazed and gay. I wrote original songs on my keyboard; they sounded like perhaps a five-year-old was playing. The highlight was casting my two straight (?) guy friends as lovers who were breaking up and giving them a split-screen duet. Judy doesn't understand why Frankie is so upset that his friend went away, until she realizes Frankie is GAY! She gets very excited!

Wow you're a gay person! I knew you existed but I have never met one before!

Oy vey.

I had the distinct honor of having been in George Kuchar's famed movie-making class. George is one of a pair of twin brothers from the Bronx who made movies from the early 1950s up until he died in 2011. Mike is also an amazing artist. George was a huge influence on John Waters and many other trashy, camp film mavericks. His class was legendary, and anyone could join. It was in a white box studio room, and

5 *Take The Art Bart To Station Broken Heart,* Video, 1997. See appendix.

the entire semester was dedicated to making a film with him in that room. He would write the script by hand in his giant scrawl and direct the movie. The students would act, shoot, do set design and lighting, and help George with whatever else. He made films with perhaps the most perfect titles ever to be movie titles—*Dingleberry Christmas*, *Hold Me While I'm Naked*, and *I, an Actress*. I wrote a show in 2016 called *I, an Moron*, in honor of him. I also made a Christmas card in honor of *Dingleberry Christmas*.

On the first day of class, he would give a few students $100 to go to Thrift Town on Mission Street and buy all the props and sets for the film.

He would cast the handsome straight boys in the leading roles and make them gay romance each other, directing them in his heavy, Bronx accent with words that sounded like he was joking, but he wasn't. Or, sounded like he wasn't joking, but he was?

OK now put ya hand on his buttocks and stwoke them lovingly like youah petting a beeyootiful cat.

He would put straight couples together in mock display of heterosexual sex norms, much like my other idol, John Waters.

Ok you ahh a mysterweeous vixen, you are sensual, he can't resist your chaaahms even though he is a haaaahdened cwiminal.

I was in the movie called *Demon of the Tropics*, about the goat-eating monster of Mexico, the Chupacabra. I played a singer in a nightclub in Tijuana. I don't remember what else happens except there are strapping young men hunting the beast with cardboard machetes through the wilds of Mexico.

I never got as close to George as I wanted to. That was the semester I had a mental breakdown and went on medication. Depression got to me finally. I was on the MUNI bus to school one day, and I saw myself from above—a person who I was not attached to, mentally. Like my friends in that art piece with the goggle faces. I was witnessing myself going through motions of being a person, but I couldn't connect with my body. It was scary. This has happened frequently over the years when I am in a major depression.

A year earlier, Marta had been killed in a boating accident in Turkey. She was swimming in the Mediterranean Sea, when she swam into the propeller of a motorboat and it sliced her arm almost completely off. The boat was idling in an area where boats were not allowed. She could not hear the motor because her ears were underwater and she was swimming on her back so she didn't see it. She was in a very remote part of Turkey with limited medical resources. By the time her friends got her to a treatment center, the hospital couldn't save her because she had lost too much blood on the journey there. This is not really my story to tell, but it deeply affected me, and I had no outlet for talking about it or grieving. I was glued to Saara's side after Marta was killed, helping her and her sisters out at the Oregon house, but I never really gave myself a chance to mourn the loss of Marta. I felt like I didn't really have a right to it, since she wasn't my real mother. My own parents were not sympathetic. I remember telling my dad she had died, and he said, "Oh, that's too bad." My mom wasn't safe to tell anything to, so I probably glazed over it and pretended I didn't care.

The grief about Marta, and the unfelt feelings of my whole life, were catching up with me. It was 1998, and Prozac had yet to sweep the nation. I had been in bed for one month and had stopped working on my new film. George was my advisor, and I couldn't even show up for meetings with him. I stopped going to school and stopped talking to anyone. I was living in San Francisco on filthy Capp Street with a bunch of friendly man bike messengers, hairy cats, and cockroaches. You couldn't walk down the hall without getting a full carpet's worth of fur and debris on your socks. Capp was a small street just east of the lively commercial Mission Street in San Francisco. It was crawling with busted prostitutes and near-death junkies. We had a pimp on our corner with vitiligo who everyone referred to as "Patches." Rent was mindbogglingly cheap, however. I think my room was $150 a month. It was run down and scuzzy and dangerous. If I was out late at night, I would sometimes run home so it looked like I was already being chased or assaulted, therefore I'd be less likely to get chased or assaulted. I think this was pretty good logic actually. Saara came over one day to check on me. I told her I thought I had mono (why did everyone have mono then?). She looked at me, took a long pause, and finally said gently, *Jibz, I think you're depressed.* This concept, this *word* was startling. People didn't fling it around all the time like they do now. Me? No. That's my mom's thing and that's a really, really bad thing. I was terrified but it felt true, and I was grateful that she saw me, she knew me, and I trusted her.

What can I say about depression that hasn't already been said? It's awful of course, but it's also a bit indescribable. It's somewhat like sadness, but it's very much not sadness. Sadness is a relief when I feel it—it's got a reason, a root, and trajectory. Depression is a lack of trajectory and an absence of feeling. A directionless vibe, dense and immovable, and that somehow is your fault. And there isn't really a way out. Even suicide seems like too much effort, feels too decisive. Like, if you can get it up to kill yourself, you might as well go jogging, too, then brunch.

Most people I roll with are depressives, so I don't have to explain it often, but once in a while, a unicorn will appear and say something like, *I've never been depressed*. Or, *I never was depressed my whole life, and now I am and it's fucking awful.* The latter is more satisfying, partially because one of the worst things about depression is that you gaslight yourself into thinking you are not depressed, just a loser. A lazy loser who is anti-social, boring, not creative, not fun, not funny—actually, you are a bad person who doesn't contribute to your community, and a liar because you lie when you can't show up to things because you are depressed.

I finally saw a psychiatrist in a weird, corporate office building. He looked like Geraldo Rivera and wore a thick brown toupee. He prescribed me Prozac. I felt a bit coked-out for a while, but then I got used to it and became functional again. I was admittedly very upset that I was on meds, like mother! I learned later from a therapist that depression is anger and grief turned inward, and apparently, I had a lot of it. I had never dealt with any of my feelings or talked about what had happened to me as a kid. I joked about being a "teen slut," joked about my mom being fucking crazy, joked about my dad being an asshole, but I had never felt the grief of these things. If someone hurt my feelings, it would just implode inside of me. It has been a lifetime project learning how to squeeze out a tear. After putting in some major hours in therapy, and a million hours into recovery, I am proud to say I am now a weeping little bitch.

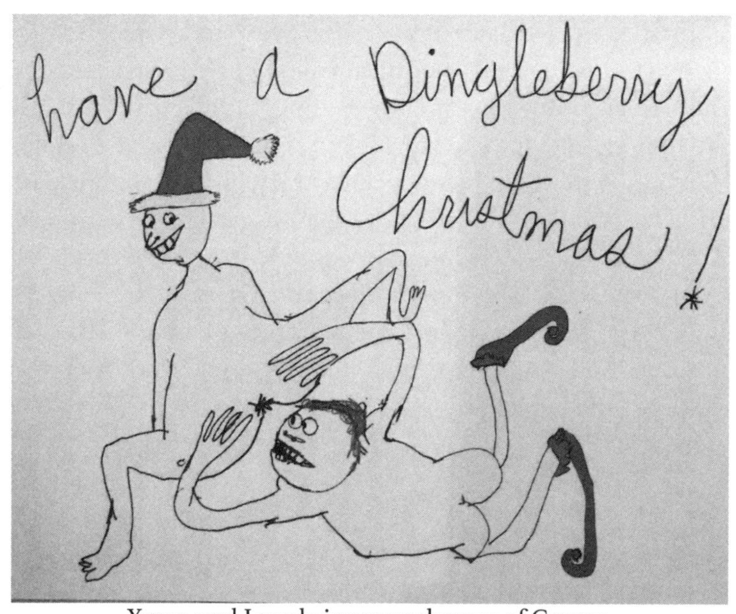

Xmas card I made in remembrance of George.

NINE: LAUGH TIL YOU CRY, LIVE TIL YOU DIE

It was 1994. I was 19, and Mom was suddenly going to marry this weird guy. My sisters and my brother all flew to Hawaii the day before the wedding and hated him immediately. They came to meet us at the terminal in Hilo, Hawaii, near their home. We hadn't seen mom in a few years. She was wearing a brown, floral dress and had prayer beads in her hands and on her wrists. Her thin gray hair was dyed a dusty pomegranate red.

OOO OOO OOOH, it's my kiddddsss, she wheezed.

My mom had a high voice. When people called our house and she answered, they would ask if her parents were home. She frequently pronounced words weird and wrong and had the beguiling habit of talking until she ran out of air. She'd start a sentence sounding like a cheerful ten-year-old girl, and end it like she was dying of emphysema. Then she would take a huge gulp of air and start from the top again.

Welcome to Ha-wahh-ee, This is Doytenanda, we borrowed a car from my friend Shirley, she's got the health food store in town, she's got a little car, it's old, you know, it's funkeh you know, but she let us borrow it, it runs.

Then gasp, *HUNNNNNNNNNNNNNGGHHHHHHH*

Hi Hi Hi, said Doytenanda impatiently.

He had a petite, wiry frame and thinning brown hair that gathered into a limp ponytail at the back of his neck, home to more prayer beads. He was wearing ratty shorts and flip-flops. He was jittery and had the uneasy energy of someone who is immediately trying to convince you how easygoing they are. Think Dennis Hopper in *Apocalypse Now*, but shorter and more paranoid with a decades-long coke habit. We got into the little car. There was a hole in the floor where you could see the asphalt blurring by as we drove. Doytenanda began to tell us young ladies that we shouldn't walk anywhere alone because native Hawaiian men would snatch us up and have their way with us. A racist and misogynist Hari Krishna troll. As usual, we began to joke the pain away.

Would that mean we won't have to stay with them?

Sounds like a dream.

Sign me up for abduction!

In a mental breakdown, my mother had decided to move to Hawaii one day and just left. She abandoned my little sister J'nai out of the blue, all their stuff was hauled to a dump, and J'nai, 15, was forced to live with my derelict father.

Not long after she arrived, my mom met Doytenanda on a black sand beach. He was part of a large number of white Hari Krishna living in that area, where there are many a literal and figurative unmarked road. Not even a grid to be off. In considering manifest destiny, soul searching, moving out west to find oneself, California is land's end. That is where we grew up, I knew that brand of settler. But imagine the emptiness that motivates a broke, mentally ill, disorganized hippie to cross an *ocean*, to find a ride to the other side of the island, then locate a community of like-minded souls to hunker down with. A hard gentrification by tent and tapestry. That is some fierce free spirit ambition. White people are truly limitless in their capacity for busting moves to get away from themselves.

At the ceremony, Mom stared straight ahead as she walked down the aisle. Her eyes were nervous and goofy and separated by a bindi. She wore an ill-fitting sari.

Im sari yer mom is so fucked up

Im sari your mom is marrying a psycho troll

The Hari Krishna celebrated their union while we squished together on a rank old couch in a corner of the large community room. We were disgusted and sad and scared for mom. The wedding guests chanted "Hari Rama Hari Rama" while we chanted,

Hairy Ball Sack!

Hairy Ball Sack!

We whispered fart noises to each other when anyone sat down. After the ceremony, we joined the rest of the people on the floor to eat vegetarian Indian food. A skinny, blonde woman wearing a peach-colored sari plopped some coconut rice and dal on my plate and smiled gently at me, *Blessings, we are so happy for Amrita*.

Did you know they all call mom Amrita???

Amrit-er? I don't even know 'er!

This sucks, am-i-rite-a or am I reeta?

Their house was really a room on stilts, typical for Hawaii and its frequent floods and other natural perils. It consisted of one room and two small decks on either side for sleeping. The main room had a junky, pastiche kitchen, a small couch, and a mini, outdated combo TV/VCR where Doytenanda could watch his favorite action movies. He was a big Steven Seagal fan. There was no bathroom, just an outhouse. For bathing needs, enjoy the ice-cold bag shower under the stairs to the "front door."

We slept in tents under the house. It rained hard the night before the wedding. We sardined inside, damp and muggy, making fun of Doytenanda's name, which legally was David.

DORKI-NUMBNUTS HAHAHAHA!

GROSSANANDA HAHAHAHA!

SCUMMY-PONDA

Would you please DIE-A-NOW NOW NOW

OH GOD, was this really happening? It was.

Crises with mom kept us together. Our gallows humor bonded us and kept us relatively sane through suicide attempts, homeless situations, and frightening episodes. We were a proud, tiny, elite team of comedians, called to action, using well-worn code language, such as, "It's mom." That meant it was time to gear up and frantically try and get her hospitalized. Sometimes it would be, "It's mom—she's doing great!" which any of us would know was definitely a joke. It gave us a boost of energy, confidence, sense of purpose, and little badges of self-pity. Especially when we became busy in adulthood. We took turns saying things like, "I don't have time for this;" or, if you were my brother, who has a wife and kids, you could say, "I have a wife and kids!!" Then a side conversation would ensue between those of us who didn't have a wife and kids, so we could talk about how annoying the person with the wife and kids was, having to always mention their wife and kids. What about us? We had dogs!

After I left home at 15, I didn't see her much for years, but her mania penetrated my life with paranoid phone calls. One of her greatest hits was phoning one of us girls to tell us a guy named "Steve" was coming to get us. I found this mostly irritating. We followed these calls up with phone calls to each other.

Mom called. Looks like good ol' Steve is coming to kidnap and rape me again . . .

Oh, that's weird! Me too!

Looks like he's making the rounds—you're in Oakland and I'm in Houston, seems like a big effort to come get both of us.

Yeah, expensive!

He must be independently wealthy.

Maybe he has a special "traveling for rape" savings account.

That's a tax write-off in Florida, I think.

After she got married, still in Hawaii, she called my brother and told him she had to get away from Doytenanda, who had been chasing her with a knife. Totally plausible that he might do this, but equally plausible that she was making it up, or that it was something not true but that she believed. My brother tried to persuade her to check herself into a psych ward there in Hawaii. Instead, she got on a plane to LA and showed up in a full schizophrenic meltdown at his Venice studio apartment. He couldn't convince her to go to the hospital there, and in California it is nearly impossible to 51/50 someone, which is when you get someone admitted to the mental ward. He put her to bed hoping she would sleep off some of the crazy and sat in a chair nearby to monitor her in case she escaped. He fell asleep, and when he woke up around 3:00 AM, she was gone. It was raining hard in LA, a gift to the landscape but a nightmare for him and his search efforts. He got in his truck and drove around the west side, through the deluge. He found her walking barefoot on the skinny margin up the Pacific Coast Highway. He called me in the morning at 7:00.

Found mom finally, she was walking up the PCH in the rain, barefoot.

Did you honk and keep going?

No, I ran her over.

Phew!

Mom showed up at my sister's house in LA once, off her meds and convinced J'nai's boyfriend was beating her up. J'nai managed to get her to the hospital, making her late for her shift at the children's department of Fred Segal. She called me on the way, stressed.

Dude, mom showed up at my house.

Oh shit, how did she get there?

Who knows? Greyhound? I got her to the hospital but it was rough.

Oh fuck, how did you get her to go?

I told her all her kids were there, about to be raped.

Hmmm, maybe I should go down there, I haven't had any in a while.

Yeah, Steve really knows how to lay the pipe.

I could hear J'nai doing a spit take of her iced coffee over the phone. I remain grateful to have such hilarious allies in our War on Not Enough Drugs for Mom.

Ok, bye, I gotta go to work. Jamie Lee Curtis is coming in today to buy clothes for her ugly grandchild.

TEN: BLAME IT ON THE ROOFIES

After I discovered performing again at SFAI, I was desperate to be on stage. The first band I was in, a garage rock outfit called the Roofies, started around 1998, right before I graduated from San Francisco Art Institute. Everyone seemed to be in a band in San Francisco, why not moi? Despite not having a drop of singing capability, I knew I could entertain by losing my mind and writing funny lyrics. And though my own musical skills were wanting, a lot of my friends were talented. Everyone seemed to have access to a practice space and equipment, and there were hundreds of live shows and alt-spaces to perform. I also had seen so many bands, that I knew there were more ways than one to be a singer. I knew how to do death metal *and* cartoon screaming—how hard could it be?

I asked my two close friends, Eli and Oran, what they thought about this band idea. Eli and I had lived together in Berkeley, and Oran and I had gone to Camp Winnarainbow as kids, only later to meet again through Eli and other Bay Area friends. Eli is a lively goofball who plays bass and many other instruments and is bossy; Oran is a wildly talented jazz and metal drummer, perpetually grumpy and stubborn. They fought constantly but were also best friends, and we all adored and respected each other insomuch as 20-year-olds can, so it was perfect.

I wanted to do trashy garage rock—60s covers and wall-of-sound-adjacent dance music. My vision for the Roofies was that it be a body shaking sound onslaught that made you want to lose it but was also funny and a "show." Eli and Oran were much more elevated musically than what I had in mind for a band, but they were game to try it. They were already in a complicated math rock jazz band called Optimists International, so maybe they needed to have a little more fun. And maybe they wanted to play shows with more than ten music nerds nodding in vague comprehension. Soon we found Andy, who played a 1963 Farfisa keyboard, and a stoner, guitar-shredding maniac named Brent. We had a band! All dudes, though. I wanted back-up singers—I loved that sound—and I wanted girls in the band. I enlisted Saara, who couldn't carry a tune for shit but was a great dancer, my friend Diana, who I was working with at a restaurant and who had a beautiful voice, and another friend, Corrina, who I had a crush on and who was in an emo band and could sing.

At first, we mostly did covers of old 60s dance and R+B songs. One of our numbers was a version of "Blame It on the Bossa Nova," which I rewrote as "Blame It on the Roofies." The original song has Eydie Gormé who I adored, falling in love with a handsome guy, but apparently it was all the Bossa Nova's fault. In my version, it was the roofies that were to blame:

Now I'm proud to say, I am a girl no more
and you can tell—by the stain on the floor
oh the evening was going so awful slow,
until I was date-raped and didn't even know
blame it on the roofies, that crazy pill

We covered the Sonics's "The Witch," changing the lyrics to "Bitch," wherein I dragged a person in our friend group who was always kinda cunty, my most scathing lyric being, "If I were a guy, I wouldn't let you suck my dick." A writer from the SF Guardian called our lyrics a "topical minefield."

We ended up writing original songs, too. At first, they were largely obnoxious, raunchy story-songs I wrote the lyrics for. The song "Frankie the Shoe Fucker" was inspired by an article I read about a man who jacked off in construction workers' boots left on porches.

What the hell is in my shoe?
It looks like Elmer's Glue

I also wrote a song called "Mean Mean Man" that was about a pedophile harassing girls at a sleepover (Eli played the mean mean man). "Fleshy Surprise" was a sarcastic lounge number about my pussy being wrapped up like a present. Good god. For original songs, Brent came up with guitar riffs, then Eli would usually spearhead the arrangement. It was a shared effort, though. I was not great at being in charge, but I brought a lot of songs in to listen to and see if people liked them. If they did, we would cover it. They could learn a song in 15 minutes, it was incredible to me. I have never had the patience to learn to play an instrument well and would rather let someone else do it for me, which feels like magic.

The Roofies were good, really loud, and had a lot of power. I worked extra hard at being nuts on stage to make up for my lack of singing skills. It's a cliché, but I can't think of any other way to say that my body became my real instrument. I was dissociated in general, but onstage I felt a full-on somatic release while performing. It was liberating to be able to do practically anything I wanted. I believe people want to see wildness because they need to see it, not just because it's entertaining. It can be a release for the audience as well as the performer, just like how I am heavily inspired and moved by Iggy Pop and Tina Turner, who are driven insane by the violent, mind-shattering sounds of their bands. Watching someone—a woman, no less—move their body freely is exhilarating, and almost enough to hold together a show. The wilder I was on stage, the more strongly people responded. I also brought in my improv skills, freestyling new lyrics and razzing the audience.

It was pure fun being a front man, but it was also a channel for my rage. I hadn't found many outlets for the stored-up anger I was toting around; in some ways, I didn't even know it was there. Songwriting became a conduit, especially for my fury towards misogyny. The lyrics of "Trash Can," for example, were inspired by being slut-shamed:

Everybody talks about me and they say that I'm a trash can
(Trash can, dirty)
Anything goes, you just shove it in.
(You do it with the garbage man)

It was the first time I felt able to be angry about things in a safe environment. Another song, "Monsters," was about my depression, which I hadn't ever really talked about.

I run this way, and they follow,
If I stop, they'll suck me hollow
But how can I run, when they're in me?
Will I have to join . . . their . . . army!?

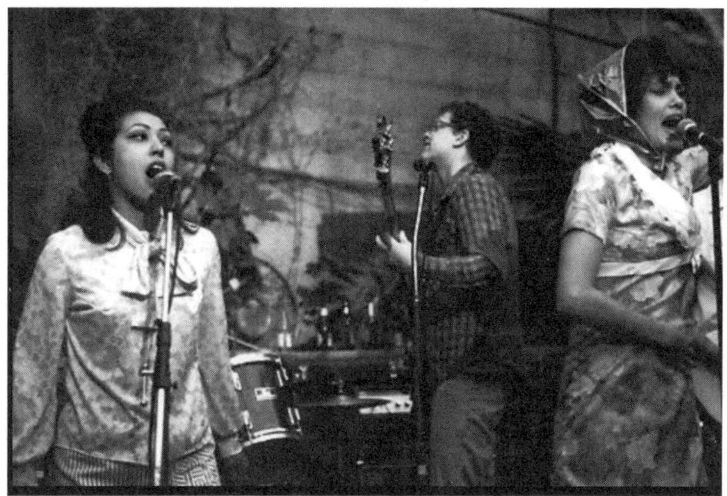

The Roofies at El Rio, 2001.

I also used songwriting to exorcize some of my humiliation and shame. "Love Darts" was about a dude who had played me really hard. Incidentally he was the first person to ever eat my ass, which was amazing. I had lost my fear of errant dingleberries! I thought we were going to be a couple. I was going to be in his art films and get my ass eaten regularly. But he completely ghosted me. It ended up being worth it for the catharsis I felt by getting to scream revenge lyrics:

You ate my asshole! I guess you are what you eat!

Who cares about that guy, anyone can eat your ass, which I also made sure to tell the audience.

I could be powerful and shocking, and I made people scream back at me *and* laugh. I was also ridiculous and campy, so it never got too dark. Some might beg to differ, but that has always been the case with my work.

> *The Roofies skate the thin line between funny and offensive, usually making great big lazy loops on the offensive side. Vocalist Jibz Cameron has a great psycho girlfriend voice, and plenty of attitude to deliver it hot and steaming into your ears. This is funny and crude with no brakes on—if you're easily offended, skip it.*
>
> —Ink19.com

In addition to the prestigious Ink19.com, the *Village Voice* also got a hold of our record:

> *The Roofies are the kind of band you'd want to play for hours: a soundtrack for your perverted prom, where everyone actually drinks and fucks.*

We rehearsed in Eli and Oran's basement studio on 16th and Mission—which was in a crusty storefront below a transient hotel. At one point the sewage pipes of the hotel burst, and it rained hobo shit into everyone's makeshift bedrooms.[6] The rehearsal space was nicknamed "The Wet Spot," cuz it was always mysteriously damp down there. There was the chaos of every type of small crime happening on that corner, along with many people who lived on the street or were in a crack spiral. My friend Jake, who lived at the storefront, had procured a bunch of B.U.M. Equipment clothing at Thrift Town and gave sweatshirts to all the winos camped in their doorway. The bums laughed, *Yep we're bums!*

We also had a practice space at my place when I was living in the Tenderloin, one of SF's most drug-decimated neighborhoods. The rehearsal room was the only room that had walls; it was essentially a box built into the side of the living area, with no windows. It was small and would get really steamy and gross, sometimes there were seven of us in there. The place was a storefront that used to be an old grocery store—the bedrooms were built by my friends, and the walls only went up about six feet, then there was a giant gap that went up to the very high ceiling. We slept in large, freezing cubicles. I started dating my friend Corrina, who was in the band and who was also living there; we had to have muffled sex, because you could hear absolutely everything.

Living with conceptual artists was the best. One morning I came into our kitchen and saw my roommate, Will, binding together a bag of flour with rubber bands. Then he hung it on a hook from the bottom of a kitchen shelf. I looked and saw that there were already several bags of grains and beans all hung in a row, like where you would hang coffee mugs. This

6 For more details on this notorious Mission Street dump and the scene therein, read Beth Lisick's hilarious memoir *Everybody into the Pool*.

was his way of taking care of our mouse infestation. As if they couldn't reach the food if it was hanging up one inch in the air? I just shrugged and moved on with my day. It did look amazing. He also managed to catch a bunch of mice and put them in a cardboard box and deliver them to the police station down the block. Will Rogan forever.

Both the Tenderloin (the TL) and 16th and Mission, our stomping grounds, were the junkie hotspots of the times. The TL was hardcore, but 16th and Mission felt somehow more dangerous because it was mixed in with normal life. There were people trying to go to work, other businesses, and the BART train, which meant there were more variables to navigate. The TL was more *Night of the Living Dead*, but it felt a tiny bit safer because every single person was literally nodding off as they walked. People were so far gone I'm not sure they could even see you. If someone tried to rob you it would be in slow motion, and you could get away fast. In the Mission, people were all kinds of desperate. I was having Turkish coffee at Cafe Istanbul once, and right on the other side of the window I saw a man get stabbed in the stomach. The assailant ran away, and the stabbed gentleman stumbled after him. I kept sipping my spicy coffee but saw the blood trail when I left a while later. In the TL no one could think or move quick enough to stab effectively. They could take a healthy human shit in your doorway, though.

The drummers of the Roofies rotated, as drummers do. Oran had a major heroin problem, which was inconvenient and terribly hard.[7] We also had a revolving cast of back-up singers, some of whom could sing, some of whom could not at all sing.

---

7 Oran got clean and wrote a memoir about his crazy life as well, *Long Past Stopping*. His father is deadbeat dad Jack Canfield of Chicken Soup for the Soul fame. He wanted to title his book *Give Me Some Bread with that Chicken Soup* but the publisher wouldn't let him.

I think we went on exactly one tour, to the Pacific Northwest and to Canada. We were supposed to play at UC Santa Barbara, but the school cancelled it because they had an actual roofie problem and thought it would be inappropriate. Vancouver is the only show from our tour I remember, mostly because the venue was in an old tittie bar. There was a stripper pole on the stage that still had the handprints of strippers past. The crowd hated us. A beer was thrown. By the end I won them over through a combo of my demonic performance and crazed dancing. It's not hard to win men over, you just have to appeal to their appetite for violence. Simply spitting on the floor can do wonders for a relationship with a male audience member. In the crappy motel by the strip club, Brent removed all the bulbs from the lamps in his room and replaced them with colored bulbs so we could have a psychedelic vibe for our afterparty.

It was a special moment. You could rent a room in a Victorian for $150 a month, work in a cafe or whatever, be in a million bands, and live on one huge, delicious burrito a day. This nostalgia may be bullshit because I was also insanely depressed most of the time—but the moment in San Francisco was unique, especially when you consider what is possible today in that city. Much of it had to do with being unburdened not only by the hard gentrification that has since come to define the city but also by phones, news, and media recognition. The outside was not let in as much, and the agony of world pain was not relentlessly penetrating like it is now through social media. Our consciousness was smaller, more intimate and more local. In San Francisco, at least, there was freedom in what we were creating, because there was no way to get famous. Self-promotion was making a flyer at Kinko's and stapling it to a flagpole, hoping someone would see. The big thrill was opening up the *SF Weekly* to see your name in the lineup of bands playing at the Bottom of the Hill or Hemlock Tavern. Once in a while, a band would kinda blow up. My friends in Erase Errata went on tour with Sonic Youth, the Osees are a major force now, and there are more, but the Bay Area wasn't really a place where people sought out the next big thing, so it felt very who-the-fuck-cares.

It was never my dream to be in San Francisco. When I lived there, I always felt haunted and unsettled. Part of my discomfort was that I never actually wanted to live there, or anywhere, really—all my choices were based on where my friends were, or where people would have me. Yes, San Francisco was a very creative place, a fun place, a wild place, but it was also dreadful. There is profound darkness in the city, a literal and metaphoric fog of melancholy. There are the ghosts and the grief of thousands who died of HIV and AIDS. There is mental illness, poverty, brutal segregation, and drug addiction every-fucking-where.

My friends and I lived in these fucked-up neighborhoods because we were broke artist kids, and we were the gateway gentrifiers. But we were not separate from our environments. Some of us were mentally ill and some of us were sex workers. Some of us became thieves and some of us became violent. Some of us became the junkies we were dodging on our way home from the bus stop. People slept in our cars and smoked crack in our cars and sucked dicks in our cars. But we did the same things.

The city is shockingly different today—the gradient has nearly disappeared between the worlds. Extreme tech wealth is completely dissociated from the wretched poverty, drug addiction, and unhoused nightmare. Yet, I would argue there is still a relationship between the very destitute and the very resourced. As in, the non-relationship is the relationship. A tech bro with giant headphones on a Segway who practically runs over a person sleeping on the sidewalk is still communicating something. There is still an energetic exchange, but the exchange pulls them apart even more. It's so extreme that the inhumanity is actually exaggerated on both ends.

ELEVEN: BYE, DAD

My dad passed away September 5th of 2001 and was buried on September 10th. All of my family was in the Bay Area for my dad's services, and then they were stuck because there were no flights out. Yusef couldn't go back to Morocco for a month because of the immediate travel bans to Muslim countries and the doubling down on Islamophobia. The world was in a haze of grief and unknowns, as was I. It was impossible to decipher what was collective pain and what was personal pain. My dad had been a talker. It was never a conversation, though—more like a one-way street of facts and opinions till you shriveled up and died. The trick was getting him to talk about something you wanted to hear about. The thing I kept thinking during this strange moment in America was that I wished my dad would explain what was happening.

On the morning of August 6th he had gone to see his acupuncturist in Berkeley. He sat down and said to his doctor he wasn't feeling right. Then he had a heart attack right there on the table. Luckily, the hospital was around the corner from the acupuncturist's office. He was rushed down the block to the emergency room.

For the next month, I visited my father in the hospital every day. He was brain dead. The room stunk like death. The nurses came in to swab his mouth with a watery blue sponge every ten minutes. I hated going there and spent most of the time sitting in the hallway, frowning. His doctors said he was most likely going to be a vegetable (this just autocorrected to "vegetarian." Fat chance, computer). I just wanted him to die. But this time it was more impatience—knowing the grief was gonna come and just wanting to get it over with—less the *god, please kill my dad prayer* of my youth. It was agonizing having to go there every day and wait for my sisters to catch up with my resolve to yank the plug on him. He would be so upset if he wasn't alive with his brain functioning. It was all he had. He didn't have his health, that's for sure. He walked with a cane because his left knee wasn't working anymore. He had a constant rattling cough from a pack a day of Camel Straights for 40 years, Hepatitis B and C, and all of his teeth were gray. It was annoying and boring to have to sit there day in and day out. My older sister kept thinking he was still in there because he would move his skeletal fingers sometimes or have a brief eye flutter—which is not a sign of brain activity, just the body doing stuff, apparently.

A variety of disheveled and strange young men showed up to his hospital room in distress: his AA sponsees, which annoyed me. Who is this dirtbag, all freaked out that his sober guru was dying? Oh, poor him, he's *my* dad, loser. Go take a bath and get a job. Dad had been sponsoring men in prison, and most of these guys were formerly incarcerated—newly so, and freaking out. I glowered as they paced the hallways in anguish, asking for information that I stingily withheld. I was envious they had my dad's care and attention.

Finally, my dad was transferred out of the ICU into a sad little room with no windows, like a pre-morgue. He was translucent. His California arms (the left one gets sunshine while driving, the right remains pale) and face-tan long gone, now the color of the flesh under the wristwatch he wore for 30 years. His shriveled frame was lost in a light blue hospital dress. His legs were like bent driftwood poking out, and his face had sunken into his skull. His lips hung open, his mouth a black hole. By this time, he was breathing on his own. He could have lived like that. He wasn't officially on life support. I am astonished that people prefer a loved one to exist in that condition rather than let them move on. I have no idea what it felt like to believe he might return one day. I supposed it would be cool, especially if he came to with psychic powers, like Christopher Walken in *The Dead Zone*—he'd had to wait five years though, and it didn't go well. After roughly four weeks we sisters came to the consensus that it was time. I was technically his first born, so I had to do the job of telling the doctor. KILL HIM! Just kidding. I don't remember what I said.

My dad's financial affairs were a disaster. He hadn't paid his bills, he'd immediately maxed out his credit cards, he had never paid child support, never had a new car lease, didn't own a house. He worked for many of his clients for trade, and later in his life he was doing a good chunk of pro bono work for poor people accused of small crimes facing harsh sentencing. He was in debt for roughly $300K to the IRS. After the funeral we went back to his tiny house in Walnut Creek to go through his things and clean it out. J'nai was looking in his closet and found an envelope with $5,000 cash in it. Knowing my dad, she said, "I bet there is more here." We began poking around in the pockets of his suit jackets and found envelopes of cash stashed in nearly all of them. At the end of our search there was a mound totaling $70K. We stood around it, staring at it. Because he didn't own anything else of value, we were not set to inherit anything. In California, the law is that if you do in fact inherit cash, or anything at all, then you are responsible for the debt of the deceased as well. Naturally we didn't want to tell anyone about all this money. We gave a bunch of it to my dad's brother, Yusef, and we each kept $10K, which we put into safe deposit boxes.

Yusef lived in Morocco and had severe brain damage. He was also a devout Muslim and couldn't have sex unless he was married. When my dad was in the hospital, Yusef began spending a lot of time with my dad's girlfriend, Julie. In Julie's grief, she converted to Islam and started making wedding plans. She also decided to move to Morocco with him, Inshallah. They didn't go through with the wedding, thankfully. I thought this behavior was insane, and my siblings and I laughed about it, but I didn't really care. Julie and my dad had met in AA, and about a year after my dad's death she made amends to me for this behavior. I had always liked her. She was a lot younger than my dad but had been around the block—that is to say, she was a sober alcoholic bail bondswoman. My dad once described her as a beautiful porcelain teacup with a big crack in it. She was the first person I ever saw to have a portable phone—although portable is not really what I would call it. It was the size and weight of a car battery. She needed it for her job, and she took it everywhere. I went to a restaurant once with them and it got its own chair.

As we looked through my dad's closets, we came upon another exciting trove. One of the closets had women's lingerie in it, including a red teddy nightgown. *One of his hoes probably keeps stuff here*, J'nai said. Then we noticed the men's size 11 patent leather pumps. Next to the teddy hung a few whips, including a cat-o-nine-tails and a small leather crop. There was also a feather duster. Photos, too. One was of my dad in a bustier, lying on a bed with his ass exposed, being whipped by a curvy, tall, blonde woman.

No one was that surprised to find the contents of the closet. Jyoti did some lackluster pearl-clutching, but gave up when she saw no one else was shocked. In fact, I felt proud of my dad. It was interesting to me that people could change sexually and find liberation when they were so ancient (56). It meant my father was mildly queer. Never in a million would I have guessed that. Classic, mid-century kinky—“wearing women’s clothes” kinky. I loved it.

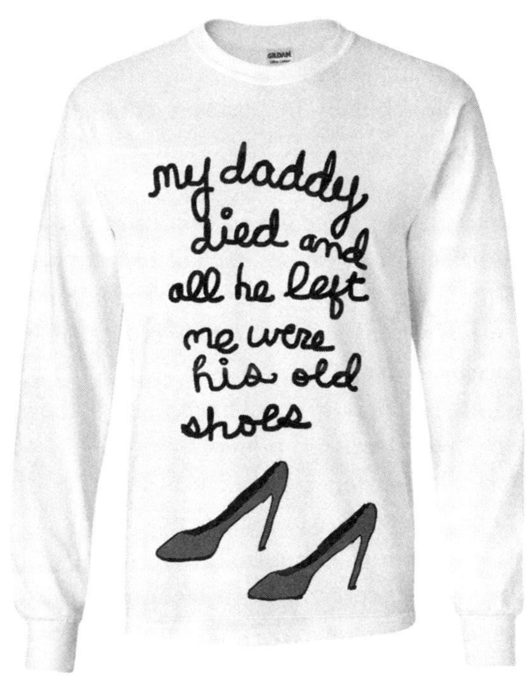

A shirt I made for the Tom of Finland art fair in 2021.

One year, when I was around ten, my dad took my friends and me to a hotel for my birthday. We were swimming at night in the pool, and dad was sitting nearby, sipping whiskey and musing over cinematic memories. He leaned back in the pool lounge chair. We had been talking about whether or not we liked Marylin Monroe.

I think she's really cool. I heard she's also not stupid.

I like her too. I like her clothes.

Madonna copies her.

Why would she kill herself? She was so pretty.

Then my dad chimed in. Phrases came and went in through my ears. What the hell was he talking about?

My dad knew her. He had lots of famous girlfriends, sure. My dad dated Jean Harlow. My dad built a lot of Palm Springs. My dad owned Herbert Hoover's old house—he had a small island built in the middle of the lake in front of his house, where he put a Model T Ford car. He would row a boat out to it so he could sit in it and read his newspapers and drink.

I looked at my friends, checking to see if they were as impressed as I was. I was also deeply confused. Could I be Hollywood royalty? Later, I would see startling photos of my father's childhood. My glamorous grandmother, holding my dad and his brother in front of an enormous Christmas tree in a large mid-century modern living room. Everything pressed and neat and shiny. My grandmother looked to me like someone who had never changed a diaper, or even seen a diaper. My mother looked like she changed diapers all day long, like she lived in a house made of diapers.

I had a complicated relationship with my grandmother, whom we called Gran. She was a bit of an alien to me as a kid. We visited her gigantic three-story home in Maine a few times and I had a hard time understanding who she was. We lived so differently. She had moved there in 1970 from Pasadena, to solidify her WASP glow-up. She was glamorous and beautiful. She wore her silver hair in a perfect bob with the bottom curled in. She had luxurious expensive clothing, a million pairs of shoes and hats, fur coats, and a big vanity in her bathroom with a tray full of lipsticks. She changed her clothes sometimes three times a day according to the occasion. In the morning, she would come down to the kitchen, make a pot of coffee and put it in a special carafe. Then she would place one scoop of Häagen-Dazs coffee ice cream into a tiny bowl. Then she would take it all up to her sitting room on a tray along with *The New York Times*. She frequented the yacht club for luncheons, and she loved to drink. Lunch was always paired with white wine. At 5:00 PM, it was "teeny tiny time" where she would bust out the martinis, brie cheese, and Triscuits. At dinner it was back to white wine. She ate very little and gave a mean side eye to anyone she thought was being "piggy." She would also stab you in the thigh with a fork if you misbehaved at the dinner table. She loved to lay by the pool. She wore a one-piece and a head scarf and smoked her Marlboros and did crosswords for one hour of tanning per day. I found it weird that she smoked Marlboros instead of something like Benson & Hedges or Capris. Marlboros were like a cowboy cigarette. She told me that when Marlboros were first introduced, they were advertised as a ladies' cigarette but the campaign flopped so they switched up the branding and started selling them as a rough guy on the range cigarette. But by then she was addicted, and they remained her brand for 50 years. I loved going to her house because it was so big and fancy, and there were always crackers and sodas, mostly Tab. She also had more than one of one thing. For example, when snooping around the cabinets I would see she had backup items. There were many bars of soaps. She had extra boxes of her hand cream at the ready. Under the sink was a box of new sponges. We never had supplies or an abundance of things. This seemed insanely luxurious and has always meant wealth to me. Now as an adult it fills me with absolute delight to have a backup of toilet paper, or "some more bubble water in the garage—I'll just throw it in the fridge!" I'm rich!

I loved visiting this world, but Gran wasn't particularly kind or snuggly. When I got a bit older I stopped being invited because I was a ratty punk. This hurt my feelings but I suspect my dad was trying to shield me from her. In college I began writing her letters, I think because I wanted some connection with a parental figure, someone to tell my accomplishments to. We had a steady correspondence for several years before she died in 2002. It wasn't exactly intimate, but it was something. She had a wicked sense of humor and liked it when I told her dirty jokes. I even sent her a Roofies CD, and she loved the song "Bitch." Game recognize game. It was tricky for me because she was a real cunt to my younger sister, who I always defended, but I still felt guilty about my relationship with Gran.

Here is what I know about her life. Ann Miller was from Colorado Springs, Colorado. When she was 18, she fell in love and married a pilot in the navy named George Wimsatt (an ugly Americanized version of the French Wimsette). She got pregnant right away. In letters I now have, he wrote to Ann's mom. I guess this wasn't unheard of back in the day, for the daughter's beau to write to the parents. His letters are warm and funny. He fills her in on visits with other family members, the scrumptious steaks they ate at a fancy restaurant.

In her early pregnancy, George was on a training mission to Pennsylvania with his squadron. Their plane ran out of fuel and crashed into a mountain and everyone on board was killed. Her baby was born in July 1945. She named him James.

When James was one year old, a bobcatter came to town.

A bobcatter is someone who prospects on other people's land in order to drill for oil and minerals, like Daniel Day-Lewis in *There Will Be Blood*. His name was also George; George Cameron. He started out in his late teens as a roughneck working on oil rigs in Texas. A roughneck is someone who works on oil rigs, like James Dean in *Giant*. He bought a small plot of land with brother Arthur. They dug 30 wells before they hit a dry one, like the hillbillies in *The Beverly Hillbillies*. They became enormously rich.

One question my siblings and I always had was, where did all the money go? Why were we poor? The Cameron family was exceptionally dysfunctional, but it also had a mystical air about it—it was hard to believe I was related to these people, though the drama and alcoholism of my weird life isn't that far from what went on with these people—it was just more punk, more gay and poor.

One story was that my dad's brother, John, stole everyone's inheritance. This is an unverifiable story, but to my understanding, when George Cameron died, he still owned several oil wells. Out of spite he left only one to his four children, for them all to share. The kids had a joint account, and Uncle John had access to it. Apparently, he took it all and spent it on coke and sports cars. I believe this is at least somewhat true. When I was very little, before all that happened, Uncle John came to visit us in Annapolis. I had never met this guy before. He was handsome and disheveled but clean with nice clothes. His 80s bangs flopped over his eyes. He was tan and a bit chunky. He drove a Porsche and took us for rides, speeding through the narrow, windy Northern California woods. A big kid. Apparently, John had been singled out by my grandmother as the child that she disliked. Mostly because he was "fat." My dad told me she was positively cruel to him. Just chose him to be the scapegoat for everything and taunted him about his weight constantly.

But she must have loved him somewhat, right? He was her kid!

No, no, I don't think she did.

My father thought my gran had borderline personality disorder and might have been a sociopath, as well as a drunk. He said his grandmother spoke to him about his mother, told him—

Even as a child she has always been mean. Just a mean girl.

George was looking for more land to drill in Colorado when he met Ann. He was 15 years her senior. His father, George Sr., was a minister, and his mother, Stella, a devout Baptist, so devout that Stella married George Sr. thinking he would be chaste and respectful, and therefore she wouldn't have to have much intercourse. He was neither of those things. He was a miserable alcoholic who raped her at least twice, and that is how she became pregnant with George Jr. and his older brother, Arthur. In our family retelling, it was law in Texas during the early part of the 20th century that sex with a woman who was nursing was prohibited.[8] So Stella nursed Arthur until he was 12 years old. At any rate, the story goes that after 12 years obeying this law, George Sr. raped Stella again and that is how she got pregnant with George Jr., whom she nursed until he was ten, and then she "dropped dead." For some reason, these poor Texas Cameron boys who sucked their mother dry in a shack in Texas became millionaires.

Ann needed a way out of her situation. Being a 19-year-old single mom stuck in her hometown was not what she had planned for herself. Luckily, she was stunning. She had movie star good looks, with lustrous blonde hair, a "perfect figure," and a beautiful smile. She was a catch for this old guy.

---

8 According to my research it was more a societal taboo than an actual written law.

George and Ann moved out to California. Although George Cameron was my father's stepfather, he adopted him, and my dad called him dad. Ann and George settled in Pasadena and had three more children—George Jr. (Yusef), John, and Nancy. He began expanding his empire—mostly in the Coachella Valley. He purchased *The Desert Sun* newspaper and KDES Radio in Palm Springs. He developed a shopping center there as well. I have picked up bits and pieces of information about him over the years, but my father didn't talk about him much. He was cruel and he had a major drug problem. His relationship with Ann crumbled under his drinking and philandering, and they divorced in 1956.

George Sr. died of an overdose of pills at the Flamingo Hotel in Las Vegas. Yusef thought that he was murdered by the mafia. The deeper I dive into this Cameron history with Palm Springs and Rat Pack-era gangster foolishness, the more I could see it happening. The photos of George from the Palm Springs Historical Society look straight out of a 1950s *LIFE* magazine. Here's George posing with Desi Arnaz at his radio station. Here's George flanked by gorgeous gals in pedal pushers with bouffants, sipping cocktails. He was a flashy business guy—*The Desert Sun*'s remembrance piece states, "He created one of the finest and most modern shopping centers in the nation right in the beautiful south end of Palm Springs." In one photo he stands in front of an empty piece of desert land, leaning on a fence in a cowboy hat, like Monty Cliff in Giant, surveying the barren desert and imagining all the burbling black gold lying beneath him. He once took the entire clan of Cameron children uranium mining. In the photo, they stand grimly in little suits in front of a passenger van with *Cameron Family Uranium Mining Expedition* painted on the side.

Ann began seeing another astronomically rich developer a few years after George died named Bill Pfau. She got pregnant again, and married him, although according to family lore she did not love him. With Bill she had three more children: my uncle Will, who is in my life today, and my aunts Lisa and Kari, who have been unceremoniously ostracized—Kari for trying to change my grandmother's will so she would get everything, and Lisa for being unbearable to be around.

I don't know much about my father's life growing up in Southern California. There were moments in my childhood when he would get drunk and talk about it, but it always sounded like he was making shit up. I just couldn't picture it at all. Our life seemed light-years away from this world I had only seen on TV. We had an outdoor kitchen and when I was five my dad shot a snake that was trying to crawl into a can of beans. I guess the Old West ran in him along with alcoholism.[9]

I have been watching *Mad Men* recently, a show I somehow missed back when it first aired. It's brutal. Through all the intrigue and slow, brilliant storytelling, the surprising thing that keeps coming up as I watch is compassion for my dad. The secrets, the sexism, the money, the drinking, the smoking, the violent whiteness, the demonic capitalist post-war American dream charade. I have been so critical of my parents' intensely irresponsible parenting, their lack of credit in the straight world, their avoidance of their families, their inability to have stable housing and jobs, their general dysregulation. I have come to understand my upbringing as "systemically reactive." In spite of their problematic fuckups that majorly lost their cool in later years, in some ways I applaud these baby boomers. What would I have been like if that were me? What if I had grown up with that kind of oppression, as opposed to my brand of willy-nilly neglect, which was damaging of course, but at least had some semblance of integrity, or at least the

9 See appendix for Cameron family photos.

intention of integrity. They couldn't know what they couldn't know. The one thing my parents did know was that they did not want that life they had grown up in. My mom and dad both wanted a family, and they wanted to do it all differently. But they didn't know how to be parents or even people, really. And if you are a drug addict and an alcoholic, well, good luck. And if you were severely mentally ill and living with the trauma of unacknowledged abuse, also good luck.

When I was around 24, Uncle John died of a heart attack. He had never married and was living in a condo with his beloved pit bull in La Jolla. I hadn't seen John since I was that tiny kid in Annapolis. A lot of the Cameron family I hadn't seen in ages came to the funeral. We knew my grandmother probably wasn't coming, but I couldn't help secretly hoping she would show up at the last minute to prove she wasn't a total demon. She didn't though. The other person people were waiting to arrive was Suzanne. This was my uncle Will's ex-wife. Several years before, John had come to visit Will and his new wife Suzanne in San Diego. John ended up running off with Suzanne. When she eventually showed up to John's funeral, everyone avoided her. I kept my eye on her. She wore a big straw hat, and her shoulders shook while she sobbed as the Rolling Stones' "You Can't Always Get What You Want" played.

My dad and I milled about after the ceremony. A shiny, tan middle-aged guy wandered up to us. He was wearing a pink Lacoste shirt with the collar turned up and pressed khaki shorts; aviator sunglasses crowned his brown bald head.

Jimmy! He said to my dad.

Hello, Cameron, how goes it, said my dad limply.

Oh not bad not bad, you know, got a few things cooking, been working on a movie with an amazing director, yeah, we'll see, getting the financing together, should be a hit.

He prattled on. Who the fuck was this guy? He made movies? I wanted to be in movies. He looked slimy and absurd, and clearly my dad did not like him, but I was intrigued.

My dad made an excuse, and we walked away towards the parking lot.

Who was that? I asked.

That was Cameron. Cameron Cameron.

Who is he?

Well, he's my brother.

Your brother? And his name is Cameron? And his last name is also Cameron!? Cameron CAMERON?

Yep. He is my dad's kid from his second marriage. He's an asshole. You don't need to know him.

And that was that. These kinds of bombs were dropped flippantly throughout my life and made it impossible for me to know what I was supposed to care about and to value. I suppose they were secrets. In some ways, I respect my dad for just shutting this guy out and never introducing his kids to him. He was all the stuff my dad wanted to get away from. But on the other hand, major abuse and trauma, huge PTSD moments, shaped both of my parents' lives and were never dealt with. If they were spoken of, they were mentioned glibly, with a shade of distaste.

Uncle Arthur was so rich that if someone looked at him sideways, he would find out who he was and ruin his life.

What do you mean?

Oh, he would get his private investigators after him and learn where he lived, get him fired, just, you know, ruin his life.

That's so mean!

He would sometimes come pick us up and take us to the movies in a limousine. But if he couldn't find free parking we would miss the movie. He would just drive around and around. He hated to pay for parking.

But he was rich! I replied.
Rich doesn't mean not crazy.

My mean grandmother did not come to my dad's funeral either. She said she was not well enough to fly, which I didn't believe, but she paid for the service—with the caveat that it be in a "proper place," a Forest Lawn industrial funeral complex on a hill in Lafayette, California. They erected a tent for shade above the hole. My dad was wrapped in white cloth and buried naked without a coffin, in traditional Muslim burial fashion. Yusef said a prayer from the Koran that lasted roughly 100 years. Then Wavy Gravy spoke, and talked about my dad's giant pensive eyebrows, a storm of thought always brewing behind them. It was so odd to think of my dad having friends. For many years I thought that my parents' friends must not know them well, or else they would not be friends with them. Or I felt resentful, thinking they should have saved us kids or intervened somehow. I realized later in my life that they actually did intervene. Most of our housing came through friends of my parents, and my mom stayed at the Hog Farm frequently when she didn't have a place to live. And I have friends whose parenting I don't love. A friend of mine recently admitted they have a rage problem and regularly yell at their children. What can you do? I wish I could have witnessed my parents with their friends more. But I know my dad loved Wavy and Wavy loved my dad.

At the funeral I was almost totally dissociated. I didn't cry. In fact, I don't know that I have ever shed a tear over my dad's death. Partially because he lived a lot longer than I thought he would, and definitely longer than he thought he would. When he passed away, he was actually doing well, despite having Hepatitis B and C and various other health issues. He was, I guess, happy.

My father had definitely changed in the years before he passed away. I hadn't seen him enough to be able to tell, until the person I was dating at the time started hanging out with him. I think my dad aided him in some legal stuff or something, that is how they got to talking, and he thought my dad he was really funny and smart. When my band had a show, he'd say, "Let's invite your dad!" What? So, we did. Suddenly my dad was coming to my shows, and he would even wear a Roofies T-shirt. He loved "Frankie the Shoe Fucker" especially. I had a pie baking contest one year and invited my dad to participate. He loved chocolate desserts and brought a decadent mousse pie with a fancy, stainless steel whipped cream dispenser. I had about six months with my dad that were pleasant and almost fun, where he showed up, finally. I bought him the Buena Vista Social Club CD, which he swooned over—imagining himself in a Panama hat being romantic in Cuba, I'm sure. He could have a conversation—sorta—and when I spoke, he listened—at least a little bit. I didn't feel bad for my loss or his when he died. I am grateful for that shitty relationship, for the miracle that took place with my dad. I appreciate my dad now. I would love to hear what he has to say about the state of our "democracy," and if he would still be getting dommed and wearing silky nighties at 80.

When I got sober in 2005, my sister J'nai explained something. I was talking about how I was grateful I got to spend some relatively good time with him before he passed away.

Well, you know why that is, right?

She always has the family tea.

He finally got a sponsor who didn't fall for his bullshit. He got a hard-boiled fisherman or some kinda surly man in Alaska who told him he hadn't done shit in all the time he'd been in recovery. Said he had been talking the talk all these years but never walking the walk.

It was true; my father was very involved in AA and even a circuit speaker. When he passed away my older cousin gave me a couple of his speaker tapes. I sort of wish I never listened to them. One of his stories was about something I thought for many years was a dream. He had left me in the car while he went to a hotel in the nearby town to watch a boxing match with his friends, because we didn't have TV. He was drunk driving me home and we crashed. He stumbled out of the car and then suddenly remembered I was still in it. He came back to get me out just before the car blew up. He also talked about putting a shotgun to his chin to kill himself but thought of his kids and didn't go through with it.

Now that I know what being sober is, what having sober humility looks like—it makes sense that he had that, finally, during those last few years. I see it. I also get to have that, the openness and the gift that AA gives you of not being so afraid all time, of learning how to listen,[10] of not thinking you are the most important person in the room who is also worth the least, so you must keep proving something. Of being held lovingly accountable for your bullshit. What a wild circle to close for me.

10 A favorite AA saying of mine: "Take the cotton out of your ears and stick it in your mouth!"

TWELVE: DYNASTY: THE BAND

After the Roofies, I started a new band called Dynasty with two of my close friends. I had been singing with Diana in the Roofies, and we wanted to keep doing stuff together. Diana is a 5'2" weirdo from Pennsylvania who shared my total obsession with music, especially Prince and Bay Area rap—Andre Nickatina, E-40, P-Lo. She turned me on to contemporary country music, which I didn't know anything about. Diana is silly but also very analytical and gets shit done. A tiny Taurus. Her hair is really thick. She's gorgeous. She does all kinds of weird shit with puppets and dioramas and makes up songs. She always identified with the Bay Area and made rural Pennsylvania sound like a hellscape. We had different but equally insane backgrounds that we laughed about. She decided to learn the bass guitar.

Indra is quiet, mostly because she's shy. She's tall and stunning. This combo leads people to think she's stuck-up, which she wrote about in a song called "I'm Shy." She screams it in the song. Ha ha. She is 6'1", and from Wisconsin. Both of her parents are giants from Latvia who immigrated here during World War II. She has that midwestern, low-key goofy sense of humor where nothing really shakes her too hard. She has great style as well, but she doesn't wear heels because she would be a million feet tall, and you can't play the drums in heels.

The three of us made up Dynasty. Our sound was early 2000s post punk/dance, reminiscent of Delta Five or the

Raincoats if a third of their members couldn't play their instruments. We were stripped down. We had no guitar. I played the keyboards, which I played like I play and do everything—I just kinda . . . do it, without knowing how, and learn-ish as I go. Like how I think I might know how to write a book (this book) because I have read a lot of books or write a TV show cuz I watch a lot of TV. Who cares? I wasn't good at my instrument, but I could bang out a melody. Luckily, Diana only learned around three to four notes on the bass, so we were resigned to keeping it simple. Indra was a consummate punk drummer and could also play disco beats. Indra had a big old van to haul our shit around, and her other, more successful band, Numbers, had a rehearsal space that we probably paid around $20 to use. We played all original songs; most of it was pretty light and a lot less raunchy than the Roofies. Some songs we wrote had actual depth, like "Loneliness," in which Diana sang the opening line from Yoko Ono's song "Loneliness" as the intro. "You've Got Problems" was a break-up revenge song, but much more sophisticated than the one I wrote for the ass-eater. We had a song about an obsessive girl who was stalking a friend of ours and stealing his clothing. The song definitely made fun of the girl, but it was less brutal than simply calling her a crazy bitch. I was maturing.

We wrote everything together; it was a full collaboration. We didn't have much at stake, certainly not our talent. With the Roofies there was always someone "shredding," or one of us going off and being musically virtuosic, which is great, but it was relaxing now to be in total partnership. I was the lead singer in Dynasty, but I was behind the keys and locked in, trying to remember what the fuck I was doing. It was purposeful. I had a job beyond just freaking out and being disgusting. Indra held us together—she was definitely the most skilled musically. Diana brought beautiful backup vocals and steady bass and is a great songwriter.

We spent as much time, if not more, getting our costumes together than we did rehearsing. Once we played a show dressed as a family of monkeys. I was the mom monkey—I had a pregnant belly with a monkey face drawn on it—and Indra wore a monkey mask and a flap of cloth over her pants that had a big dick drawn on it. I guess she was the dad monkey, and Diana was the wet nurse? We also did a cavewoman look, not realizing the Slits had done that already. For that show we grunted all the lyrics instead of singing. We dressed as mummies for another show—but it got shut down by the cops before we went on. We also had an all-lace look, a lá Vanity 6.[11]

We made a really weird record. We had recorded a rehearsal with just a room mic. We gave it to our friend, an electronic music synth guy, to mix and master it, and he kinda just re-made the record. He added filters and synths and played bass over Diana's bass. He even cut together the drum parts to make them perfectly synced. In the end, it sounded like we had made a fancy album in a studio. Now I wish we didn't put it out that way, because the original mess recording is better. But that is what happens when people make things better—they ruin them.[12]

I recommend anyone between the ages of seven and 90 to be in a band with their best friends. It doesn't matter if you get good; it's better if you don't. We didn't make a major dent in anything, but it was huge for me to be in this band. For one thing, we were all women. There was a chillness to the rehearsing that felt so relaxing after being in a band with dudes (wonderful, amazing dudes I loved, but . . . you know). We got along so well, had so much fun, were so stupid, laughed

---

11 Dynasty playing at a warehouse party, Photo, 2002. See appendix.
12Dynasty studio album and live recordings, 2001-2003. See appendix.

constantly, and were as excited about music as we were about each other. Outside of the band I was having a terrible time—my dad had just died, and I had left an abusive relationship. These nutballs really saved me.

During this time, I had started acting again. My theater-fag flame had been relit by performing in these bands and wanted formal training. I completed the summer intensive course at American Conservatory Theater in San Francisco. It was kinda revolutionary for me—I wanted to learn something, and I went and learned it—on purpose! After that program I was in a few plays in San Francisco, and I even got an agent who told me I was "special," but wouldn't go anywhere if I stayed in San Francisco. I needed to move to New Yawwwk, she said. Didn't I know it.

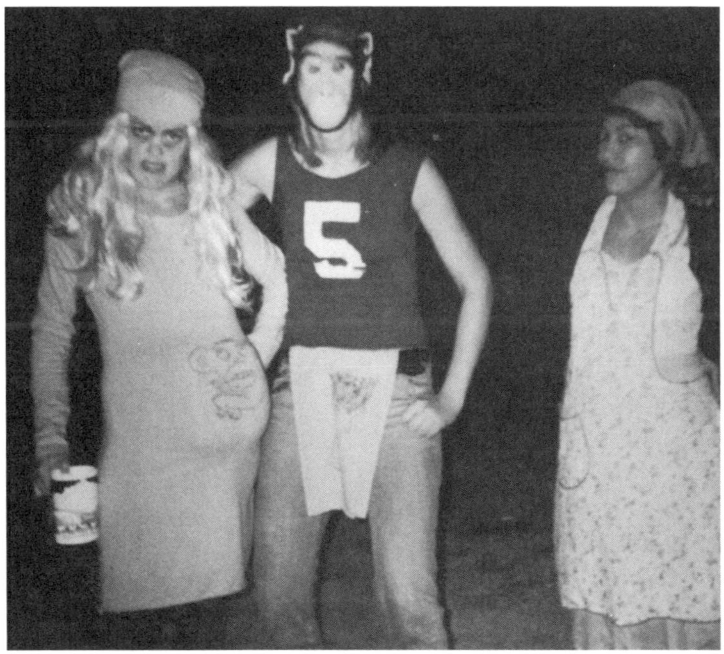

Diana gives solid side eye while Indra crouches to fit in the picture. Has anyone seen that wig BTW?

PART II

I thought art was supposed to be beautiful.
—My aunt after seeing Weirdo Night

THIRTEEN: A BAG IS BORN

When Dynasty Handbag slid out of the womb covered in hair gel, I was trying to get out of a bad relationship and in suppressed grief about losing my dad. I was 25 and I had just gotten a marriage proposal from a man. As for my queerness, I was out, but for some reason I'd decided this dude was my ticket outta this dump! I told him all I wanted to do was move to New York City and be an actress, and he said he could make that happen. But we had to get married. Why, said I. He gave a bullshit reason about his grandma, an old Catholic Puerto Rican lady who would be very upset if we lived together without being wed. I think he just wanted control. I had never thought about getting married before. Never crossed my mind in fact. I thought, why not? He was a charming handsome mean guy that looked like a lesbian. I liked him a lot at first. But he became a bully very quickly. I got stuck, and I was afraid of him. He berated me constantly and tried to control my performance life, my friends, and my familial relationships. Needless to say, the marriage did not work out.

Months before my dad died, in a rare intimate conversation with him, I told him vaguely what was going on.

It's not going great, he is trying to tell me to kick Eli out of the Roofies because we dated when I was 17! And he doesn't like the play I'm doing, he said it's not good enough for me.

I didn't tell my dad he called me a bitch and a whore on the regular.

Well, he is jealous of you because you're a real artist, and that is what he wants to be. But he will never be a real artist, and you will always be one. Always have been. He will always envy you.

This shocked me. I couldn't believe I was being seen so clearly by my dad. My dad, who I thought couldn't see anything besides his own massive ego. And what he said rang true. It wasn't a *me* problem. It was the insecurity of this guy I was with. There was a slight shift in my consciousness, and I started to see this guy I married as pathetic. Still scary, but also maybe a loser. I have always been grateful for this perspective from my dad.

I was ready to get out within a month of the wedding, but then my dad fucking *died*! I was too numb and tired with grief to leave the relationship, but I knew I had made a big fucking mistake and I was really embarrassed. I found myself in this bizarre place—an adult situation I had zero tools for. And I found this . . . funny? I found it funny that I was going to be a divorcée. Funny that I had failed at a thing I never even wanted in the first place, but still felt shame about flunking. It made no sense. Growing up in the 80s, divorce had heavy significance—conjuring loneliness, horniness, sadness, and desperation—women on the verge, as it were. The ultimate failure for a woman—whose identity is to hold together the scaffolding of the man's family, no matter how big of a loser or a dickhead he is. TV movies with recently divorced women who lost their minds because the husband ran off with the secretary and faced zero consequences.

I needed somewhere to put all these fucked up feelings. So, I put them into a 4-track, and called them Dynasty Handbag.

I heard the first Julie Ruin record around 1999. I knew and liked Bikini Kill, but I was not that into Riot Grrrl; it seems like an obvious niche for me, but it didn't speak to me at the time. I didn't quite understand it. I thought it was dorky, and the little-girl-nostalgia aesthetic grossed me out. I never wore barrettes or any dumb decorative things in my hair as a little kid. The lunchboxes perplexed me. My "lunchboxes" were enormous paper grocery bags my mother would roll all the way down into the shape of a baguette. My lunches had no twee value either, they were usually a soggy tofu salad sandwich, and like, one big hard orange. I never got a juice box or a drink in a fun pouch. If I got a drink it would be water in an old peanut butter jar that was still kinda oily. Anyhow, I did like a lot of the Riot Grrrl music, and the Julie Ruin album was hugely influential to my first Dynasty Handbag recordings. Kathleen Hanna had made the record by herself with a 4-track. I imagined her sitting on her floor alone, with her deep private thoughts and feelings, doing whatever the hell she wanted, surrounded by her gear, notebooks, snacks, cigarettes. She sang about fear of men and police violence, romance, and friendship. The sounds were enchanting and soulful and inventive—she sampled the Clash and Lesley Gore and was generally getting weird. The intimacy and analog warmth of it filled me with possibility. I felt I was sitting right next to her on her bedroom floor. I was also struck by how tender and honest it was. Everything I wrote was always cloaked in humor. Julie Ruin gave me permission to write more directly what I was feeling, and to do it all myself. I am always inevitably trying to impress my collaborators, whereas my solo work allows more honesty, from me at least. Back to the poetry closet of my youth.

In the depression purgatory of grieving my dad and hating my husband but being unable to do anything about it, I retreated to a tiny room in our house and began spilling my drama into a dusty 4-track, on the floor of course. With the Roland synthesizer I borrowed from a noise music nerd, I began recording songs about how hopeless I was. Soon I had a handful of pedestrian clunkers with simple beats and dreary melodies. The feelings coming out of me were intense, but the music and singing were so bad it gave me freedom to be as melodramatic and dark as I wanted. I was able to be really honest because it was hard to take the whole thing seriously, and that was a relief. The stupider it all sounded, the funnier it was to me, and that kept me from getting bored with myself. This is still what keeps me making work.

My first show as Dynasty Handbag was called *Miami Funeral Vacation*. It was at a small gallery in San Francisco's South of Market neighborhood. I pictured myself as a widow in Florida, who had perhaps murdered her husband. I wore a heavily pleated nylon, black, sleeveless blouse monstrosity over matching pants. I had my signature smeared lipstick and wore enormous dark sunglasses—a salute to both Yoko and cataracts. I had a tiny, gold Chanel purse I bought at the Salvation Army on Fulton Street for $8. My hair was teased into a humongous rat condo. I wore a Band-Aid on my chin. That became a signature look for me in the early days.

A Band-Aid is a great micro-costume. It's an intrigue, a tiny mystery. Not nearly as fun as a cast, but definitely cause for concern—*what happened to her chin*? A peep for help. Dynasty Handbag's Band-Aids indicate a dermatological problem rather than an injury. The Band-Aids also denoted a part of me that always wanted to be sick or injured as a child, mostly because I wanted to be rescued or at least cared for a little bit, preferably by a kind, midwestern, upper-middle-class adult who would feel sorry for me, murder my parents, and take me away to their McMansion in the leafy green suburbs, with a canopy bed and a refrigerator full of juice boxes and packaged snack items.[13]

13 *The Neighbor,* Live Performance, 2025 (Original Performance, 2008). See appendix.

Back to the performance—which included my divorce revenge ballad, "Oh, Baby."[14]

Oh, Baby
When you walk in the room
My stomach flips
I start to sweat
My skin crawls
My teeth fall out
My breasts shrivel up
My eyes crust over
My nose it bleeds
My mouth it foams
My ears drip puss (drip puss!)
My bladder explodes
My knees they crack
I piss and shit
And roll around
In a sea of waste
Just seeing your face

Something else began to happen during these early recordings that would become a hallmark of Dynasty Handbag performance work. I started interrupting myself as I was recording with some of the various peanut galleries of my mind. For example, during the song "Uniform Lust," a woman with a heavy midwestern accent interrupts my singing:[15]

Hellooo hello? I'm sorry to interrupt, this is God. (recorded)

You know I don't believe in god, if you were god you would know that. (live)

Ok ok, I'm not God, I'm your conscience, and I am just wondering why you haven't called me lately? (recorded)

14 *Oh Baby,* Live Performance, 2024 (Original Performance, 2001). See appendix.
15 *Uniform Lust*, Live Performance, 2001. See appendix.

Oh I am really busy and I've been doing a lot of home projects, etc. (live)

Are you sure you're not... depressed? (recorded)

I mean maybe . . . I dunno Ok yeah maybe uh yeah a little . . . (live)

I understand I understand, I just want you to know—you can call me anytime. I'm here for you. OK, I'll let you get back to your little project. (recorded)

The audience always laughs hard at that last part. Then I finish the song. Looking back, I'm almost embarrassed at the level of mental illness I was ru-vealing about myself. *I don't feel like I am real. I feel like this is a show of a show.* I now clearly see that this interrupting consciousness sounds a lot like what a nice mom might sound like. A parent saying, *Hey, how are you? Are you doing ok? I'm always here for you!* It also oddly sounds like what my mom experienced during her bipolar schizophrenic periods: voices.

By this time, I was on Prozac, but still had major depressive disorder and what is now called bipolar disorder II. Which is a less bat-shit version of bipolar I. People with II exhibit more of the depressive symptoms and less of the manic behavior. We're lazier. Ha ha. I would continue to float above myself and observe this stranger who looked like me in the world, knowing that her existence was a lie or at least felt like a lie; that she wasn't actually normal, that she was running around doing this and that—having friends, drinking, not drinking, being a lesbian, not being a lesbian, being in bands, being in plays, fighting, having friendships, drawing, making art—all these things weren't really her. The real her was a complete darkness, a vacuum of joy. Throughout these times of misery, I would have moments of happiness or joy, but I couldn't truly feel them. I had a running narrative in my brain, *Bitch, you better not get used to this, don't forget what a piece of shit you are.* On this rickety platform, a bag was born.

FOURTEEN: INTERNATIONAL HANDBAG

In 2003, when Dynasty Handbag was just two years old, I took her on tour opening up for Indra's other band, Numbers. It was a six-week affair. Indra needed another non-man companion along the way. We were going all over Europe: France, Spain, Portugal, Croatia, Italy, Germany, Hungary. I was concerned about how my work would translate; after all, it's very wordy, and at that point the Dynasty Handbag repertoire consisted of many tracks where I talked back to a pre-recorded voice, or one interrupted me during my songs. I got the idea to find people who spoke the languages of the countries we were going to. I had them over to my house and recorded them saying in Italian, French, Portuguese, etc.:

Good evening, my name is Dynasty Handbag.

I am a disgusting American here to entertain you. I hope you enjoy my offerings.

The first song I will do for you tonight is about—

Then I recorded myself imitating that recording, as opposed to actually learning how to say stuff in these languages. I can always find a way out of having to do actual work; in fact, the entire Dynasty Handbag project may just be an exercise in doing the least amount possible. I only learn things if there is no other way. Armed with my iPod and a tiny suitcase crammed with costumes—1980s shredded secretary's dress, a Mickey Mouse leotard/T-shirt combo,[16] white pumps, and many pairs of tights—we set out from San Francisco to

16 Dynasty Handbag, Croatia, 2003. See appendix.

Heathrow. Our group consisted of me and the band Numbers: Eric, keyboard; Dave, guitar; and Indra, drums—all from Wisconsin. They had known each other for years. Dave and Indra were a couple and were classically good-looking, with early 2000s hipster fashion vibes. Dave was hilarious in that special dry and dull-edged yet sharp midwestern way. He was a sorta good-time guy, in a cheerful mood much of the time; Eric was notably more misanthropic, with some Eeyore energy—his shoulders sagging forward, freckled, tall and Nordic, with a bit of a boxcar hobo repertoire up his sleeve. But he was also insanely funny and an incredible musician. The northern and eastern winds blew around their pale frames and last names, BROEKEMA, LANDMARK, DUNIS. I loved them.

Then there was Ethan Swan, our manager and driver. A deep music scene nerd from Providence. The kind of guy who knew all the indie punk and weirdo bands from every corner of the earth. I didn't see him eat anything but candy or take a shower for six weeks. He drove the entire time, sometimes through the night, with a gigantic atlas of Europe sprawled out on his lap while one of the guys helped to navigate. How did we ever find anything? Certainly not with the help of Indra and me, who spent most of our time in the van cackling at the boys maniacally from the backseat and being annoying bitches.

We had rented a white utility van/torture chamber in the UK, the kind that pedophiles in British detective series drive around in. It had two rows of seats and a big storage space in the back. There was a tiny window that you could look into the back through, which came in handy when people started to sleep back there. The seat backs shot straight up and wouldn't recline. We rode around like LEGO people, in agony.

By week two we were all desperately sore and out of our minds with exhaustion. Eric put out a call to see if anyone along our journey could loan us a mattress. We stopped to pick one up from some stringy-haired musician in the Czech Republic. The guys expertly loaded the van so that all the gear lay relatively flat. Then the mattress went on top. From then on, we took turns sleeping in the dark, abduction part of the van, rolling around on the crusty mattress.

The general set-up when touring out of the country is that the promoters of your show—those who find the venue/work for the venue/ arrange the show—also take care of your housing and payment. You meet all kinds of freaks who are genuinely happy to see you and show you around. Sometimes—rarely—you get a real turd. When we arrived in Budapest, we were supposed to meet the promoter at his apartment. We found out that he had to go on a last-minute trip to the UK and had gotten his grumpy girlfriend to take over our hospitality. This woman could not be less excited to have to babysit a bunch of goofy Americans. She got in the van with us to guide us to the venue, because it was truly impossible to navigate the streets of Budapest with a map. EV-ER-EE time we were supposed to turn she would miss it, and say in a voice coming from the dead, "Oh you miss-ud the turnnnnn." She sounded like she was on an Anna Nicole-level of pills, but also mad at the same time, with a Hungarian accent.

We arrived at the venue and played an unmemorable show that was poorly attended. The venue hated us. The sound guy made a big show of yawning throughout everyone's set. The bartenders made us pay for our weak drinks. The third band, which was the headliner, was a metal band who all had long dyed-black hair, shredded jeans, and man-energy. We were *all* going to stay at this woman's apartment?

When we got back to her place, everyone was exhausted and didn't feel much like partying. So . . . where were we all sleeping? She had two bedrooms. Since she wanted to fuck the singer in the man-band she took to her bed immediately, with him, and left us lingering around, looking for shelter and warmth. There was one other blanket in the apartment, which Dave took. Indra and I slept under towels on the tile floor of the bathroom, using our filthy jackets for pillows. In the morning everyone was sore, obliterated, tired, and very pissed at this woman. In our only means of retaliation we demanded that we do all of our laundry in her tiny, Euro washing machine as payback. We hauled our sacks of smelly tour garments and began a three-hour washing machine torturescape. Every time a load was done, she would lumber over to the machine as though she were hauling bricks up a mountain, slump over the machine, drag out our socks and T-shirts one by one . . . and mutter, "Morrrre wet clothes-es," repeatedly.

Since it was Europe there was no dryer. We took our wet sacks to the van where Ethan and Dave had strung clotheslines above the mattress in the back. Now when we napped we could stare up at damp boxer shorts and holey gym socks flapping around, like a dirtbag baby mobile lulling us into a hungover sleep as we rocked, cradled in the loving arms of the utility van.

We stayed in some lovely places, like a beautiful barn loft in southern France, where they cooked us a gigantic French meal and we all sat around a huge wooden table enjoying ourselves. We also stayed at a hotel that looked like Marie Antoinette's bedroom, but more brown, with the stench of a few centuries of cigarette smoke in the walls.

In Italy we performed in a pizza parlor in a remote mountain town, up winding green hills into Noweheresvillialinni. The audience consisted of local families trying and failing to enjoy their dinner while we expressed ourselves on the floor of the restaurant. The promoter was a very young guy who didn't know what he was doing. They didn't have a mic stand so they fastened a mic to a broom handle with duct tape.

The restaurant was so offended by us that they shut off the power during Numbers' set. After the show, we followed the promoter back down the hill to the place we were to stay that night. It was over an hour away through the nauseating hills of northern Italy. We were exhausted and humiliated from the pizza parlor tragedy, and all in terrible moods.

It was a tiny little house. Very soon after we arrived, we learned that this young man may or may not have had permission to let us lodge there for the night. And, like the electroclash sloth of Budapest, he, too, could provide no blankets. We were only allowed access to the kitchen and a small living area that consisted of one skinny, hard couch. For some reason the bedrooms and the bathrooms were locked. It was very dark and cold. Maybe if we had been plane crash survivors in the North Pole we would have been overjoyed to stumble upon this shack with running water. But the amenities were severely lacking, even for this band of scumbags.

Dave had an immediate meltdown. This was well into the tour. By now everyone else had already had one or two solid freak-outs, yet Dave had managed to keep up his good-time gal attitude until this moment, when he was faced with the possibility that there was nowhere for him to take a shit. He lost his mind. There was absolutely nothing we could do. There were no hotels. Dave was so angry that he slept in the unmerciful van, freezing his nuts off and wallowing in self-shitty-pity.

We played a lot of shows in Germany, most interestingly in rural Germany. The towns all looked like the village in the Herzog film *The Enigma of Kaspar Hauser*, where Kaspar is locked in a shed his entire childhood and made to sleep on hay. One town we were in was so isolated and provincial it was completely unimaginable that anyone even lived there, let alone that it would hold any type of punk weirdos who would come out to a show. That venue/anarchist squat had the accommodations attached to it, which is common in Europe. "Accommodations" is a stretch, though. We slept in a large room that resembled a children's infirmary from 1942. Or a Dickensian orphanage. It was large and freezing, with child-size metal beds lined up against the graffitied walls. It was fun, however, and felt like we were in summer camp, albeit a summer camp for youth being punished. That evening, the punks miraculously crawled out from the basements of their mitteldeutsches Hauses, and came to see us play.[17]

By far the worst audiences were in Paris. For the first time (and the last time, as it turns out), I walked off the stage during a performance. We were in a sweaty packed club somewhere. I was a complete unknown; I'm positive there was no one there specifically to see me—which was the case for most of this tour, but in Paris the crowds seemed particularly incurious and demanding to be impressed. As I was doing a song, three frog bitches started heckling me in the front.

WHO ARE YOU!? YOU ARE SHIT! YOU THINK YOU ARE PEEEECHEEEHHHZ

Oh no, you better didn't just say I am trying to be Peaches. That was an insult to me. Not because I wasn't a devoted Peaches fan (still am) but because I really was trying to do something VERY different than Peaches. I wasn't trying to make people party! I was trying to make people uncomfortable! *MY* on-stage underwear looks were supposed to repulse and suggest geriatrics, infirmity, and despair, not queer sass and all night Berliner debauchery.

So, I stopped the show on that Paris stage that fateful nuit. I turned off my backing track. I looked down at these French assholes in the silence and screamed, "Ok, it's your show, you

17 Dynasty Handbag, Ethan Swan, and Dave Broekema in the torture beds, 2003. See appendix.

want to come up and do this—here's the mic!" And I walked off. Then I went to the green room and cried.

But I was back on the scène the following night, more determined than ever! At this point in my performance life, I tended to see the audience as adversarial. I was combative, in a funny way, but I definitely did not yet have the concept of being in energetic flow, let alone gratitude. My communication was very "us vs. them."

I could get people on my side by fascinating them. I had vulnerability in that I was doing something weird—but I was still very controlling with my act. For example, I had a very tight grip on my persona. I didn't want to have to interact with the outside world at all when performing as Dynasty Handbag, so when people asked me to host things, or interact with other performers in any way on stage, I would strategize how to still remain in my reality. If I was hosting an event, I would never actually be in reality with the performers. I would just make stuff up.

Instead of saying, "Now, welcome to the stage, Erin Markey—comedienne and chantoozer from outer space!" I would say, "Now, welcome to Bank of America, here's your first client who wants to open a savings bank for her woman eggs, which are all rotten and won't yield anything worth saving."

Or something like that. It's funny, haha, yes, but it's not generous, and takes away from the other performer. There was something ego-driven about being in that closed space that I had to learn to dissolve.

I would also fight with hecklers. If a man ever said anything, or heckled me I would say something to the effect of,

Oh, I'm sorry, did you need some attention sir? Everyone be quiet! A man has a need!

Delivered in a very cunty-spirited way. Whereas now I would say something in a kind posh British accent, to the effect of, *Please quiet down, a man-person has something important to say that we can all learn from. Sir, you have the floor.*

The difference is subtle. It's not meant to shame the heckler into the ground and it's goofy enough to make me the butt of the joke a bit as well. I think, for the most part, it's actually more fun for me and that's what it comes down to. If I get activated by someone in the audience, my heart rate goes up and I lose focus. My energy funnels to the defenses in my body, and it takes over. We performers sometimes call this being "taken out:" being taken out of the moment you're in, your flow disrupted, the attention divided. Being taken out on account of a heckler or some flimsy disturbance is the worst because when your body is defensive you shrink and close down. Of course you don't want to be vulnerable, that would expose you to hurt. For me it's a big boner killer to become defensive on stage and be taken out of the world I have created, which is meant to be unflappable idiocy and true disarmament. I believe in disarmament—not to say I don't think violence is sometimes necessary, sure, give me revolutions and grandmas on the porch fending off poachers and evil ex-husband cowboys, etc.—but not at the alt-comedy show with 35 people in the audience.

Touring Europe gave me the confidence to perform practically anywhere, under almost any circumstances. It gave me "chops," pardon my French—the experience of learning by doing. When obnoxious people tell you, "There is no way to leaaarrrrrrn a new language except by going to the country of origin and being among the people"—it's like that. There is simply no way to become a consummate live performer without the experience of weathering audiences, travel discomfort, weird venues with multitudinal seating arrangements, stages, lighting, heat/AC, space, facilities, and limp string cheese in the green room. I played nearly every single show I was offered for at least the first ten years of performing Dynasty Handbag. Maybe 15. It's the reason I'm good.

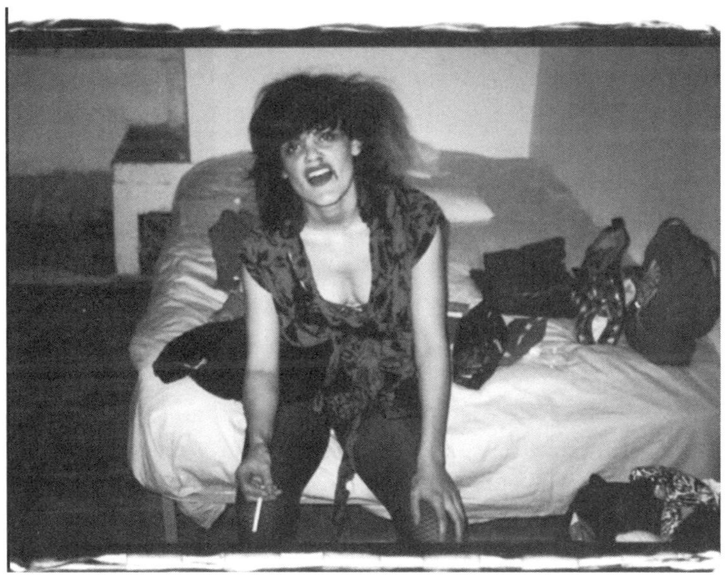

Dynasty Handbag, Lisbon, Portugal, 2003.

FIFTEEN: HOW DO I DYNASTY

I never in a dillion years thought that performing Dynasty Handbag would be my career; that this crazy hoe would follow me through my 20s, 30s, and 40s, and let's face it, my 50s. That my real job would actually never show up. This might be my real job?

I have always struggled to describe Dynasty Handbag. I usually say I am a performer, in order to qualify that I am not a wretched *performance artist*, or merely a comedian, or the ghastly clown, or simply an actor. Then the dreaded question inevitably comes . . . "Oh, what do you do?"

Well, I perform as this alter ego. I do songs sorta and stand-up kinda and ummm I look insane. Yea. It's like, funny performance art, or artsy comedy. It's like my insides on the outsides. Sort of an alter ego that is moving crazy saying all the things you can't really say, but in a leotard and also looks like they got run over?

I know that when I am actually doing it, it is indeed powerful, but there is no good way to describe live energy. It's the annoying truth—*Oh man you gotta see them live!* In many ways it doesn't matter what I say about my art—art shouldn't have to tell you what it is. It should tell you what something else is, or move you through an unnamable thing; after all, it is another language. The annoying thing about art is that when it becomes interesting or popular to people, suddenly you have to know how to talk about it. Or at least the public wants that, and funders want that. People want to know that you know that something is happening here, and that it's not a mistake that the work is complicated. It's on purpose and it's aware of itself. It has meaning. This is a terrible premise that creates a classist bullshit system of separating fine art from folk art, craft from "outsider art."

If I try to make work with meaning, if I start from that place, I produce boring and didactic work. When my ideas are transmuted into a song, a performance, a film, or a drawing, an infinite number of little things come together. People are witnessing a bunch of decisions I've made based on my entire life experience, or one overheard conversation that gets mutated by my entire life experience; all the dumb things I think, and all the smart things I think and everything in between. Including taste, which I have heard there is no accounting for . . . actually, there probably is, but it would take too long to account for it. Like how it's actually possible to predict the weather, but it's too hard. It would be inefficient! And boring. How would people who just met get caught in a rainstorm and fall in love?!

When I direct myself as Dynasty Handbag, I'm simply making choices about the way my brain synthesizes my experiences, which in turn becomes style I suppose. I can't really know if they are good choices. I can know if they feel good in my body, feel right, as it were, but that's about as far as my ability to know anything goes. This expands into all areas of my life. The major questions I'm always asking myself are, Is this the truth? Am I trying to force an idea? Is my ego in the way? Is this fun for me to perform? Am I trying to make people think I'm smart? That last one is the topmost destroyer of good art IMHO. I'm Hoe. Ha ha.

I occasionally teach workshops and college classes. One time at Pratt, I taught a segment in my directing class on the movie *Showgirls*: a legendarily terrible movie about an ambitious stripper in Las Vegas. I got in minor trouble for failing to give a trigger warning before asking my students to watch this sexist, homophobic, racist, and rape-forward garbage pile of a film. I felt terrible about it. One student was very upset. She was genuinely disturbed by the violence and racism in the film and wanted to understand why I would assign it. Fair enough. The reason I assigned the film, I explained to her, was to investigate the logic of director Paul Verhoeven by attempting to unpack his decision making, the emotional logic of the characters, and why their reactions to events and conversation are radically outsized and bizarre. The film goes beyond "bad acting" camp—it's not simply exaggerated or heightened emotion, it's demented emotion. The scene I respond to the most is when Nomi and Molly first meet. Nomi tries to steal Molly's luggage, they get in a slapping fight in the parking lot, then Nomi throws up, runs into the street, almost gets run over. Molly saves her, they embrace, almost kiss, and go get some French fries.

When Molly then asks Nomi about her past, Nomi gets so frustrated by having to answer questions that she slams the French fries down and they explode all over the table. She doesn't clean them up. Molly doesn't say, *Jesus, calm down. Or, Are you ok?* They just keep talking. Then Molly becomes her best friend, and is consistently thrown under the bus in every way—raped, racially demoralized, stepped on—in order to serve Nomi's bonkers storyline.

It makes me consider the logic of Dynasty Handbag in terms of what I would say or would not say, do and not do, why a costume look is right for her or not. Her logic was somehow there from the beginning, but I only began to unpack it when I started having to write about my work for grants. Hers is crazy logic—as in, mentally ill logic—which I am intimately familiar with because of my mom. It is also traumatic logic—the logic of responding to horror. Like I said, my mother's crazy thoughts and actions were totally reasonable to her. In my case, crazy things happened around me all the time, and no one responded appropriately, which is also true of society at large. Our country's emotional response to rape culture, racial violence, poverty, child abuse, environmental disaster should be more like Nomi's response system. Dynasty Handbag is an attempt to speak to that.

Dynasty Handbag's aesthetic logic is pretty straightforward as well. She is meant to look ugly. More specifically, she is trying to look like a beautiful woman but fails. She is my response to women's clothing and beauty standards being historically hideous, restrictive, uncomfortable, and expected to be either sexually "appealing" or sexually repellent (controlled). Dynasty Handbag stuffs herself into ill-fitting, cheap women's wear, or is in some kind of get-up of undergarments that attempt to conceal lumps, bumps, and "imperfections" but end up highlighting them, seemingly by accident.

Unfortunately, fashion has gotten progressively illogical, and now everyone is into ugly clothes. Much of Dynasty Handbag's standard wardrobe is now fashionable, and there is very little to claim as actually ugly anymore, which erases the significance or coding, which is one of the most interesting and important things about fashion. I used to wear leotards, aerobics gear, crop tops, acid wash, but that stuff has long since lost its sting and become meaningless. Much of it has already cycled in and back out of irony.

Fashion seems to be on a 20-year cycle—it must run a whole generation or the looks are too close for comfort. The key to Dynasty Handbag looking awful might lie in being 15 years behind instead of 20, and to make sure I am buying clothes for "women," not for regular people.

When I started hosting my variety show *Weirdo Night* in 2016, I thought that Dynasty should look the part of an MC more, so I started wearing suits. They don't fit and look hobo/bank teller circa 1986 but I love wearing them. Women's suits harken to something tragic, bygone and middle management. This capable lady will help you get that small biz loan for your dream bakery! Or help you run for prez a million times and keep losing! I suppose since I have aged a lot through Dynasty Handbag, suits these days also speak to my maturity, professionalism, and stature in the community.

Dynasty Handbag is me trying on middle-aged-woman drag. I don't know if you have ever been hanging out with a middle-aged butch or masc NB person and imagined what they would look like as that same person if they never "went Gay." If they had a husband and three beautiful children? Or a wife and three ugly children? It feels like a hate crime to do this, and probably is—maybe that's what homophobes are doing all the time.

When I am in Dynasty Handbag business suit drag, it's a press-on nail away from how I could . . . if . . . I . . . wanted . . . to . . . *look for real*—instead of who I am, a womanish person of 51 who dresses somewhat like a 15-year-old-boy crossed with an art teacher. But it's a scientific fact that Gay people age differently. At this moment I am wearing a tie-dyed Chucky T-shirt, stupid cotton pants with a 90s pattern, and soccer slides from the dollar store. My hair is a half-inch long, shaved, and bleached blonde. Who am I? Lesbian Eminem? I don't know what I'm supposed to look like, but I also don't believe in what I'm supposed to look like. Mom's (buckwheat) spaghetti!

Before I wrote this book, I thought my love of the word Dynasty was mostly related to the TV show and its outrageous fashion indicating the absurd, baroque 80s. But I don't really care about that show. I do care about camp—and I care about the 80s, and in truth I've always been fascinated by the brand of family represented in that show, because I actually came from a family like that. In fact, the show *Dynasty* was about a Colorado oil family—a failed oil dynasty, complete with intrigue and drinking and drugs and lying and wife-stealing and people all trying to grab the family pot. I didn't grow up in that, but I felt it in the air—a residue, or proximity, a mist of it—my dad being someone who knows they will always be bailed out to some degree. He stopped being helped by his mom after he got sober, but she owned a house, she had money—there was money in the family. That's a very different consciousness than when people are broke broke, like my mom—when you get to the end of the month and have zero, and there is zero coming anytime soon, there's no trust or a house coming down the pipe when a parent croaks. I have to say that although I don't have a pot coming to me or own a home, I am relieved that my parents kicked the bucket with neither of them owning anything. I just love a failed rich white family. Because we don't usually deserve a dime of that money.

The word Handbag has always been funny to me, too. It suggests maturity and womanhood—two elusive concepts. Also, it suggests a pussy, one that's on the outside of your body. A handbag—well, a handbag is a woman's everything. They can be aspirational wealth and status symbols and cost more than my car. Some are cheap knockoffs, dirty with broken handles. Just like pussies! As a kid, there was something that normalized my mom when she carried a handbag. Hers was soft light brown leather with ink stains at the bottom. Ha ha. It contained a pack of Big Red gum, keys, a change purse that didn't zip all the way up, and her checkbook that she painstakingly kept balanced at $0 in her careful cursive. And it meant something. It symbolized a regular person. The leather smelled musty and gave her a hint of legitimacy. I would dig around in it for loose change. A quarter was a big find. Real women have purses. Purssies.

The busted-ness of my mom is a source of both grief and pride. The contradiction of these symbols of capitalism—Dynasty and Handbag—crashed in me to create an absurd and delightful agony. Now, as an anti-capitalist adult, I celebrate things that symbolize brokeness and the unrelenting resourcefulness of the less monied classes—like Dynasty Handbag using a frazzled bungee cord for a belt. Or how I use car tape. For those of you who don't know what car tape is, it's tape you use to hold your car together instead of getting it fixed. I am currently using classic silver duct tape on my front under-bumper. One of the many reasons I love my partner Mariah so much is because she understands car tape. The creative MacGyvering she will labor over instead of simply buying a replacement item or hiring someone to fix something broken is astonishing. Once, she held her rear bumper onto her car with an old USB cable. I love trash cars, too. It makes me so mad when people complain about them in their neighborhoods. I like to complain on Nextdoor about rich peoples' ugly houses. *Get this monstrosity out of my neighborhood, it's been parked here for ages!*

Although I now have a great reverence for the sloppy and unrefined, as a kid, I sometimes wanted my mom to look better. Mostly because I didn't want people to make fun of her and I wanted her to have nice things. Her attempts at dressing up were pretty pathetic and made me sad, but I did like it when she tried. I can still see my mom's toes in pantyhose peeking out of her floral-patterned wedge sandals. The sandals were a huge deal because other than the occasional job interview, my mother, rain or shine, only wore those flip-flops with the rainbow straps. Dynasty Handbag *always* wears pantyhose.

It's almost as important as her hair. If there are runs in them, or if the feet are all brown and gross and have been shredded to pieces, all the better. Sometimes if they are really filthy and shredded I tie them up and the ends of my feet look like they are encased in little nude garbage they look funny as hell.[18] Pantyhose is an indicator of a woman's success and failure in our society. Essentially a fake layer of "better" skin. The holes and tears and dirty soles of Dynasty Handbag's pantyhose reveal the sickness and rot under the façade of American aspirationalism.

It's not difficult to understand Dynasty Handbag's makeup. Women with smeared lipstick, runny eyeliner, too much rouge, are immediately suspicious. Either whores or hysterical (and also whores).[19] When my mom put mascara on it would *always* be clumpy. She never learned how. It embarrassed me as a kid, but as an artist it makes me proud. She had so little, which still breaks my heart, but I also think it's ok to not have stuff. Why have stuff?

As for performing, the stage is my comfort zone. It's the only place I feel safe being as powerful as I am, or want to be, or pretend to be. This could be because of the agreement inherent to theater—as in, the dynamic that is understood, a social contract that makes sense to me and the public. In thinking about the stage as a container, the audience knows they are required to agree with the reality that I am presenting, as long as I am confident in its existence. That is what confidence in a great performer serves. Live performance is a balance of control and vulnerability. My task is to demonstrate to the audience I am in control enough to not abandon them in the reality I've created.

---

18 *Pantyhose Toes*. See appendix.
19 *Fascist Dictatorship Makeup Tutorial*, Video, 2016. See appendix.

I need to be vulnerable enough for the audience to enter that world and risk feeling something. After all, if I'm not risking anything, why should they?

I believe I was born to be on the stage. I have innate theatrical talent, much like how Olympic swimmers are born with giant hands and stumpy legs. Through rigorous training, Olympic swimmers' legs become stumpier, their hands gianter. So too with my own neglect as a child—it was the training that sharpened my observation skills, instincts, and my ability to ingratiate myself to strangers through humor. The only way to get attention from my dad was to entertain him. As mentioned, Father had a silly, raunchy, iconoclastic, baby boomer sense of humor—this is my dowry as Dynasty. I was shown from an early age this idiotic sense of humor was the way to his heart. He especially enjoyed my takedowns and impersonations of my horrible elementary school teachers. Ms. Donna was a mean femme Phys. Ed. teacher who was decidedly against me; I made up a song that rhymed her name with piranha, naturally (piranhas had cultural currency in the 80s). There was also Mr. Shimon, the mean eighth grade math teacher who despised me. He had a nasally irritated way of barking at us as he wrote on the chalkboard with his arms bent in goal shape. I later learned he had been injured in Viet Nam, which is why he couldn't straighten his arms out—the skin around the elbows was pulled tight with scar tissue. My dad cackled as I mimicked Mr. Shimon writing algebra equations on the chalkboard with my arms poised like a cartoon cactus. I would not make fun of Mr. Shimon's disability today, but as a kid I was more than willing to throw him under the bus in order to squeeze a chuckle out of my dad.

Being the center of attention is what I want, but it's not as simple as that. In fact, attention is very uncomfortable for me unless I am in control of it. For instance, I dislike my birthday.

The focus is on me for just being me, which feels drab and pedestrian. The sincerity of admiration in a loved one's face as they approach me with a bouquet of flowers and look into my eyes while I am in civilian clothing is ghastly. *Happy Birthday!* I immediately feel the dread of a social contract being fulfilled. Why would they want to show up for this? They aren't getting squat! It's too tender, too fragile—they are basically naked and it's repulsive, as am I. If I'm on stage, however, in a costume, dazzling and stupefying you, and you approach me with a bouquet after the show—well, that I can receive! *Thank you so much for coming! I am soooo glad you enjoyed the show, truly my pleasure!* Don't get me wrong, those sentiments are true. If only I could turn the civilian exchange into that. *Thank you for coming to be my friend. I am so glad you enjoy me as a person, it is an honor to be a person with you.* I am actively working on this part of myself. After all, I am now mid-century modern at 51, in the hellscape of 2026, so I should probably appreciate every non-violent thing that comes my way.

I did a show at a warehouse in Brooklyn once, hosted by Eric André. I am a fan and was honored to be asked by him. I brought a bunch of dykes for security, cuz I knew it would be a weenie-fest. I had been told I was going on at 9:00 PM (lesbian midnight) but then he changed it up and said 1:00 AM, so I was already irritated.

OK, do you have a green room or a place I can hang out?

Not realllllllly, but there's a closet over there you can change in.

It was a smelly janitor closet. Not my first mop closet rodeo, but there was something about it that night that really depressed me.

After I got changed and put on my makeup with a handheld compact, I crept out of the dank closet to see what was happening on stage. It was a large warehouse space and was very cold, which I hate. The lighting was bad, it was too dark, and there was nowhere to sit. There were about 50 people scattered in front of the stage area, but the majority of the space was empty. The sound bounced around the high cement walls, and I wanted to die. Eric was on stage, on-brand antagonizing the audience by spitting milk all over the place. Why was he going on before me? He was the headliner! I pictured the turnover between him and me, and I couldn't imagine him cleaning up the stage—or I couldn't imagine him doing a good job of it, anyways. So, I left with my small gaggle of support dykes before I went on.

Never had I left a show before performing. Never had I even considered leaving a show. I may have cancelled a show once or twice from being sick, though I don't even remember doing that. But to get somewhere and leave? In proper showbiz, such as theater, or film/tv, you are never, *never* late. And you never cancel. But leaving? I had never heard of that at all. It may not seem like that big of a deal, but this incident moved a small mountain in me. It gave me a meagre shred of agency in a business that tells you that you have to do everything that is asked of you whenever it is asked, that you are weak if you don't show up and work and work and work for no money and slide around dangerous wet stages and feel humiliated. I don't bounce out on shows this regularly, in fact I think I have only done it one other time, where I was asked to perform for free in a similarly humiliating unprofessional sketchy shithole. I don't mind a shithole, don't get me wrong, but when all elements of a show suck, the shithole part tends to feel more magnified.

For me, the hardest part about performing is actually getting to the show. It's torture. All day, waiting around for shit to get going—waiting to arrive on the stage and be in the fun part, and then to feel the satisfaction of completing this task, like jogging off the court after a great tennis match! Ahhhh, now we can relax! But the day of? It's hell. I'm anxious and keyed up all day. I mistake that for a good-ish feeling, and usually don't eat, or have a really hard time eating. I typically have a low-grade stomachache as well. Sometimes (every time) I will buy a pack of cigarettes and really ruin my life. I will sit around trying not to get worn out, but it's not restful—and if I am unprepared, I generally berate myself for it, instead of actually doing the work to prepare. If I have written something new for Weirdo Night I will childishly refuse to rehearse, or I will, but I won't do a very good job of it. It's like I'm too anxious to even do that. Or, perhaps I am holding onto that anxious buzz by being stressed? I don't know the show, and I know the stress is keeping me alive?! WHO KNOWS.

OR . . . On show day, I am so tired my eyes are crossing. Or I am so depressed I not only don't want to put on pantyhose and dance around like a monkey, I can't believe how stupid I am, how shameful it is to be doing what I do, and asking people to come see it—for money! Or I have my period, and I am in agony. My gunt (gut + cunt) is protruding and the hell that is womanhood is upon me, and I can't imagine anything worse than stuffing myself into a form fitting unitard and thrusting my pelvis all over the place. What is this life, I say, who am I!? Why did I choose this, what is the point, why why why, every single time, why!?

No one will come.

Everyone is sick of me.

People are saying things like, *"Here she goes again, why won't she quit, ugh, give it a rest, cryptkeeper" "I can't look...it's like watching Madonna's halftime show."*

The only defense I have found against this line of unhelpful inner dialogue is to put it in the work. When I bring my anxieties into my performance it generally harvests gold. People really respond to self-deprecation—but it's not simply deprecation, it's actual, real thoughts that people have all the time, yet still somehow surprise and delight when they're expressed freely. As long as the powers that be are at work destroying us from the outside in, there will be that brand of material.

For instance, the first performance of my show *Titanic Depression* was in March 2023. It is now May 2026, and I am solidly in pre-menopausal *Twilight Zone* years. My body is changing in all the ways that they say it will. I get targeted ads for wrinkle creams and things to combat "meno-belly (TM)," which apparently is a whole new, second spare tire that appears. More gunt, Madame? In *Titanic Depression* I wear shapewear for a good portion of the show, meant to indicate that I am naked—it has boobs and pubes drawn on with Sharpie. It was already hard to feel confident in that outfit three years ago, but I feel even more insecure in it now. I also know I am not going to do anything about it. Ok lord, I am ten pounds heavier. I honestly can't imagine trying to change my life at all to combat the reality of my changing body. I'll just get a bigger naked costume, I've decided, so I don't have to think about it. The most important thing is my presence on stage. If I'm thinking about how I look at all, or worried about sucking in my meno-belly (TM), I will be taken out of the experience, which would be a disservice to the work and to the audience. Maybe I can even say something on stage about it.

I bet you were expecting to see more of my actual body, but it's actually sacred, and I am 51 years old, and not every queer loser theatergoer gets to have that privilege. My boddy oddy has changed in ways you can't imagine. It's a temple of secret lumps, and it's holy. So don't try me.

SIXTEEN: NYC

I got a divorce and finally moved to NYC two years later in 2004, in the hopes of becoming an actor. I didn't need a man person to get me to the Big Apple! Dynasty Handbag would be my little side project. I was gonna take over the town. Satan had a different plan for me, however.

In New York, the first thing that I did was start partying like it was 1989.

My bender allowed me to immediately get involved with a marginally famous butch who was a chronic cheater. I was still long-distance seeing someone in San Francisco, so I was also cheating. But she was worse I swear! JK, we mirrored each other. I would get wasted in order to assuage the guilt of hooking up with her, blasted high on desire and her relentless pursuit of me and everyone else with a pussy. We cycled in and out of chaotic drama for a few months, chasing each other down the drain, until the humiliation of her lies forced me to end it for good. But not without hitting an alcoholic bottom, upon which I will elaborate shortly.

Through my acting work in San Francisco, I'd made some connections to directors in New York. The plan was to get an agent there and go on proper auditions. But I was too hungover or in sloppy lesbian drama to show up. I blew all my auditions and meetings.

For money, I worked in a never-ending stream of stupid French bistros in Brooklyn. To my astonishment, I kept getting fired. My grandmother had just died, and since my dad was dead, I got a third share of the inheritance money—roughly $60,000. This was a fortune for me, which I drank and snorted away in my first six months in New York. But it got me there and into an apartment. Without my grandmother's money I would not have been able to move. I had never in my life saved money; I didn't know how. And if I hadn't moved to NY, I would have never bottomed out and gotten sober there, which was critical to my being able to tolerate going to AA, which has given me a life. There is no way I would have gone to meetings in San Francisco—I was too prideful, I knew too many people there and was too concerned they would "find out I had a drinking problem." As though people didn't already know. I thought, idiotically, that I had been hiding it. Alcoholics are ridiculous.

The marginally famous butch introduced me to many New York performers, including Murray Hill. Murray was *thee* downtown (drag) king of performance. He was a consummate variety show host, donning burgundy polyester suits, a thick mustache, and a seamless, brilliant Borscht Belt comedy persona that was unlike anything I had ever seen a lesbian do. They were also a huge support and inspiration during my first months in New York, and still are.

I had come to New York with a solid Dynasty Handbag performance cachet and a small queer following. Murray put me in the Miss LES (Lower East Side) Pageant, a mock queer beauty contest that featured the lesbian weirdos of the day and a panel of celebrity judges. The year I was a contestant (2004) it took place at Fez, a cabaret club on Lafayette and Great Jones. I had been watching beauty pageants on TV since I was a kid and was absolutely over the moon to give it the Dynasty Handbag treatment. For the talent portion I wore a purple spandex bodysuit with one sleeve, given to me by Marta in 1994, who had aerobicized in it in the 80s. I think she could see my future. My ex-hairdresser friend had given me an extra huge, ratted 'do. I sang a brutal, original dance number about a friend dying of a heroin overdose. For the interview section I wore an ill-fitting Chanel-esque suit and carried a clipboard with fake notes. I answered all of Murray's questions with the perfect cadence of a pageant girl trying to sound smart, but I didn't pronounce any actual words.

And what would winning the Miss LES Pageant mean to you, Dynasty?

Wehhievl, Ir mont mogwoegntt je blurp United States of America.

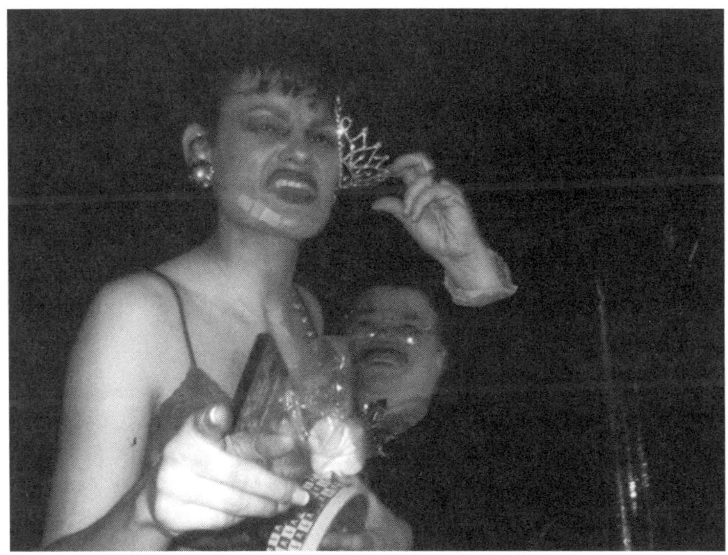

Crowned by Murray. Photo by Linda Simpson.

I was definitely in the zone. I didn't care so much about winning, I only wanted to bring the house down, show them something they had never seen, and I brought my best. I was up against a bunch of other weirdos—my friend Kim Ann came in second by performing as her mother-in-law singing a Thai pop song. I don't remember much of the other performances except it was high spirited, funny, gay buffoonery with many dyke jokes. I crushed it dead. The dykes were blown away, and I won! The Miss LES Pageant launched me into my own marginal fame, introducing me to at least 75 new queers. Alan Cumming was there and told me I was "very funny." I was gonna ride this train all the way to the top!

That didn't exactly happen. As I said, the aforementioned butch and I crashed and burned with some big consequences for me. I had a therapist who more or less demanded I go to AA. At least for a week, she said.

I have talked about my teen drinking a lot in this book, but not so much what it looked like in my early adult years. After the haunted house rape when I was 15, I stopped drinking entirely for about three years. Then I went back and forth with it for the next 15 years or so. I had always been able to stop, to pull it together, so I didn't think I had a real problem. I thought a true alcoholic drank 24/7 and couldn't simply stop and start. I didn't know this was a thing, but I was what they call a controlled drinker, or binge drinker. One pattern I had was to drink and go nuts in between relationships, then sober up when I found a new person to date. This is also very common alcoholic behavior. I learned quickly in AA that if you have to control it at all, it's a problem (duh). This toxic relationship brought out the absolute worst parts of me, and I finally got to a place where I couldn't stop. I tried but couldn't. For the first time. Which was a jift from jodd.

I had also started cutting myself, something I had never done before. My wonderful therapist, who looked like Greek Kelly McGillis, told me to go stay with Saara, who was living near me in Brooklyn with her boyfriend. They took care of me.

I got sober. I was humiliated and angry, but relieved that there may be something I could just surrender to. I am not going to go into my sober journey story too much, I promise. Who wants to read about someone getting sober? Snore. It always ruins TV shows, that's why Nurse Jackie had to die. Spoiler alert! If anyone is curious about how I did it, you are probably an alcoholic, so go to a meeting. Just kidding! I am always happy to talk to anyone about my (learning to) eat, pray (eew), meetings (zzz) journey. But you know already. It's hard as hell. It is so hard. Then it's amazing.

This was also when I was diagnosed with bipolar II. I had been experiencing a new depression that had more of a crazy seasoning than regular Prozac brand depresh. I couldn't hold onto a thought, I was paranoid and manic, and my brain skittered around like a chipmunk. The bird's-eye view and dissociation of my body was relentless. I ended up going to a city-funded outpatient rehab in Manhattan. To complete the rehab, I was mandated to go to therapy there every single day. My therapist looked like Bea Arthur and wore ugly leather sandals, which showed off her remarkable feet. Her big toes both crossed their neighbor toes, creating a toe X on both feet. Maybe regular shoes were uncomfortable. She was helpful and kind to me and talked about trauma turning into anger which, when turned inward, becomes depression. I had no idea about these concepts. Could I be angry?

Group therapy was also mandatory. It was with about six other young women who were all bat-shit crazy but I loved them. I heard terrible stories of incest and abuse there. One girl was working at a bar with her father who was *still fucking her*. Most of us had deadly eating disorders. Of course, I thought I wasn't as bad as everyone else, but I was there, too, so go figure. I was prescribed Lamictal, which is a mood stabilizer given to epileptics and bipolar patients. It was a new drug at the time, and there was no generic version, therefore it was outrageously expensive. The rehab psychiatrist, a lovely gay man, gave me giant paper bags filled with sample packs from the drug company that I procured from him in secret at the rehab. It was a lot like scoring drugs come to think of it. It's got a generic version now, thank god.

The humiliation of it all was excruciating, but I have come to love my wacked out brain and I am so lucky to be medicated. Bottoming out in New York just as I got there, thinking I would light the town ablaze with my talent, was exactly the humble hair pie I was meant to eat. I am so lucky, because New York is full of incredible sobriety. There was no way my whiny ass could get away with complaining it wasn't cool enough, or there weren't "my kind of people" in AA. I mean, Lou Reed was in AA (public knowledge). My first sponsor was an ex-Chanel model who had gotten married to her drug dealer at the Palladium. What could be cooler than that!? She was incredibly kind to me, but it was truly her good looks and hot fashion that got me to even talk to her at all. I heard Joan Wasser of Joan As Police Woman speak at a meeting during my first year, and she is a complete weirdo—I could barely understand what she was saying at all. But I was starstruck and felt reflected, too. Could it be glamorous to be sober in NY? I mean, no. But just as in New York there is the proverbial melting pot of every kind of person, so is there every kind of person at meetings in New York. Regular-ass people, celebrities, Hasidic husbands, teenage prostitutes, famous fashion designers, firemen (lots of them), murderers, gangsters, East Village baby boomer health-nuts, drag queens, bums, ancient Upper East Side old ladies.

I went to a meeting at Perry Street once where someone was holding a sink over their head. No one said anything. And there were just so many fucking meetings; one on practically every stop of my subway line, at all hours of the day.

In early sobriety I had to put Dynasty Handbag on the shelf for a minute. I was in too much pain at first to be out and about in New York. My sponsor said something to me that I still recall whenever I feel too fragile to participate in the world: "New York will always be here." I had to learn to turn off my fear of being forgotten, to take care of myself. I also had to learn to perform sober, which was terrifying.

I started taking classes at Upright Citizens Brigade so that I could practice performing sober, and so that I wouldn't be on my own while doing it. I thought this might be a good way to get away from drinking and hectic lesbians, but in all honesty a big reason was that I secretly hoped I would get discovered there. Many of my female heroes from SNL had come out of UCB, and I missed doing improv. I started at the bottom level. It was fun at first but quickly lost its charm. There were too many dick jokes, fat jokes, and homophobe jokes. It was a stark reflection of early 2000s culture; when all else fails (because of your lack of imagination), make a stupid joke about someone's race, weight, gender, or sexuality. Then pass it off as making fun of racists and bigots.

For example, when playing the object-changing game, it was common for a man to grab the sandwich or the binoculars and just make it into a giant cock:

I love to suck dick!

Oh ha ha ha a man who likes to suck dick.

Or, a pair of boobs. Ha ha. BOOBIES.

A joke, and everything dies. Jokes murder an improv scene. You can have jokes throughout a scene and it's funny if they are quick and don't make the audience responsible for affirming them. But a joke is a closed system that doesn't really have anywhere to go.

No one ever jumped in and said:

Yes AND, it's just one of many dicks protruding from an alien who is forcing humankind to give it blowjobs or else it will destroy the earth.

And no one else jumped in with a French accent and said:

Yes and, we must start a mutiny, I will be the leader of zee resistance!

These are dumb examples, but I don't want anyone stealing my good material.

One day a friend texted me and asked if I had been watching *SNL*. I hadn't really watched it in years. They said there was a new and unfunny character on the show called "DJ Dynasty Handbag." What the fuck? The skit was terrible, it starred Kenan Thompson and I felt violated watching it—my special name! I brought it up with my improv teacher who had a lot of friends on *SNL*, and he told me they were "notorious poachers" and had probably seen my name in some newspaper and stolen it. This debacle eventually faded away because the sketch was dumb, but it got confusing for a minute. People thought *I* had ripped off *SNL*. As if! I even spoke to an entertainment lawyer about it, and it got accepted as a case in a list of cases that needed pro bono help. But no one would touch the case because everyone had a conflict of interest with NBC and all its myriad conglomerates. I mean, it would have been different if I had a business making jam or if I was a landscaper named Dynasty Handbag, but I was a comedian. RUDE! It really annoyed me. I can't count the number of people who have told me throughout my life, "You should be on *SNL*!" Well, I was, I guess!

While at UCB, I had a revelation that in order to be "discovered," I would have to make this world my world. I would need to hang out at UCB all the time, go to shows there multiple times a night, and perform there as much as possible. I couldn't bring myself to do it. The improv comedy world felt stifling to me: there were just too many straight men, and it was too white, therefore, boring. So, I teased my hair, slapped on a beret and stretch pants and marched back to the queers.

When I was ready to start performing as Dynasty Handbag on the regular, the queers of New York carried me. I got love there—and as they say in recovery, go where it's warm. I performed in lots of early 2000s clubs: The Slipper Room, Mo Pitkin's, Ars Nova, Knitting Factory, Galapagos, Canal Room, Dixon Place—which is still kicking, though the earlier iteration, in Ellie Covan's living room, is no longer with us. It looked like a . . . well, a living room. A shitty one. There were flea-ridden couches and rickety chairs, clip lights, and a mishmash sound system. Large windows looked out onto Bowery and Houston before Whole Foods was the captain of that corner. I did many shows there—a split bill with Faye Driscoll, and many variety shows with the regulars of the day: Erin Markey, Joseph Keckler. Ellie had been in the East Village for ages, she was an old theater dyke and a bit nuts. One time she was so mean to me I cried. I'd created a performance for a festival at Dixon Place in 2010, and it was a huge mess. I had to stay up all night before the opening and rewrite it. It turned out great, and I was really proud. I thought Ellie would be as well, but in the lobby directly after the show, she began barking notes on my lighting in my face, in front of my adoring fans and friends. I was so ashamed. I should have listened to her notes, probably. But cheers, Ellie, you bitch, for your unrelenting determination to continue supporting downtown gay performance art—for better or worse. I also met Martha

Wilson around this time. She is the founding director of the Franklin Furnace FUND, the only organization that funds solely performance art. Martha would become my champion, and Franklin Furnace gave me my first ever grant in 2008.

Whether I knew it or not, what I was doing on stage was part of a legacy. Many of my biggest inspirations were NYC freak women. Yoko Ono, Laurie Anderson, Sandra Bernhard. But I began to see that I was following in the footsteps of others who'd paved more obscure paths: Holly Hughes, Carmelita Tropicana, Ethyl Eichelberger, women from the WOW Cafe, the Five Lesbian Brothers, Bongwater, Klaus Nomi, Joey Arias, Vaginal Davis.

In 2006 I was asked by a guest curator of PS122 if I had ever written anything narrative for Dynasty Handbag. I had not. Although there was some relief in finally being sober, in the beginning I truly felt that I was in hell. A hell of my design, of course, but hell nevertheless. Hell got me thinking about hell, and I remembered Dante's Inferno, which I had read at SFAI and really got into—it's so extra and makes no sense. I mean, he didn't know what to do with all the people who didn't know about god, because they were born before Christ, so he put them in Purgatory? The logic is flawed. But I loved the ghoulish, gay drama of the torturous eternity he came up with. I decided that I would insert my own narrative of hell into the structure of Dante's hell. I called the show *Hell in a Handbag*. I wore an outfit that suggested I was on a hike, or a sporty journey. I wore pink Reeboks, jean shorts, a stupid, tasseled tourist T-shirt that said *Jamaica, No Problem!*, a visor, and a backpack that had imaginary "snacks for my journey."

I looked at Dante's version of the levels of hell and asked myself what those were to me. I was learning about addiction—what it did for me, what purpose it served. The third level of Dante's hell is Gluttony; its most base classification is "more."

The song for this level had a sort of Philip Glass dirge vibe, and I sang the lyrics like I was under a zombie spell rocking back and forth from heel to heel with my arms sticking out in front of me:[20]

More more more
Give me more more more
I want more more more
But you've already had eight
I don't care I want more
But you've already had ten
I want more more more
But you've already seen the results of more
Doesn't matter I want more
(shameful, bad-on-purpose beatboxing)
I see ten cookies and I want ten more
I want to eat so many that I can't get off the floor
(dissolve into weird robot dance)

Inferno's level two is Lust and level seven is Violence. In *Hell in a Handbag*, these were the same level. The way the bad butch and I circled the drain was addictive, so much so that our relationship turned violent. This addictive vibe pervaded all of our interactions, which were mostly sex. Writing the show in the wake of all this, I was contending with wanting to hurt myself. I had started cutting: sloppy, shallow slices with my Leatherman tool. Getting sober is painful as it is, but I was also in agony over the breakup, rubbing self-pity lemon juice into my wounds, positive I was suffering worse than anyone in the world. At the same time, I knew it was silly, and I could make fun of it. I had to.

When I get to this combo-level in the show, I open the scene in conversation with the audience. Telling them I actually just barely made it to the theater that night, because I was jumped

20 "More More More", from *Hell In A Handbag* live performance, 2006. See appendix.

. . . by a girl gang! The leader of the pack pulled a knife out of her hair and threatened me! A nod to all the John Waters bad girls and the bad girls from films he was inspired by.

She said . . .

You better get out of here, or I'm gonna cut you

And I thought, I better get out of here. But you know I am the kind of guy that when it's time to do the right thing, I do the wrong thing

So this is what I did
I bent over like this (ass to audience)
And I said
Come on then. Cut me.
Come on
Come on
Slice me
And dice me
Come on come on
My face
Is ready
Come on come on
My eyes are ready
Come on come on
My lips I painted
Come on come on
My legs I shavey
Come on come on
My pfffffft, I waxy!
Waxy till it's raw

To my surprise, writing a narrative suited me. I liked that there was a structure in place and I enjoyed employing "what would Dynasty Handbag do?" as a way of reimagining stories. With *Hell in a Handbag*, I tried to be sincere in asking, what is my version of hell? I didn't simply want to lampoon Dante's *Inferno*. There's not much fun in that. I have continued to write in this way my whole career: *Soggy Glasses, A Homo's Odyssey* was my version of the Homeric hero journey, but through my own body; *Titanic Depression* took the narrative of the sinking ship and gave it the ol' DH workover. I also created a show that used the structure of a TV morning show, but with information I would find useful for getting through a day, like how to combat paralyzing fear, rather than what morning shows tend to offer, such as a new cobbler recipe.

After I performed *Hell in a Handbag*, the *Inferno* show, at PS122, queer scholar and chair of performance studies at NYU, José Esteban Muñoz, wrote about my work in his legendary book *Cruising Utopia: The Then and There of Queer Futurity*:

Dynasty Handbag's queer failure is not an aesthetic failure but, instead, a political refusal. It is going off script, and the script in this instance is the mandate that makes queer and other minoritarian cultural performers work not for themselves but for distorted cultural hierarchy.

OK! What? Could it be that my life's work—entertaining myself/working through my demons in synthetic women's wear—was actually a political refusal?! Yes. I accept. This filled me with glee. After all, don't we all just want to be seen and heard—even better when it's by someone who is incredibly smart and writes books? Up to that point I'd never had a review or much of any thoughtful critique to establish that what I was doing had cultural significance beyond just being insane, funny, or gross. It was the first time someone reflected what I was doing in a way that made sense to me.

Something broke open, and I considered that what I was doing was beyond being a freak in a world of freaks that mirrored each other's freakiness. I noticed a snottier contingent of queer art world people trickling in to see my shows (you know who you are, shitty art queers of the early aughts). In 2007, José was asked to curate the alt program of Outfest and asked me to make a film. We had zero dollars and about one week to make it. I asked a new friend, filmmaker Hedia Maron, to make it with me. We wrote *The Quiet Storm* in two days.[21] It's a short film in which Dynasty Handbag takes a vow of silence because no one understands her anyway. We shot it on green screen in a friend's warehouse in Williamsburg. Later we filled in all the backgrounds and supplementary characters with images from the internet. It was like thrifting, digitally. Whatever we could imagine could be produced. Or vice versa: we could look an image up, and a whole story would come to us from that image. This technique speaks to Kembra Pfahler's term "availabism:" use what is available. I had been making collages since I was a kid, and this was just another way of using found images to make a new world.

Making this film also deepened my interest in sound effects, which I could listen to all day. I have a cross-sibling who is a sound editor in Hollywood, and he gave me a drive with a gigantic sound effects library that I still use. It includes the Hanna-Barbera sound effects library as well, which must be used sparingly as they are iconic and immediately recognizable and make you think of Fred Flintstone's feet scrambling around to power his car made of dinosaur bones.

Sound and physicality might actually be the basis for my whole performance life. I am so inspired by music, I couldn't possibly ever list all of my influences in this book. But I'm not a musician really, so how does sound inspire me? And inspire me to what? It's almost embarrassingly simple: sound makes me move. Not just dance—movement. My hands will start floating to the string section listening to "Mass in B Minor." I am thrust down the street, pelvis first, while walking my

21 *The Quiet Storm*, Video, 2007.

dog listening to Sexyy Redd. Why does sound move me so? I don't know. But I do know that my obsessive music listening and the compulsive memorization I have done since childhood come out through my performance.

It's not hard to make things this way, it's already in my body. One night, I was on stage at Club Deluxe in the West Village, doing a show where I played the set myself from my laptop. I accidentally hit play on "Love Me or Leave Me" by Nina Simone, a song I had listened to hundreds of times. Her piano solo is one of my favorite pieces of music ever. I started doing air piano to the song with my hands, but it quickly moved to the rest of my body; the pressure she applies when she really goes crazy sent me into unbridled shadowboxing, where I slapped my own face and air piano-ed my legs all the way up to the top of my head. Later I worked that piano solo into a piece that includes a cover of Janet Jackson's "Control"[22] and also Lesley Gore's "You Don't Own Me," along with a soundscape I built from my SFX library of a car crash, wherein paramedics pry my head open with the jaws of life and find a swarm of bees. What I am getting at is that much of Dynasty Handbag's work comes from music that's already in my body and what that music makes my body want to do. I just let it do it.

José Muñoz and I became friends and deep admirers of each other. Much to my disappointment we never got super close, I suspect because I couldn't really hang out that hard. He liked to party and socialize; I was trying to be sober, and I was afraid of people. I would go to dinners at his house with performance world luminaries and queer scholars but leave just when things were starting to get sloppy and fun.

RIP José. You helped me more than you will ever know, and you were brilliant, kind, and so so so gay.

22 "Control," Live Performance, 2018 (Original Performance, 2011). See appendix.

José also gave me my first teaching job. I was working in a tiny Spanish tapas restaurant[23] in Chelsea when he asked me, very casually, if I would like to teach a class in Performance Studies at NYU. I was gobsmacked. I had never taught before. He said, *Just tell them what you know.* What do I know? Hmmm. I guess I know how to put on a show. But where do my ideas come from? I like talking about why things are good or bad or funny or smart. So that was something. It is really something to suddenly be reframed as someone interesting and smart who knows something that others want to know. Institutional validation is intoxicating. I left the meeting with José and walked down the hall to the elevator. Karen Finley was heading to her class with a wheelie backpack.

I need a backpack, on wheels, preferably, with stuff in it. What stuff, exactly? Books! OK, I'll do that. What books? And notes. I gotta get some notes together. I gotta read some theory—and write notes about what I read. I need to read about what I am doing.

I didn't do any of that.

I came up with assignments that I thought would be fun and help students find material and information that was already in their bodies. One exercise was "Personal Ad for Dad," where you write a personal ad for your dad in his voice, how he sees himself. Then you write one for him the way you see him. It always made me laugh, but it was sometimes too harsh a toke for the student, if they, say, liked their dad. Or had never thought critically about their parent.

We also did "Dance Like Mom," where each student teaches everyone in the class to dance like their mom. I always kick this one off, because my mom had such a specific dance move. She would ball her fists up and sort of pump them up and down at her sides, and march delicately in place.

23 People always think I'm saying "topless restaurant."

Then her arms would go up over her head while fists were still pumping, exclaiming:

Get up stand up stand up for your rights

Or

Just a little bit just a little bit! R E S P E C T woooow!

My aim with these dorky exercises was to help students recognize how the material that makes up their lives can be transmuted through their bodies and into artwork. That their stories can be fascinating if they leaned into the details, then leaned in more. Of course, there are students who are well-adjusted and boring, but not many—they don't end up in art school.

SEVENTEEN: BYE, MOM

My mother's suicide is not the worst thing that has ever happened to me. There were many, many times in my life when I'd wished she would die—wished it for her sake, and ours. Though I would never presume to know what my mother's mental agony felt like, I've touched the edge of it, and it is a perfectly good reason to leave this realm.

She made many suicide attempts throughout my life. The first one I remember was in 1999, when I was 24, although that wasn't her first time trying. She was living in Colorado, on a mountain somewhere, growing weed with her rotten little husband. She OD'ed on pills and had a grand mal seizure, I always chuckle at "grand mal seizure"—French for Big Bad Seizure. Another good band name. It has been renamed as a "tonic-clonic seizure." Also a bonkers-sounding name. It was unnerving, because by the time I had heard the news she was already back in the woods doing her same old thing: not taking meds and tending to her garden full of weeds and weed.

In January 2010, my mom overdosed again on pills. She had, by this time, been on lithium and a million other meds for so long that it was increasingly hard to tell if she was stable or not. However, I knew something bad was coming that week when she told me on the phone that she was worried her husband was "having an affair with a six-year-old little bitch" up the street. I can only imagine how bonkers their fights looked if they started with a jealous rant from my mom about the child he was absolutely not dating. D was awful, surely, but that was over the top even for someone demonstrably obsessed with child molestation.

They were now living in Santa Cruz. She was losing her mind on the regular and he couldn't handle it, as usual—such was their pattern. She would stop taking her meds, helped along by his semi-legit, anti-big pharma conspiracy theories. On this particular night, he chased her around the house with a steak knife; she left, and checked into a hotel and took an entire bottle of something that could kill her. The manager discovered her lying on the bed in a pool of piss.

This time the consequences were more serious. She was in a coma, and it seemed unlikely she would come out of it. I flew out to Santa Cruz after being convinced by a friend in AA that she really could die, and that I would regret it if I didn't go. There were so many near-death disappointments in those years; I honestly thought I would just hear one day that she was dead. Killed herself, or her husband killed her. My reaction to this attempt was mostly surface-level annoyance at being faced with another drawn-out scene we had to participate in and make decisions around, and that took me out of my life in New York. It was too sad to truly feel what this was doing to me.

But she came out of the coma. It was a miracle according to her doctors. Hallelujah, I guess? We were exasperated, but also scared, and tried to convince her—now, surely, with her husband trying to stab her and all—surely, she would reconsider their union? We gathered around her bedside in the hospital.

Mom, we want to get you a place of your own and we can all help you do that. It's time to start taking care of yourself, David is dangerous.

You can come live with me and Roumen in the back house.

I don't want to live in Houston! Too many meat eaters and republicans.

Fair enough.

I want my HUZZZZZZBANNNND

And that was that. She went back to D, and we slunk away defeated to our various corners of the United States, waiting for it to happen again.

I wrote a song called "Death Wish"[24] right after this that summed up how I was feeling.

I want you to die
But only cuz I want you to live
But you will never really live
So maybe it's better if you die
(next part sung to the melody of "Sympathy for the Devil")
Rape! Murder!
It's just a thought away it's just a thought away
Rape! Murder!
It's just a thought away it's just a thought away
Rape! Murder!
It's just a thought away it's just a thought away
Rape!

I like to introduce it like this:

This next song is a little thing I wrote about my mother.

I strike an exaggerated muscle man pose and wind my arm around like a pitcher a few times and belt out:

I WANT YOU TO DIEEEEEEEEE

It shocks people, and I look nuts, so they laugh, but people also relate to this. It's the tale of mental illness, disability, frustration, depression, addiction; of trying to change

24 "Death Wish," Live Performance, 2020 (Original Performance, 2010). See appendix.

someone who is sick. Because surrendering to the reality of their pain, which is then also your pain, is too much to bear. So, there is nothing to do but fantasize about the freedom of non-existence for them, for you. I guess she felt that way, too, finally.

In January 2011 she tried again, and she succeeded. Another OD and coma. It was almost the exact same week of the following year, and the exact same thing had happened in the same place—she was even in the same hospital. But this time when we heard she was in a coma it was worse, and somehow we knew it.

One difference was that this time my mom had an apartment outside of her house—her own SRO. It was a government-subsidized building near where she lived with her husband. She still mostly lived with him, but that was her little alone time space. I guess they got into a fight, and she went to her apartment and took a ton of pills. Her neighbor in the building, a woman named Dina, who was in a wheelchair, kept coming by and eventually called 911. She hadn't seen my mom leave since she arrived a few days before. I am grateful to this woman who kept checking on her, maneuvering to her apartment several times, which could not have been easy.

My sisters and my brother and I all gathered again in California. We stayed in the Santa Cruz Holiday Inn, a few miles from the hospital, the same one we had visited the year before. My brother is an editor and brought a bunch of work with him, thinking this might be another false alarm. My sisters and I were pretty out of it. The hotel was gross and brown. The dread was that it was another waste of time. I wanted her to hurry up and die. Every morning, we would go down to the brown continental breakfast room, squirt some brown waffles into the machine, drink weak brown coffee, and head to the hospital up the road.

We all slid into our respective family system roles. In crisis, we put up our most effective shields. My older sister coped by being detail-oriented to an agonizing degree—micromanaging the doctors and wanting to know everything about each medication and procedure.

I don't like Dr. Bilson, he has a really gruff manner. I really don't like that nurse Jennifer, she is an idiot, doesn't seem to know what she is doing. Are you sure that zarapzalapam is safe? I don't think it's been tested nearly enough... What was that drug she was on two years ago? I don't think she should have been prescribed that.

My brother was methodical and businesslike, making sure he was in touch with work and managing family life back home in Colorado. He was measured and dissociated. He was probably thinking about when he could get some tennis in but was too embarrassed to say it out loud.

J'nai, who doesn't front when it comes to feelings, was miserable. She had on an "I hate this" face pretty much 24/7. Refreshing. When everyone else is trying to control their emotions in some way, J'nai will simply say:

This sucks. Mom sucks. This hospital sucks. Suicide sucks. Fuck everyone and fuck everything.

I was perfect. Just kidding. I was doing my usual thing of squirming around being unable to sit in a room with anyone. I was outside a lot, on the phone with my sponsor or other people in recovery. I was itching to leave all the time. I didn't want to be mad or irritated at my siblings, so I wandered off. There was a turtle pond at the hospital that I liked to sit and look at. The turtles sat peacefully on a log and stretched their little necks out, soaking up the sunshine. I liked the cafeteria, which included its institutional salad bar—crunchy lettuce and blue cheese dressing. My brother said a really kind thing to me after this was all over. He said I was so calm, and I handled it all so well and seemed to float above all the drama. I was not above it, but I was doing some black belt Al-Anon and trying my best to "detach with love, not an axe."

Doytenanda David ding dong husband would come to the hospital every day and make a real stink. He usually had on some drapey, linen situation and beads and a long slimy braid from the back of his head. He also had paint on his face that I guess was some kind of Hari Krishna makeup, who knows. He would walk down the hallway of the hospital in his flapping sandals, crying out:

Where is my sweet honey ambrosia? What are you doing to her?! You can't trust these doctors, man! They are all sick, man, and my sweet woman needs to get out of this place now and come home, mama needs to come home.

We would collectively scatter when he would come by.

Scummyponda's in the house! Hit the deck!

My sisters would stay up drinking wine into the night, talking about mom, talking about our fucked family, processing. I would go to bed early to read and hear them through the wall. It sounded like they were bonding. I wanted to come out and join them, but I couldn't do that kind of bonding. It was a weird time. I don't know what else to say about it. She left. She didn't want to be here anymore. Why would she?

About a week into her being in the coma and on three different kinds of life support, the doctors told us her condition was not going to change, and it was time to make a decision. We all agreed immediately it was time to pull her plug. The doctors said it could take a couple hours or up to two days for her to pass after shutting down the life support. We said our goodbyes and went back to the hotel to wait. Early the next morning we got a phone call. She had passed when none of us were at the hospital to witness, which we were grateful for.

I am still struggling to forgive my mom. The process has been drawn out, excruciating, and liberating. I still have more rage to go through, in case that wasn't evident this entire book. Only within the last five years could I even admit to the terror she put me through, admit to the idea that I had needed a mother at all. I have a tightness in my heart around my mom, a deep freeze that is still thawing. A dead parent is one thing, but a suicide parent is quite another. Suicide is sad as hell. I mean, she was already in her 70s. Couldn't she have waited a bit and died a tad less ghoulishly? It's just so fuckin dark. I know from other friends who have had a parent die by suicide that the manner of death really confuses the actual grief process. It's a whole other trauma that's happening alongside the regular grief of a loss of a parent. I have experienced a lot of grief in my life, but my mom's death is the only death that has had a tinge of repulsion. The suicide part is gross.

We went to her apartment after she was gone to clean it out. Immediately to the left of the door was her futon mattress, covered in a tangle of blankets and many, many pill bottles. There were pills scattered in the folds and on the floor beside the bed. There was a broken glass in the sink, along with powdery pill residue. Why was the glass broken? Did she try to drink water after taking the pills? Was the residue just a loose pill, or did she spit them all out and drop the glass? Did she suddenly think better of overdosing and change her mind, but it was too late? Maybe she was just out of it, and everything went as planned.

Whether she wanted to die or had changed her mind, it is grisly and unbearably sad imagining her lumbering around her one-room apartment drugged. A part of me never thought it would actually happen. Like it was simply too dramatic. Maybe the reason it hadn't succeeded in the past was because maybe, just maybe, she didn't actually want to go, she was just being extra. But I knew that wasn't true. The fear and torture in her eyes when she was in her manic episodes was enough to show how inescapable her hell was. And I don't blame her or anyone for taking their life. Life is terrible, unbearable, cruel beyond words for many. That we—us survivors, let alone thrivers—that any human being can stay here with the amount of suffering around us is almost the biggest miracle of all. These may seem like contradictory thoughts, and I suppose they are—but these conflicting feelings are part of going through losing a loved one, a parent, a mother, to suicide.

I had suicidal ideation frequently throughout my life. My only real, decisive action toward it was purchasing a fun-size bottle of Tylenol, in case I got brave enough when I was living in the Tenderloin. Oran was struggling with heroin, and I was cheating on my girlfriend and feeling utterly hopeless and disgusting. I had a constant low vibration of "kill yourself kill yourself kill yourself" buzzing in my head. It really was true hell. I would periodically look at the Tylenol bottle and think, is today the day? Then get scared and go get a burrito or draw a sad picture.

My mother's family history is a bit of black hole. She rarely talked of her family, and we didn't know them at all growing up. She had been close to her grandparents when she was little and once told me how her grandmother would walk in a field and suddenly stop, bend down, and pick up a four leaf clover without even looking for it. I have tried this. It is not genetic, as it turns out, but I still give it a shot sometimes.

My mom often sang to us. Her songs always had a gothic, 1800s barnyard darkness to them that made it seem as though mom herself came from another time and place—out of one of these creepy songs, perhaps. One song in her repertoire, "Billy Bardo," was about a bunch of people getting high on "grass" and whisky, finding out one of them was a narc, then throwing them in the river to die. That was by Johnny Paycheck, but in my mind it came from pirates and surly old cowboys. She sang us "The Fox Went Out on a Chilly Night," which was scary because the fox graphically murders a big, gray goose to feed his family. There was a nursery rhyme about a woman who had whooping cough.

According to my Aunt Liz, who I visited in my mid-20s, my mom left for college in Detroit at 18 and never returned. She was a stranger to Liz as well. I tried once to delicately ask Liz about mom's mental illness. I was trying to see if she would say anything about possible child abuse in her family. It was clear she wasn't privy to anything, or it was an absolutely untouchable subject. About my mom she said, *I don't know anything about it, but I think she had always been a little sad.* That's one way to put it.

Looking around my mom's little apartment after she was gone—at her scant belongings, her watercolors, the same fifteen cassette tapes she had had for twenty years, her thrift store clothing, her plastic hairbrush, her ratty floor futon—I felt an emptiness that was gutting and profound. She simply could not get out of herself. I found a pile of papers from a rehabilitation center—her unfinished therapy work. It made my heart sink. A person simply cannot get well unless they want to. And even if they want to, sometimes the darkness of the trauma is just too big to overcome. How could I know what that feels like?

I got so lucky on my recovery path. Why did I live? Why couldn't my mother stay medicated? Get well? Why couldn't she ever stick to a plan of wellness? I know it wasn't something that she could overcome on her own, but so many people tried to help her. And it didn't work. I had what they call "the gift of desperation," and it was definitely not something I conjured myself. Perhaps I was moved by all the things I knew were good in the world, that even though I was depressed and mentally ill, I didn't want to miss out on what could maybe happen if I found a way to live. Maybe I didn't want to destroy my family even further. If one of my siblings decided to off themselves, I don't know how I would keep going. I guess that gift of desperation was something perhaps my mother never had.

One Christmas, when I was an early teen, my mom gave me a small gift. I opened it and found a large, wooden earring in the shape of a flamingo, wearing a rainbow-colored skirt. I was confused: where was the other one? And why on earth would she think I would wear this? Then Jyoti opened her present, and it was the matching flamingo. We both laughed, and then my mom laughed, recognizing how ridiculous it was. But she didn't have any money, and this seemed like a good solution to her. At the time I didn't even live with Jyoti. We would have had to mail our respective earrings back and forth in order to share.

At moments my mom could see her craziness and funny behavior. The second time I visited her in Hawaii, I went into the bathroom to wash my hands. She ran in and said:

You have to keep the bathroom door closed at all times!

I'm not on the toilet, mom.

Swami Prabhupada can never see the inside of the bathroom, it's insulting to him!

Swami Prabhupada was her guru, his photo hung in the hallway across from the bathroom door.

I stuck my butt in front of his photograph and said:

You don't wanna see my butt, you can't see my butt, you're a guru, but you can't see butts!

She giggled and said:

I know I know.

We had a memorial service for her at the house we rented on the beach in Santa Cruz. I thought we did a really good job of trying to honor her in spite of the fraught relationships we all had had with her. We invited some folks from the Hog Farm down from Berkeley, and we even invited her troll husband. I had learned the phrase "keep it light and polite" in Al-Anon, which is basically revolutionary when you're around people you hate. You're welcome for that tidbit. Anyhow, when people die you inevitably see more of their life. I've heard this happens for a lot of people with their parents. My mom's husband had one million kids, and a lot of those kids had babies. Some of them came to the memorial, and they called her Grandma and they adored her. I didn't even know their names, I had never seen them before or heard of them, really. This made me realize my mom hadn't been totally alone—which lifted some of the guilt I felt whenever I thought about her. I had a similar feeling when all my dad's sponsees were loitering around the hospital, or when I saw the pics of him with his dom. We can never know someone's life. With my mom, though, the truth was, she didn't want my help. I don't know what she wanted from me, but it wasn't that.

My main communications with her had been through letters. I didn't like speaking to her on the phone. In our letters we kept it, well, light and polite. I would tell her surface-level things about my life. Never anything about relationships, money, jobs, my depression, anything that could make me vulnerable to her. When I got hired by NYU in 2010, I did tell her I was suddenly a professor, after 15 years of waiting tables. Instead of congratulating me, she asked if I could sell weed to the college kids for her. In her letters she would tell me about her gardening, or what she was beading or painting. Sometimes she would send me a completely insane collage. A picture of a beach cut out of a magazine glued to a piece of construction paper with a wonky colored pencil illustration of a coconut palm. Sometimes she would send us family picture collages but with my dad's head cut out. Like Joan Crawford in *Mommie Dearest.* Invariably, her letters would include something that was clearly either made up, or not real but that she believed, such as her secret Russian boyfriend. Which I responded to by saying, Wow, otlichnaya! He sounds really interesting!

I didn't have much of a relationship with her beyond sparse mail correspondence and navigating her emergencies. In the years leading up to her death, I felt truly helpless in the face of my obsession with her mental health, and with the idea of her getting better. My incredible, older dyke therapist once said to me after my mom had been hospitalized, not long before she died:

You know she may not ever get better.

That had never even occurred to me.

My first major move with boundaries had been telling my brother and my sisters that I didn't wanna be included on any more threads about mom's dire living situations, like trying to get her into a women's shelter or into a hospital. It was the same every single time: we would all scramble to help and our lives would be completely disrupted, and she would just go back to her husband. Then she would stop taking her meds. The same cycle for thirty years.

It was very scary putting up that boundary, but transformative for me. Nothing changed with her, but I had more peace.

I saw her one more time before she died. I was in California with my girlfriend Sophie, whom my mother kept calling Sonya for some reason. Me and Sonya took her to a seafood restaurant on the Santa Cruz pier. She ordered a veggie burger and fries. As we were chatting, my mother started fiddling around with her fries. Eventually she began to arrange them in an orderly line, side-by-side lengthwise across her plate.

Mom, what are you doing?

What does it look like I'm doing? I'm building a bridge.

At her service I made a long playlist for her, with all of her favorite music: Talking Heads, Stevie Ray Vaughan, Bob Marley, Otis Redding, Aretha Franklin. We made flower arrangements, placed all over the house. My partner at the time, Sophie, helped out by renting a big house on a cliff by the beach, and it turned out to be just right. We all went down to the ocean and put flowers in the water for her. She was cremated. We all got a sack of her ashes.

My sack sat in a cardboard box in my closet for 14 years. It was deeply hidden in the closet, and Mariah almost threw it out in a bout of decluttering.

What's this, do you need it? she called out from the other room.

That's my mom.

Once I took a pic of it on my phone and sent it to my siblings with the message:

Mom's still looking for stable housing

I bet she would have laughed at that.

Only this year did I get a real vessel for her ashes. I still don't have them out in my house—I don't wanna be reminded of her every day. But it's a pretty little box with deer painted on it. Mariah was proud of me for finally doing it. I was proud of me, too.

EIGHTEEN: THE NORMA RAE OF EXPERIMENTAL THEATER

Note: The incident of assault in this chapter is public record.

Ever since I learned about them in the early 90s, I had dreamed of working with The Wooster Group. They had a mystical aura surrounding them and were the ultimate in "downtown experimental New York theater." I had heard that if you worked with the WG as an intern you would be allowed to enter the sacred chamber of rehearsals, a surefire way to eventually work with the company. In 2004 I applied for the internship, and I got it. Unfortunately, revered director Liz LeCompte and her longtime boyfriend (and Wooster Group star), Willem Defoe, had just split up—he got Hollywood famous after being in Spiderman and started dating a hot, younger actress. Liz was shattered and subsequently closed the rehearsal process. This meant I rarely got to see or interact with any of the company members. I spent my time upstairs in the office area, answering the phone and buzzing people into the building, while the illustrious actors rehearsed in the space below, the Performing Garage.

Once the show was ready it moved to St. Ann's Warehouse, where I was finally able to attend rehearsals and see how the Avant-sausage is made. For this production: a Faustian situation called *House/Lights*, many TV monitors showing black-and-white films with tinny noises. I could never really follow the show, but it was thrilling nevertheless, and the performers were excellent. Kate Valk, the longtime main actress of the company, was my hero. Kate is mesmerizing. She's so pretty and alive. When she went into a scene, her transformation was instant, and her laser focus had a lightness that let you in easily and invited you to go on this ride. She had fairy godmother energy. Her voice has an extraterrestrial, metallic, femme shimmer that was soft and inviting but still loud and powerful. She could shoot it to the back of the theater, through the wall and out into SoHo, into greater New York, and off to the sea and back to outer space from whence it came. Kate was everything I wanted to be. Though she always waved at me and was so kind, I never got to talk with her.

I was charged with sweeping the stage before and after rehearsals and cleaning up coffee cups and trash from the actors' hang-out zones. At long last I got to meet them. Mostly they were busy eating out of to-go containers and low-key joking about stuff. I desperately wanted in. If they only knew how good at joking I was! I hoped they would notice my effortless star power as I lingered, trying to get attention, wielding my broom. Like Kate, everyone else was extremely kind and thankful, but I never had a conversation with anyone, and no one asked me a single question about who I was or what I was doing there. I saw the show probably ten times. Every night I trudged home through DUMBO in the snow, disappointed at not having been made the star I so deserved to be. I worked as an intern for The Wooster Group for about six months. Then I began my internship into alcoholism and lesbian drama, so I had to give up on that dream for a bit. Hold, please.

Six years later and sober, I had the distinctly early 2010 honor of being cast in a live lesbian soap opera called *Room for Cream*. It was one of the best and weirdest theater experiences I have ever had. *Room for Cream* centered around a college town called Sappho—a lesbian haven hidden somewhere in the Berkshire mountains. The series depicted an idyllic but complex queer community that had audiences longing to live there, too. We often had legendary downtown theater icons like Wallace Shawn in the show doing cameos. I played a no-nonsense butch FBI agent, Agent Steph. In my first appearance in *Room for Cream*,[25] I was getting an enthusiastic dildo blow job from Erin Markey. Then I shot them.

It was not a real challenge to play Agent Steph; all I had to do was think of my dream date. Friends who came to see the show told me they were attracted to Steph and felt weird about being around me now that they knew she was lurking somewhere in my consciousness. It's a crazy thing about desire; I think that's why I'm such a committed switch. If I concentrate hard enough, I can make anything hot, EVEN the cops.

One day in rehearsal, director Brooke O'Harra announced that Kate Valk would be in the next season of *Room for Cream*, playing my estranged mom who had put me up for adoption. I was going to be sharing the stage with Kate Valk! A dream come true. She was every bit as warm and lovely as I had hoped, and we became friends almost immediately. She later came to see a Dynasty Handbag performance and loved it. She even consulted with me on a solo show I did called *Vertititgo*, where she gave me one of the best pieces of advice I've ever gotten about performing. When I was showing her my script, I told her, "I don't know why, but I want to be a bear in this scene." Without pause she said, "Oh absolutely, be the bear. The why will be answered once you do it."

Months later, she called me up and asked me if I knew anyone who might be right for a part in The Wooster Group's new show, a version of Shakespeare's *Troilus and Cressida*. They needed a Cressida to play opposite Scott Shepherd's Troilus. I recommended a few people, I can't remember who, but I think they were all blondes.

---

25 "Room For Cream," episodes on YouTube. See appendix.

Then Kate said, *What about you?* I couldn't believe my earholes. I was so fucking excited. She told me to learn to speak in iambic pentameter. Sure! NO PROBLEM!

There was nothing I could do to prepare for the way Liz LeCompte works. Explaining it feels simultaneously impossible and sacrilegious. Her methods in no way resembled a traditional audition, where you come in and perform one well-worn comedy and one worse-worn drama monologue to a table of unreadable people. This was more akin to a cult initiation or a fraternity hazing.

The first audition exercise was to stand center stage while four TV monitors mounted in each corner played a scene from *Avatar*. As the gigantic, prehistoric dragons or whatever the fuck they are flew dramatically around cliffs and epic landscapes, I was tasked with watching the screens and moving along with the cuts in the film. Not the camera moves, and not the moves of the dinosaur, but the cuts in the film: fast, swooping camera moves and extremely quick power-cuts, of which there were many. One wouldn't notice them unless they were concentrating hard. I did my best, hopping around manically, trying to keep up with the cuts changing at a feverish pace. This was so much harder than you might think, and I felt stupid in exciting new ways.

The second, more involved and most important audition task, was using an in-ear monitor, which is a tiny speaker such as a spy would use to get important directives from a guy in a white van, or a nerd who needs someone telling him what to say to a love interest. In-ear monitors are a big part of The Wooster Group's practice, but their employment of them was more complex than a simple instruction into the ear.

Through my in-ear, a passionate and desperate scene between horny young actors Natalie Wood and Warren Beatty from *Splendor in the Grass* played. The words I had to speak while listening to this scene were not from the film, but rather lines from *Troilus and Cressida*—and I had to speak them in iambic pentameter. The scene was played between me and Scott Shepherd, the star and darling leading man of The Wooster Group. So, I was listening to *Splendor in the Grass* in the in-ear, reciting Shakespearean text in iambic pentameter, and also trying to connect fully with Scott Shepherd/Richard/Troilus. And, for some reason, I nailed it. God knows why, because I later had such a hard time with this process. I kept going, and the scene got even more tense and hot with Scott Shepherd. I remember Kate later saying that my ability to "go up against Scott" is what got me in the room.

I got the job. But I did not end up getting cast as the lead opposite Scott. That went to his then girlfriend, Marin Ireland, a petite blonde powerhouse actress. I was relieved to not get the lead. I definitely would not have been able to handle the amount of gobbledy Shakespeare dialogue she took on. I got cast as Cassandra, the doomsayer, the lesbian whistleblower, the fun police. Which turned out to be excellent casting.

At the time I thought that getting this job was the best thing that had ever happened to me. My foot was now solidly through the door, and I was gonna make this company my life. I was going to work with my idol, Kate, who had taken me under her wing. I was going to learn from Liz, one of the greatest theater directors of my time. I was going to have security, a job, a focus, a nexus, a new family who saw and valued me, and the art world's stamp of approval. I was a serious theater guy now. I wouldn't have to stretch myself, my finances, my energy to the edge of collapse to show people I was good. I could relax! I was IN. The validation of being cast in their project was a new layer of self-esteem laminate.

Liz is brilliant and creative at getting people out of their heads and below their surface layer of personhood. The audio coming through the in-ear was meant to split one's focus, getting to deeper layers of consciousness by making you focus so hard you couldn't be *self*-conscious. Rather than being lost in "emotion" to make acting authentic, you were lost in focus, which contained emotion, yes, but also other mysterious elements. It took me a long time to understand this. When I could catch this wave, I would sort of blank out and not even remember being in the scene, and it was transcendent. Performance can be a spiritual experience, in the sense that you can reach total presence in the moment on stage—perhaps one of the only ways I experience total presence. But it was so incredibly hard to believe that I was doing anything. I was not *trying* to *act* or focusing on *acting*. Through this divided concentration, a dare-I-say "pure" essence emerged. There was no, "In this scene you feel this—so act like you feel this." Liz stressed, always, that I was enough. That what came through was enough. I didn't believe that.

I was not good at this method at all. I had a terribly hard time focusing. I would miss cues constantly. In fact, my part got whittled down to one monologue that I could barely manage. I don't know why I was able to do it so easily in my first audition—maybe because I wasn't terrified of Liz yet. When I could get there, it would make Liz proud, which is all I wanted. But disappointing Liz was always impending. For example, I act a lot with my face. One day I was in the middle of running in circles on the stage—trying to capture the essence of a mood from some scene playing on a monitor. Liz suddenly hollered at me from the theater seats, "*YOU'RE NOT ON SATURDAY NIGHT LIVE! STOP TRYING TO BE FUNNY!*" Everyone laughed. *SNL*, always there to humiliate me.

It started to feel like I was in a familiar family dynamic, like that of an alcoholic matriarch and her eight to ten children, vying for her approval and attention. We each had a role to play in the show, of course, but also as her children. Scott was the favorite son who could do no wrong, Kate, the fiercely loyal longtime company member who gave Liz advice and private conference. Then there were the cast members she barely spoke to at all, and the men that she low-key berated, and at times compared to Scott. The rest of us were just hoping we could get through the day without being a letdown to her.

Generally, creating a theatrical production takes two to three months, and is divided up with rehearsals, actors first, usually scene by scene. Then there are technical rehearsals, lighting rehearsals. Then dress rehearsals, then you open the play, then it runs for however long, sometimes with an extension or a move to a bigger theater, or Broadway if you are one of those kinda plays. The Wooster Group's rehearsal process was highly out of the ordinary. When developing a show, Liz has all the company members, including technicians, present in "the room" at all times. We met at the Performing Garage from 10:00 AM to 6:00 PM, five days a week, with union time breaks. All told, we took a year to build this particular show. It was amazing to witness but could be uncomfortable if you didn't have a lot to do.

A major factor in this particular project (and a big reason it was happening at all) was that it was being funded by the Royal Shakespeare Company in London—literally the queen's theater troupe. And it was to be a collaboration. The Wooster Group had never collaborated with another company. The only way this was possible was that Liz agreed to split up the scenes with the RSC. We would be the Trojans, and they would be the Greeks. We would only be onstage together for one or two scenes, and then with only a couple of actors from each company. This was a terrible idea.

The other gigantic, violent, offensive, elephantiasis-of-the-white-lady-ego in the room was the show's concept. Liz's idea for dividing up this work between our company and the RSC—us as Trojans, them as Greeks—was to use a "cowboys and Indians" premise. Except the RSC didn't know they were the cowboys. They were doing something else entirely, with no relationship to this concept. The other glaring issue here is that we were playing "Indians"—yes, in the deeply racist sense. Early in rehearsal I meekly asked if they had "talked to an Indigenous or Native person" about this idea—or had anyone in mind to consult with for that. The response was a quick and adamant, "No." Because what they were doing wasn't "about race," and they were more or less able to do anything in the name of "art." A typical white avant-garde excuse that reminded me of the early 2000s culture of "we are not being racist, we are making fun of being racist!"—but in doing so you are perpetuating language, cultural stereotypes, what have you, that is, in point of fact: racist.

Within our show we used dozens of representations of Native American culture in films—from movies made by Indigenous people to horrifying old Hollywood westerns. Because Liz "knew" the old films were problematic, and we were reshaping these depictions to tell a different story, the meta-concept supposedly erased all need for permission to appropriate. I knew this was not . . . right. Or good. Which is often something that appropriated material suffers from. The work is not only fucked up, it's also just not interesting, because it has nothing to do with the performers and writers.

This was a huge bummer. I was aware of racism and bullshit in the theater of course, but I thought because The Wooster

Group was avant-garde and esteemed it would be different, or that the company would have a more compelling argument for their racial weirdness, one that I'd never considered. Wasn't art supposed to be radical? And somehow about justice? Wavy Gravy definitely thought so. Cracks in the pedestal began to reveal themselves.

I was stressed over the appropriation and considered making a stink, but I was afraid to lose my job. When I reached out to some friends in my community about what was going on with this play, most of the feedback I got boiled down to, "Yeah, it's truly fucked, they are fucked, but it's a job." In terms of what was happening within work environments at the time, there was way less conversation around discrimination than there is now. It was also theater, and yes, theater thinks it can do whatever it wants.

The costumes and sets were modeled after random representations of North American Indian clothing—fringed skirts and long shirts, tipis and blunt instruments. The artist who designed the costumes was a guy from the Netherlands. The Wooster Group flew him out to New York to watch rehearsal and talk through costumes and props with Liz. He was polite and kind as he sat with Liz, admiring the tableau we created with his pieces. I remember Liz saying the word "exquisite" when she saw us suited up in our long, black wigs and weird, stiff plastic fringed skirts. The costumes were a hodgepodge of white fantasies of "Indian" garb—unspecific, unconsulted, unresearched "Native clothing." The fact that they were made of rubber was another insult to the injury. Fringe was used in clothing by many Native American tribes to repel rain and dust, and it was also a way to use all of the animal, therefore preventing waste. Our costumes were synthetic materials made from crude oil sucked from the earth's core. They have no use beyond being the shameful costumes for a shitty play and will never, ever compost.

I had a small part, but even that kept changing. Day after day, I was asked to sit in rehearsal, reading along with the script and being totally ready to hop in at any moment whenever Liz had an idea. It was thrilling at moments, and boring as hell a lot of the time. The actors working a scene might pause for long moments of deep discussion about a certain word or phrase. Because I was rarely included in these conversations, I would tune them out and doodle constantly in the margins of my scripts—cartoons such as a Trojan warrior with a giant dong sticking out of his skirt.

Having the whole crew in the rehearsal room was luxurious and incredibly expensive. The soundboard operator and the AV techs were expected to be on hand the entire time, so that if Liz decided she needed to hear audio or view film, they could look anything up for her immediately. The costume designer (not the Dutch guy, their in-house person) was at the ready, to grab whatever element Liz wanted to see on someone. And so too with all of the actors. Our parts changed frequently and we had to be ready to hop up and go, go, go. This is the fragmented way in which the play would come together.

Ok now Jibz—you watch that monitor and in the in-ear we will use Smoke Signals.

Oh, put her wig on!

Let's see everyone in the wigs!

Liz liked to see us in wigs, it helped her envision things. I understand that now—wig power is real. For nearly 20 years I used my own hair as Dynasty Handbag. It was a symbol of my power to tease it into oblivion. There was something charged and preparatory about the violence I perpetrated on my head before going out on stage—holding a big swath of my hair straight up, spraying it to hell with Aqua Net and combing it backward down to the roots, until it was a giant puff of chaos. It revved me up, like warming up on one of those dangling boxing bags before a big fight. A few years ago, when my hair started to really turn gray I began wanting to shave my head, but I held back because of Dynasty Handbag. The stars aligned when I met a witch who was also a wig designer. He sent me to a wig store in North Hollywood and told me exactly what to buy. Then I went to his house, and he cut and styled it for me exactly the right length so that it looked like my hair.

Wooster Group rehearsals *could* be incredibly fun. Especially when we, as a company, got to help build or give ideas. Everyone was funny and quick and there was a lot of joking around. On the day we heard the news that Donna Summer had died, the sound guy immediately started blasting "She Works Hard for the Money," and we had a spontaneous dance party onstage in the middle of rehearsal. I loved all of that connection, the little world we created together. It was magic.

Then there were days when Liz would come down hard on someone and embarrass them, or make the boys take their shirts off for no reason. Her voyeurism was so intensely voyeuristic that I felt like a voyeur voyeurizing her process as I was being voyuerized. Sometimes behavior is so blatantly Freudian and obvious, it is embarrassing. Liz knew this. It was part of her power.

Liz would sit in a chair all day in front of the stage, with a notebook, taking copious, elegant, handwritten notes. She loved rehearsal. I once heard her say she wished she could be in rehearsal only—never, ever in the performance phase, just process. On the one hand, this makes sense as an artist, wanting to continue to explore—just be experimenting and living in imagination, incubating forever. A baby who never gets born. On the other hand, it also makes sense because the decisions around when something is "ready" make for a vulnerable stage of the project. At this point, the messages crystallize, or are supposed to, anyway. The choices solidify and become open to scrutiny. The audience's whole job is observation, digestion, and energetic exchange. I loved this very long, very measured building-of-the-show phase. To have everyone employed equally and contributing to every aspect of the creation of the project was unique and very special. I will probably never experience that kind of rehearsal process again.

The bulk of the money raised for the company went to funding this unorthodox, full-time, year-round rehearsal and touring schedule. Funds were never used for excess anything—parties or dinners or investing in the space beyond general maintenance and operational costs. The building was a mess, but functional enough. Frances McDormand has been in a few Wooster Group shows. Once, during rehearsals, she was so grossed out with one of The Wooster Group's bathrooms, she decided she would foot the bill for a remodel. It was a crusty old SoHo building bathroom with drippy, rusty pipes—shelves crammed with cleaning supplies and mops, industrial and indelicate. Kate said that when the bathroom remodeling started, the entire chemistry of the building shifted. Men clomped up and down the stairs with tools and buckets, their bodies in motion upsetting the regular rhythms of the well-oiled avant-garde theater machine, their gruff man voices bouncing through the halls. And their disruptive questions: "Do you prefer this color paint to that color paint? Do you want a two-faucet sink or a one-faucet sink? Can we store this drill here? Can someone let us in at 7:00 AM instead of 8:00 AM?" Liz did not want any of these questions coming at her. She didn't want any part of her brain making decisions outside of the work of the play. I thought this was the coolest thing. It spoke deeply to me and validated my resistance to making plebeian life choices.

Once New York rehearsals wrapped, we flew to London where we were housed in a cluster of stately apartments that felt like they were meant for diplomats or members of the business clergy. We were a few blocks from the Millennium Bridge that takes you to the Tate Modern and very close to St. Paul's Cathedral. Our rehearsals took place in Clapham, a residential and somewhat gentrified bohemian neighborhood a few Tube stops southwest. The RSC were straight-up actory actors. Blustery with confident Big Tudor Energy. Lots of hearty guffaws and handsomeness. They were good natured and warm, but a lot less interesting and tortured than us. Liz absolutely hated their director, and they butted heads immediately.

Rehearsals clunked along. I enjoyed being in London. I loved the city. I loved how many Middle Eastern bodegas there were. I could pop in and get halva in a tin and eat it with a spoon any time of day or night. I loved riding the double decker buses around, looking at stuff from the second floor. I loved all the parks. I loved how silly it was there; that everything is "royal." So faggy. There are no civil monuments or commemorations, really, only shit named after the long legacy of kings and queens and princes and princesses and lords and ladies and dukes and colonies.

Not to brag, but I am a bit of an Anglophile. When I was first getting into punk and classic ska as a preteen, much of the glamor of it for me was that it was British. The politics of it were British, filled with new words and dynamics that captivated me. The National Front. Brixton. Lots of mentions of *fascists* (a word I still have to look up to spell). Linton Kwesi Johnson's "Inglan Is a Bitch" described all the injustices and shitty things immigrants faced when moving to the UK to escape the poverty of their homelands that had been devastated by British colonialism. People move to the UK to survive, because they speak the language, because colonialism—and then people are racist to them!? The complexity and injustice blew my mind as a kid, and I loved all the music that talked about it. I knew Margaret Thatcher was a devil. I wasn't sure why exactly, but I trusted the Sex Pistols and whoever else told me she was.

Then there is British comedy. Early on I was a huge fan of Monty Python and their ability to use humor to expertly mock class and religious repression—endless material for comedy, and they do it like no other. When I was there, I felt London was familiar, and also that I had an understanding of something—that I could see all of the things I had loved in British music and comedy playing out before me, and that was very exciting. Once my friend went to NYC for the first time and had a checklist of all of the things he wanted to see; things that had been endlessly shown in TV and films about NYC:

1. An Italian in a tank top, yelling.
2. A bum with fingerless gloves. BONUS if they were warming themselves at a trashcan fire.
3. Someone saying, "I'M WALKIN HERE."
4. A cab driving through a puddle and splashing someone.
5. A secretary in tennis shoes clearly walking to or from work, where she puts on pumps.

England felt like that to me, but more personal. It had lived in my imagination for years and brought back *Sid and Nancy*—the clothes, the slang, the music. I had it on a VHS until my dad recorded over it with John Bradshaw lectures on PBS. Fashist!

In spite of enjoying Londontowne, I was having my own private meltdown. My long-term girlfriend and I were splitting up. We had been living together in Brooklyn for four years, and my summer abroad with The Wooster Group was going to be a "break" for us to sort things out. This was also only one year since my mother had taken her life, and I had not processed that pain. I was frozen around it. The pressures around me, the weirdness of the play, the constant anxiety to do a good job so I could grow old and die in The Wooster Group, the tensions with the other theater company, my relationship dissolving, and the immense grief underneath it all were taking a toll and I was starting to unravel. And I was doing all of this sober, which was not easy.

Things were tense in the room as well. Besides the fact that we all knew the play emerging would most definitely be bad, Scott and Marin were having some intense friction that seeped into the space. Marin was not a company member for this particular show, but a contracted player like me. She was Scott's girlfriend, and they had palpable chemistry. You could feel their pale-skinned horniness for each other in all corners of the rehearsal room. She seemed to be in awe of him, but also oozing with the frustrations of a woman who knows their man needs to be locked down—he was getting ass thrown at him from all over, because he was a super cool experimental theater star with abs. This had been bubbling up in New York rehearsals, but in London it got much worse. At the same time that Scott was rehearsing the play with us, he was also starring in another play in the West End, and he was getting major attention. It was called *GATZ* and it's basically *The Great Gatsby* read aloud. The play is five hours long. He's the star. And he crushed it. Not a dull moment, if you can believe it. I know someone who has seen it five times. He was the toast of Londontowne.

Scott and Marin often came to rehearsals in a cloud of fraught energy. Marin was not good at hiding her feelings, which made her amazing to behold in the play. Her skin was alive with emotional turmoil zapping around under her flesh, like a very fragile bubble filled with screams. It was as though one poke could bring it gushing out all over you. Within *our* interpretation of *Troilus and Cressida* there was a scene wherein Troilus punches Cressida. This was Liz's big boner idea, from watching a film that she loved, where a Native American ritual with some physical violence (between men, for societal power) took place. They acted that out as the monitors played the film scene. It was actually scary: Scott shirtless and stinky, while Marin cowered, barefoot in her plastic skirt, bird-like, terrified, with fire in her eyes, *I dare you motherfucker!* And he punches her.

One early morning, around 7:00 AM, in my apartment in Blackfriars, I woke up to a text from Marin asking if she could come over. We were becoming good friends and I really adored her. When she arrived she was visibly shaky and distraught and had a black eye. Last night she and Scott were drunk and arguing, and he had punched her in the face. I didn't know what to do. I was panicked and triggered and a bit hysterical and just wanted to do whatever she wanted to do—she who was also panicked and triggered. She wanted to go down to the rehearsal space and blow up the scene. She was enraged that rehearsal was going on as usual that day, that Scott was down there as if nothing had happened. I told her it wasn't a great idea to do that. I said we needed to tell someone in the company what was happening, and they can stop rehearsals and help us figure out what to do. She reluctantly agreed. I wanted to call Liz, but Liz didn't let people call her. I called the stage manager.

Hey Jibz, what's up?

Uh, hey, Scott punched Marin and we need help, can I talk to Liz?

Oh. Uh. What?

She has a black eye.

Oh my god. Ok. Um. Hold on a second.

She came back on the phone after a pause and said Liz wasn't available (!!!) but we could talk to the producer. Uhhh, ok? The producer's only solution was to suggest they move Marin to a separate apartment. She didn't offer any other help or ask if Marin needed a hospital, something that hadn't occurred to me either. I was in a big domestic violence trigger in hindsight. She said she would call us back after rehearsal that day. What the fuck.

I took Marin to a cafe where we could get some coffee and food and talk about next moves. She insisted on going to Clapham and stopping rehearsal, and she needed me, so off we went. When we got there, she went into the theater and I waited in the hallway. I heard some yelling. Some of the RSC members came through and asked what the fuck was going on. I said to one of them, Scott Shepherd, assaulted Marin. Confused, they replied—

WHAT?? Is she ok? Where is he now?

He's in there.

And where's Marin?

She's in there.

Why is he in there? What are they doing?

I dunno.

Did you call the police?

Uh no. I don't know.

What are they talking about?

I don't know.

What the fuck is wrong with you guys?

A little while later Liz sent everyone home. Marin was taken back to someone else's place, maybe Kate's. The air was thick with disaster. Back at the apartments that evening, me and my roommate, The WG's costume designer, talked into the night. Something huge had happened. Something altering the whole experience. Heads were gonna roll. Shit was gonna change. Would the play be called off? I honestly could not imagine that happening. In fact, I could not imagine Liz really doing anything. But the thought of her not doing anything was also unimaginable. I was distraught and spinning out—which was a familiar panic in my body. I knew this sensation. I was in disaster mode. But it was exciting, too, because I saw revolution in the distance. Were we going to witness the fall of a great white man!? My roommate, on the other hand, had a calmer sadness to him, probably because he knew better how shit worked in this empire.

The next day all company members, staff, and contracted players were called to rehearsal. I thought, for sure, we were all going to talk about what happened. We arrived after lunchtime. Everyone was quiet and nervous. We settled. Liz, Kate, and the stage manager sat behind long tables, facing the stage; the rest of us were in chairs on the periphery. Liz got on her god mic.

OK, everyone, please mic up for ACT 2 SCENE 2.

The called players began to go suit up. Rehearsal was starting. She was starting a rehearsal. No one said anything, just proceeded to silently don their in-ear mics and make their way to the stage.

Bursting with rage, my heart pummeling inside of me, my hand shot up.

Yes? said Liz into the god mic.

Is anyone going to talk about what happened? I said.

What happened? she replied, as if nothing had happened.

Scott punched Marin in the face, and she has a black eye, I blurted.

That is a private matter, and this is a work space. If you can't handle that, you need to leave.

My stomach sank. Then an extraordinary force shot me out of my seat. I believe this force was the freeze-dried jumble of rage and grief that had been accumulating in my body my entire life—the shock of witnessing my mom being smacked around, the injustice of misogyny, my unfelt heartbreak about my mother's suicide, lesbian self-righteousness, and just straight up refusal to sit in this bullshit. It didn't feel like a decision, but—like I said, a force: something internal that launched me out of my hard plastic chair. I grabbed my backpack and, scared and raging inside, began to make my way to the door. The trouble was, I had to walk all the way across the stage to get to the exit. It was dead silent, and everyone was watching me. When I was center stage, Liz got on her god mic.

Wait.

I stopped. I faced the magistrate.

What do you think we should do? She asked as though there was actually nothing that they could do.

I waved in Scott's direction.

Kick him out of the play! Arrest him!

This isn't a kangaroo court, said Kate.

I stumbled around in my brain. There wasn't much there. I turned to the company members.

Is anyone going to say anything? Is anyone here upset about what happened?

There was one other woman non-company member, Jennifer Lim—the only person of color in the play, I should add. She said:

I am not ok with what is happening.

A few other people mumbled their discomfort.

I looked at Kate. Please say something, Kate.

You're right, I think we need to talk about this.

Liz, in her masturbatory observation, was watching the whole thing indignantly. I got the sense that she realized letting this unravel might be more titillating than rehearsal, so she agreed to stop rehearsal and let people "come talk to her" while she posted up at a bar somewhere for a few hours.

Anyone is welcome to come and say whatever they want to me.

How on earth would it have been helpful to sit on a bar stool next to Liz while she savored your discomfort and her Chablis, filing it away for further performative output? It was dawning on me that corporations have laws, HR departments, sensitivity training, to protect employees, yes, but mainly so that they don't get sued. But no one in this hostage situation would sue their own avant-garde mafioso family. Many of the people working in the company—if not all—had very specific full-time jobs there. Jobs that would be very hard to find or that simply didn't exist otherwise. There was Kate, who had dedicated her whole life and career to this world, did incredible work, and owed a lot to Liz. Some people had their work visas sponsored by the company and were not about to get deported over this shit. I had nothing to lose, really, and I was still terrified to face her.

But I did. All I remember from my own meeting with Liz is trying to tell her she was fucked up while being charming and funny about it so that she still respected me. UGH! And the one clear thing I recall from our convo was that she said:

I love you, but I hate you.

Phew, at least she still loved me a little bit.

My mom had told me once that she hated me. I was eight. We were living in some woman's house I didn't know. Mom was drinking a glass of wine. She didn't really drink—she was on too much medication. I was sitting on the floor, playing or drawing, and she looked at me with disgust and said flippantly with a slight slur,

I hate you.

I felt nothing. I felt nothing about that for decades.

There is a coincidence magic that happens on collaborative theatrical projects. Circumstances, signs, puns, and weird occurrences that reinforce either the fate of the show—"it's meant to be"—or the connections of the players—"we are meant to be." This has happened in every play I have ever been in, and certainly with bands and touring. Liz loved this. I love this. It puts an enchanted gloss on the world you have built with the project.

One such parallel was that, as I've mentioned, my role in the play was Cassandra:

Cassandra is a Trojan priestess who was cursed by Apollo to tell the truth, to prophesize doom, but she is never believed. An original #METOO-er. My full name is Jibra'ila, a mutilated Arabic version of Gabriel, messenger of god. Liz really liked that, too.

As Cassandra I was on stage for most of the play, but I didn't have many lines. My big moment in the show was to emerge from the rubber tipi and warn of the downfall of Troy in a dramatic monologue that I could never quite remember. You can imagine her delight when Liz put together that I was the Cassandra of Troy and now the Cassandra of SoHo fringe performance art as well. The truthsayer! The doomspeaker! She pronounced this revelation to the entire cast shortly after I blew the whistle.

The first words of the monologue, which I could never master were:

Cry, Trojans! Cry!

I could never get it to come out the way she wanted it to.

After that fateful day, which I can remember like it was this morning, the events that followed are a bit of a blur.

There was a stiff, British group therapy-esque thing that happened. Someone came and talked to us, but no one really said anything. Scott gave a limp apology to the group. Everyone was exhausted. The show was opening in a few days. I was muddled and confused by the reactions of those around me and the general lack of outrage, but I also felt committed to the show, god knows why. I became tortured by the decision of whether I should stay or not. I very much wanted to leave. I was concerned that staying would make me a "bad feminist," but on the other hand I was worried about leaving Marin. Most people seemed to want to get on with it. Marin, I thought, would surely leave, and then I could leave. But her reaction to the whole thing was to stay put and not let Scott Shepherd "win." It can't be overstated how much the credit of being a lead in a Wooster Group show meant to an actor—even having a small part was enormous for me. I know she was tortured by this decision as well. The turmoil seemed to be unbearable for her—like I said, she wasn't good at hiding vibes. This thing happens with gaslighting and lack of consequences, which is that, if the survivor is "moving on" or "staying in the relationship," everyone else starts to assume the abusive situation must not be that bad. The company seemed to be basing the seriousness of the situation on whether or not Marin stayed in the play, thus putting all the responsibility for what happened next on her shoulders. She should never have been put in that position.

A few members asked me directly to stay, they told me they needed me. Always a middle child, that sealed the deal. One actor told me I was the "moral compass" for the show, which was intoxicating to hear—I mean, who else was going to point out wildly problematic things that wouldn't be addressed?!

How could I leave them!?—but also a big responsibility. I also felt it was my gay duty to protect and support Marin. She also told me she needed me. I was her lesbian knight in shining denim. And there was the other thing, which is that I didn't have a lot to go home to. I stayed and finished out the run.

We moved from London to Stratford-upon-Avon. (Yes, that is the name of the town. England is so dumb.) I was put up in actors' apartments near the Royal Shakespeare Theatre, where Shakespeare had produced plays and died. To get back to the apartment at night, I had to walk through the cemetery where he was buried. But it was not that exciting. I didn't feel close to Shakespeare. The show veered so hard from Shakespeare's vibes that I didn't think about him at all.

We slogged through. I was stressed and keyed up and trying desperately not to drink. I avoided going out after rehearsals; after all, I had no business in pubs. But it was unbearably lonely. To really up the ante on my spin out, I even developed a vile, unwanted crush on a guy in the play, which felt out of control because I couldn't square it or get rid of it. It was another tool from my rusty old toolbox to avoid this pain I was in. It became agonizing to be in the rehearsal room.

I was reaching for anything to calm my nervous system or get me out of my pain.

After rehearsals I scurried home through Shakespeare's graveyard so I could smoke cigarettes on my porch. In the mornings, I ran. I ran and ran and ran. There were paths near my apartment that led to long, dirt roads through flat, beautiful farms. Cows and sheeps. Clouds in the sky. Never too hot. I had so much self-righteous rage propelling me through the quaint British countryside—crunch, crunch, crunch on the gravely road. Hi, cow. Hi, sheep. Hi hi hi. You seem good. You seem well cared for. Will you be eaten? That is ok. You seem good. Breathe 2, 3, 4. Out 2, 3, 4. Playing "Fistful of Love" by Antony and the Johnsons (now ANOHNI) on repeat. By the end of this trip, I could run for nine miles.

The show opened and it was undeniably bad. It was clunky and made no sense. The play went back to London, with another lukewarm reception.

Everyone started unraveling even more. Night after night we were forced to watch Troilus punch Cressida on stage. Almost comical in its irony, and nearly unbearable to watch. I continued to run all over the British countryside, crying and showing up for performances. Many of the RSC players were party boys, doing blow in the dressing rooms, which our company members joined. I got mad one night when they were hoovering rails on the vanity in the dressing room I shared with another actor.

The whole project should have been thrown in the trash. Everyone knew it. But we all stayed and acted crazy. It was just sad.

Another humiliating thing was that my crush was becoming Marin's caretaker, which was excruciating—and embarrassing, how excruciating it was. Also, hilarious—the irony here is not lost on me. Not only was I nauseously jealous of his attention to her, I felt betrayed by her for turning towards someone else, when for so long I had been the lesbian knight in shining denim. UGH this is so cringe to write. I hope you are all having fun laughing at me, my facade of impenetrable cool now totally ruined by my confessional auto-bile-ography.

Scott and I spoke just once about what had happened, one afternoon before a show in Stratford. We sat on a grassy hill overlooking the swans in the river. He apologized and told me he wished he could take the punch back. I was not interested in anything he had to say and largely avoided him. I didn't believe his regret. Unfortunately for me, in the play we were brother and sister and we were stuck together for one entire tipi scene every show. Night after night, we crouched together near the tipi door, looking out. On Scott's cue, he was to come bursting out of the tipi, and he had to shove me out of the way to get there. He would spring up from a squat, shirtless and stinky, and put his palm on my shoulder and push me aside. Before the assault he would lightly graze me, signaling me to pretend I was being pushed, but after, he got method and thrust me aside with gusto. I felt his physical power, and I felt his rage. It was scary.

Finally, after about a month of performances in England, it was time to go home. There was talk of Liz wanting us all to continue in the show. I still wasn't entirely ready to give up, if you can believe it. My stipulation was that I wouldn't continue if Scott was going to stay. Marin set the same boundary. She was critical to the show, but I knew I was pretty disposable. I think it was some sort of test on my part. I wanted to hear Liz pick Scott over me, over Marin, one more time.

In the end, Scott stayed. I left and Marin left. They reshaped the play to not include the RSC, they recast Marin and I and renamed it *Cry, Trojans!* It did not do well in the States, where it finally got some blowback about the Native appropriation bullshit. In England they were like, "we don't even know what the fuck this is."

Shortly after returning to New York, my partner and I split up for good. I felt lost and unanchored. I was also jobless. I tried to maintain a few key relationships with some of my friends in the company, but the pain of my experience with the company rendered them untenable. It saddens me. I loved so many of the company members and I loved their work. I miss Kate and the friends I made there.

Around this time, I got an email from Jack Black saying he wanted to talk to me about developing a project with him. For the first time I felt that maybe I could actually do this career on my own. That I was actually *enough*—my ideas, my skills, could carry something into the world that would support me, that I could make bigger. Which is oddly what Liz was always telling me, that I was enough. But perhaps I could take up even more space and not need this intense approval from people like her—who are geniuses, to be sure, but who don't reflect my values or my actual idea of what love is. I was excited for my adventures in Hollywood, a famously functional and healthy working environment!

What I didn't realize then, but know now, is that this experience was not just about a fucked-up theater company, it was about my grief. I was looking to be loved and approved of by these powerful women, Liz and Kate, a kind of love and approval I was coming to understand my mother had never given me, and now never could, or would, now that she was gone. But that was never their job, and their support of an abusive man was too much like my own mom, who had been beaten by my dad, made excuses for him and stayed with him, and then allowed grown men to stay in her home and have sex with her underage daughter multiple times. It was too fuckin much. I had coped with this felt abandonment with my childhood tools—obsessing about someone, getting tangled up in co-dependency, desperate people pleasing, and the misery that comes with feeling like you have something to prove. In a way, this crash and burn was the best gift I could have been given actually, because I had had enough. I started my recovery journey in Sex and Love Addicts Anonymous because of this and it has helped me beyond words really. I need a lot of help. If I don't surrender to that fact, I am doomed. DOOMED, I SAY!

NINETEEN: HELLAY

The TV show Jack wanted to make with me was based on a comic I had written with Hedia Maron about coming to LA in 2006 and trying and failing to sell a different TV show.[26] The story was sort of a lesbian performance art Larry David joint, or at the time, Louis C.K.—structurally, that is, not #metoo-y. There's an unlikely hero at the center of this docu-esque short comedy, me. The kind of show where you are "playing yourself but not yourself." A retelling of a central character's life that is very close to the real thing, but in 20-minute chunks, with punchier jokes. In the past ten years, there have been tons of these shows made. Mine wasn't one of them.

So, I moved out to LA in 2015. It was mostly to work on the TV show with Jack, and partially because I had somehow reached many of the career goals I had brought with me to New York. I had produced a handful of big solo shows and performed at places that had been dreams for me like BAM and the Kitchen.

I started working hard right away writing the pilot with my now best friend, Amanda "Bubbles" Verwey, to create the pilot and write a ten-minute sizzle reel, which Jack produced. In the sizzle, a queer performance artist named Figs moves to Los Angeles and gets discovered by a big Hollywood movie star, but has to navigate caring for her mentally ill mother while traversing the uncertain and high-stakes landscape

26 "The Dynasty Handbag Show," Comic on Triple Canopy. See appendix.

of the TV industry. Figs would be dealing with psych wards and homeless shelters in the day, then dipping into stressful Hollywood networking events at night. It was meta, because of course much of this was unfolding at the same time around me, Jibz, as we shot the sizzle reel and subsequently tried to sell it to networks. The difference being, of course, that my mom was not alive anymore. I wouldn't have moved back to California if she had been.

This show "didn't go," as they say. I was downright naive about the whole process, thinking I knew how TV worked because I had seen how it worked on TV. I considered Jack to be so famous that he would simply get whatever he wanted. I thought movie stars were the ones to make things happen, but they are not. It's the most boring people in the world who make things happen. Movie stars—they're just like us!—as it turns out. Just trying to pay the big bills and not fade into oblivion and maybe work on something not totally heinous. It was disappointing but something I needed to get used to.[27]

Hey kid, I gotta gig for you—it's too weird for me to even tell you about it. Basically, it's the people who own the Magic Castle. They have a theater, they, um, do these weird shows, you'll love it. I been tellin' 'em about you. You gotta come.

It was now 2016. I had been in LA for one year when I got this call from Murray Hill, who was in LA from NYC doing some shows. I asked *is there a ticket link*, and Murray said *no, there's no tickets*, and I asked, *am I getting paid*, and they said *no, it's not a paid thing*, and then I said, *is there any information about it online, anywhere*, and they said *no, just come, I tell you, it's worth it. I promise.* I trust Murray, so I just went.

The theater is called Brookledge, and the show, the Brookledge Follies. I did a bit of research online, but there

27 "Figs," Sizzle Video, 2016. See appendix.

wasn't much. Brookledge is inside a 1920s mansion that belongs to the Larsen family, owners and founders of the Magic Castle. Their granddaughter, Erika Larsen, lives in the mansion now and runs the theater. The mansion was originally owned by a guy who had a magic props business—they mostly made magic wands. They have to come from somewhere, right? They don't just magically appear! He had a theater built in the lower part of the mansion, where they held magic shows and performances. It was rumored that Charlie Chaplin had performed there. I hear that rumor about every old theater in LA.

Murray texted me the address and told me to go through the side gate when I arrived. I parked in front of some fancy houses on a dark street in Larchmont. The house was an old Spanish mansion with a modest façade. I walked through the side gate and down the stone path alongside the building. There was typical landscaping along the pathway, plants and flowers, but scattered throughout were a million billion trolls, dinosaur sculptures, little mushrooms, and hundreds of little twinkling lights.

The patio opened up to a little sitting area with gigantic palm trees and huge jungle flowers, plants, and rattan furniture. There were more lights, this time up in the trees. There were fountains and campy garden sculptures, old patio furniture with wrought iron curlicue flourishes. Further down the path a wooden bridge stretched over a babbling brook with wide-eyed, life-sized fake deer standing mid-stream. Even lower down was another little patio, with an outdoor fireplace and some seating. A ratty Disneyland. Basically, the most wonderful place on earth.

Murray was nowhere to be found. The place was in a flurry of pre-production, so no one had time to hold my hand, but Erika did come over to introduce herself. She was small, blonde, no frills, with a high, urgent speaking voice that sounded like she'd been smoking for 500 years.

Dynasty! I'm so excited you're here. Thank you for coming!

My pleasure.

OK go give your stuff to Joe upstairs, and the green room is up there, too, it's gonna be a great show.

The theater was connected to the rest of the house at the lowest point, down the back of a hill. It held about 100 seats. At the end of the long, rectangular room sat an ancient wooden stage with thick red velvet drape curtains on rope pulleys, and floor lights cradled in clamshell lampshades. On the walls hung candelabras, paintings that looked like they were from the thrift store but were probably not, and many pictures of magicians and performers. A bar ran along one side of the long wall. Behind it were shelves crammed with all manner of Americana curios: teensy, old-fashioned toys from the 50s, magic paraphernalia, pamphlets, flyers, posters, cards, matchbooks, lighters, figurines, shot glasses, teacups.

At the rear end of the theater, a skinny staircase led up to the tech booth, where they ran sound, lights, and video projection. This room was small and stuffy and also filled with crap. It was adorned with dozens of signed celebrity headshots of people who had either performed there or had seen shows there. To the right was a room called the "magic room"—also crammed with fascinating bric-a-brac—magic paraphernalia going back to the late 1930s, like Ouija boards, spell books, Houdini tour posters, games, vintage magic tricks. Definitely haunted shit all over the place. To the right again, a very narrow staircase led to a small mezzanine room where glass windows overlooked the jungle patio. Beyond that, another petite staircase led to a spacious room with a dusty green carpet. This was the performers' green room.

I found an empty spot on the floor in a corner. There were some older white magician guys who looked as though they had been there a million times, talking very casually about Vegas and how much money they made. Something like $70,000 for a gig. I was shocked. They continued ignoring me, so I kept my mouth shut, put my costume on, did my makeup and continued eavesdropping. I went over to the tea kettle for some caffeine and discovered craft services consisting of peanut butter, grape jelly, a loaf of white bread, and a greasy toaster. I loved this place.

This was the first space that I had been in in Los Angeles that had real freak theater vibes. I was seeing a layer of LA that I had a hunch existed but didn't know in what shape or form. It's hard to understand what LA underground is. In some ways, all of LA is underground (besides Hollywood—which is hidden away in its own fashion). The center of things is hard to locate, because there is none. When my partner's father visited us from Vienna, he asked, "Is there a little town squeaahh? Like a little church or some-sing, we can see the center of ze town?" We ended up taking him to the Americana, a fancy mall with a little cable car going through it. He loved it, finally somewhere you could walk around. The nexus of cool doesn't exist in LA. It is a town of, well, dorks. Nothing feels exactly "cutting edge" here, because LA's edges are fuzzy, like the edges of a watercolor splotch. Warm and melty. And there are lots of spaces between each splotch. Not much is butting up against anything, so when you do find something with energy, it feels like an anomaly, or an oasis. Like you have been in the desert (which you have) and have finally arrived at a lively party with carousing and fabulous entertainment, and think, *Where have you all been hiding?*

There was a jolly man in his 70s wearing a tuxedo and chatting with a much younger woman in a silk, powder blue gown. She had giant boobs and a 1940s hairstyle. I found out later they were a father-daughter magic act and were quite good. They had a duck in a cage that they would make disappear, which upset my gay vegetarian sensitivities, but I discovered later that they had rescued the duck from a poultry farm. I guess the duck was doing ok, though I would still argue it was forced labor.

The stage manager eventually came and gathered the performers together for places. The entrance to the stage was outside through a small doorway at the back of the theater. There was a ragtag lineup of burlesque-looking people, and me. I was simultaneously excited to see these acts and preemptively embarrassed by how dorky and circus-lame it all was. Everyone was friendly, but in their typical, anxious pre-show moods. I stood next to a gorgeous woman in an Esther Williams-style sparkly hot pants outfit with a Josephine Baker finger wave. She had a giant pile of hula hoops around her neck. I started chatting with her. She was exuberantly friendly.

Hi I'm Jibz.

Hello I'm Marawa, what do you do?

I explained my act as best I could.

I asked her what she did, and she gestured to her giant hula hoop necklace. I hoop. I didn't know what that meant exactly, but she seemed extremely confident and comfortable.

Have you done this show before?

Yeah a bunch of tie-yums, it's the beest.

She was Australian!

Everyone's aabsuhlutely insahayne.

There was a thin guy in all white with white face paint, little triangles painted around his eyes, a frowny mouth, and a beret. That's right, a mime. I gestured to him. Grimacing, she said, *That's Billy the Mime*. Then she stuck out her tongue and pretended to gag herself. I knew we would be pals.

The show started. Murray introduced me—*Ladies and Gentleman, next is a person like nothing you ever seen before*. I did something I can't remember. The place was packed and I got a roaring applause. Afterwards I made my way outside and around to the main entrance so that I could watch the rest of the show. Next up was Billy the Mime. He acted out a scene of a little boy forced to blow a priest, performing as the priest and then the child. The audience groaned and made eew noises. Some laughed. In a subsequent show he did a piece miming being sexually assaulted by Harvey Weinstein. He played Harvey and his victim. I hated Billy the Mime.

Next was my new friend, Marawa the Amazing. She performed a dazzling routine to a Perez Prado song with her hoops. She had hoops on her arms, hoops on her legs and around her neck. They spun forwards and backwards, she tossed them into the rafters, and they glittered and spun in the light, she caught them expertly and continued wielding them like extensions of her body. For the finale she spun 36 hoops around her waist in her four-inch heels and sexy outfit. Marawa, it turned out, was a 12-time *Guinness Book of World Records* hula-hooper and had been on several "got talents," including *Arabs Got Talent* where she had roller skated and hooped in a burka. Her record for spinning hoops is 200. Three of the hoops rely on the use of her long middle fingernail to provide extra length when her arms are outstretched to the side.

After the show we gathered on the patio to meet audience members and check out the "catering." Besides the plastic liter bottles of vodka and gin, the snack table looked like it was laid out for a little league team. Cheeseballs and candy and gigantic bottles of orange and grape soda, red Solo cups.

Around the table were a mix of regular-looking people and celebrities. Laurence Fishburne—aka Cowboy Curtis of *Pee-wee's Playhouse* fame—stood towering over everyone. He was wearing a dark silver wrap, a chunky leather bracelet, and a humongous snake ring. He shook my hand. *Wonderful show, I very much enjoyed it.* Kathy Griffin, fresh off of her "beheading Donald Trump" scandal, stood for a selfie with me. I would meet many random celebrities at Brookledge over the years, including Dick Van Dyke, which was thrilling for me. He came often and sat in the front row with his mile-long legs stretched out in either direction. One time a doofy lounge crooner accidentally dropped a hulking 1950s microphone on him. Idiot. Dick Van Dyke once pointed at me after a show and said, "Yer insane!" I think that's going to be my one and only blurb for this book. I also saw Priscilla Presley there, but I didn't talk to her. In fact, I turned away when she looked at me, like I would be cursed by too much fame.

The shows were secret and invite-only. It was a place where famous people could go and enjoy being entertained without being harangued by fans, but special and exclusive enough for them to still feel like celebrities. I imagine the Costco cheese puff container and liters of Dr. Pepper made them feel more human, too.

I knew Erika was close friends with Paul Reubens, and that he was a frequent attendee of the Follies. He wasn't at that first show, but I ended up meeting him there another night. Erika scooted frantically up to me, *Oh oh you have to meet Paul, he loved your set*. I was terrified and excited. Paul Reubens, the actual Pee-wee Herman. My hero, hero to so many, OUR hero. The freakiest freak to ever slip past the gates of corporate TV with his brilliant, creative, thinly veiled gay agenda. I had been waiting for this moment. He was vaping in a corner under a gigantic palm leaf. He was dressed like a regular guy, in dark pressed jeans and a little cotton jacket, pristine white tennis shoes. *Hi Dynasty, so nice to meet you*, he said. *I loved your set, it was so funny.* Puff puff on the vape. It was weed. We shook hands and chatted. He was warm and charming, cracking shady jokes and making funny faces at people. Something snapped into place—he shifted from Pee-wee to a snarky, hilarious, catty, gay, old man. I knew this man. I know this man and his kind of man. I relaxed and we chatted and joked around for a while. He gave me a look at one point that said, *Girl . . . turn around.* Colin Farrell was heading my way. He was wearing a velvet suit with an ascot and carrying a cane with a silver knob on the end. He didn't have a top hat, but he might as well have.

Dinnistyyy Handbagg you durrrty little tramp! I laughed. *Why hello, Colin Farrell.* I glanced over at Mariah. We smiled at each other, acknowledging his scandalous viral sex tape where he pauses to look at the camera to say "breakfast, lunch and dinner" while eating pussy. Just then, queen Geena Davis glided up the stairs, heading straight towards me. She shook my hand. In her flat husky voice she said, *So nice to meet you, what a great performance. Thank you Geena, it is such an honor to meet you.* She was kind and elegant and easy to chat with. I tried to be normal and introduced her to Colin Farrell, like any regular person would when they were hangin' out with regular people at a regular party. *Oh hello*, she said, *I met you a long time ago.* They had both been cast in a film that never got made. He shook her hand, and she leaned over and whispered to me, *I think I just got pregnant.*

Amanda rushed over and pulled me aside. *Guess what Paul Reubens just did? What what? He whispered in my ear, "There's no basement in the Alamo!"* The famous line from *Pee-wee's Big Adventure* when Pee-wee finally gets to the Alamo to retrieve his stolen bike. He had been told by a charlatan fortune teller that his bike was there, in the basement. At the end of the excruciatingly long tour, he finally gets to the Q and A portion. *When do we get to see the basement?* Smacking her gum and laughing in his face, the guide replies, *There's no basement in the Alamo!*

After, I screamed in the car for a few minutes, from the excitement of meeting him. Then we became friends. He loved to send me dirty memes about lesbians. On my birthday he would bombard me all day long with GIFs of old cartoons and celebratory memes. All. Day. Long. There was a performative hilarity to doing this that he was aware of. He knew how valuable he was to a plebeian like myself. He knew how to make people feel special. He was aware of his power, and also aware of the discomfort and excitement one feels around that kind of power. Essentially saying to Amanda, *I know you are freaking out right now, and I know you are a fan, and I know you have seen that movie a hundred million times, and I am going to give you a private gift of all of that acknowledgment.* It relaxed her, and made everything more normal by acknowledging the abnormality of the situation. He had a grace I have rarely seen with celebrity, or anyone else with power for that matter. He understood what he meant to people. When he passed away, everyone I know, including myself, said the same things about him. *He changed my life. I never would have survived my childhood without him. He made me gay. He was a total weirdo, how did that show ever get made?*

Once when we were talking on the phone I asked him that question and he said,

I have no idea, Jibzy. Actually that's not true. But I had to give up a lot. A lot.

When I was trying to get a pitch together for a sort of Weirdo Night variety show TV series, I asked him for some guidance. He was less than encouraging.

It's nearly impossible to get something made, Jibz, it's just really really hard. My situation was a total right place, right time thing, and a totally different time at that. You need the right manager and there are none of those people around.

What the fuck, Pee-wee!? I was a bit hurt by his reaction, thinking he should have been encouraging me and showering me with excitement. I understand now after knowing him for longer, and by learning more about what he went through to achieve his extraordinary level of fame. He was closeted, lonely, and lost many friends because he left people behind as his star rose. He also was decimated by the gay witch hunt that colored him as a pervert and a pedophile, the worst thing imaginable for him. The same bullshit that is happening to queers now. In talking to him, it struck me many times how hurt he was still by friends who had not stood up for him when he was being persecuted and criminalized. He may have been trying to protect me to some degree.

I miss Paul a lot. He supported me unconditionally and always told me how talented I am. I call on that whenever I am feeling scared or like I have nothing to offer, and it's more than enough to get me through.

After the stinging disappointment of the Jack Black TV show saga faded a bit, I decided there was no way I could survive in LA if the TV industry was in charge of my nervous system. I realized this after getting an ulcer. THE THING was happening to me. A grotesque, strategizing alien was beginning to take over my body. My creativity—for better or for worse —never contained any calculated thought related to success beyond what I wanted to make, and now I was considering the best ways to get this and that, meet that person and that person. It stressed me the fuck out so badly that I lost the plot a little. I felt manic in new, disturbing ways. I didn't want to network, meet producers, go to parties, talk about myself, but I truly thought I would have to—which kept me up at night playing out all the horrific glad-handing convos I was soon going to have to be having. In all fairness, this is how things happen in that industry, but it was also not what I wanted to be thinking about all the time.

That's what my creative life comes down to—what do I want to be thinking about? The noxious fog of Hollywood makes you believe you must care deeply about the television and film industry, and because you are around other cult members, it's all anyone else cares about, too. But if you step outside of it—for example, when I would talk to my New York friends about my sagas with the industry, what other people were getting or not getting—nobody cared or knew what I was talking about. People cared about me, but not about the world I was in. Who was selling what, what was going on over at Comedy Central. Who gives a shit. But I also love it. I absolutely love the medium, it gives me so much joy, it's so absurd.

Amanda and I stayed friends with a producer at Starburns who worked on the *Figs* pilot with us, this goofy sweet dude named Casey. He was still gunning to do something beyond the TV show with Jack. So, Amanda and I kept writing together. That was the best part of this whole TV debacle after all. We decided we would keep working only if it remained fun, and our motto for writing together was "nothing's too stupid." The stupidity inherent in TV is not something you want to forget; the entire structure and language of it is 98% trash. If television is meant to keep us engaged over certain periods of time so that we can be sold advertising, it can never be pure. It can only be television.

Amanda and I made a commitment to never take the thing too seriously. Getting money and surviving is serious, but the ideas were not. The amount of fingers that will be in every ingredient of your TV pie makes it insane to assume that you will be able to hold on to any purity of content. We do see the rare, brilliant exceptions—*Pee-wee's Playhouse*, *Twin Peaks*—we often don't hear about the pain and complexity that people face to bring a show to fruition. My friend who is a famous comedian made a live series based on her comedy special, but the network didn't allow her to be a writer on it. She was so excited to have the deal go through, but there were many things in the content she disagreed with, but she didn't have any power. Or in the case of *Twin Peaks*, the creative clashing and budget restrictions that led to its cancellation. In Paul's case, being closeted and then subjected to a homophobic media terror and criminalization, losing your community, your whole life. People have to work so hard to get things funded. We think it's possible because it happens once or twice, out of hundreds of thousands of TV shows that are utter dogshit. It is unfathomable to me how many amazing shows never get made. Every one of my friends who works in TV, or is a comedian, has an incredible idea that will probably never get realized. So, it remains imperative for me to have feet in other worlds that I am totally in control over, at least content-wise.

Amanda and I continued to write together and came up with a show called *Garbage Castle*.[28] With help from Dan Harmon at Starburns we ended up getting interest from FX—by the same woman who took our meeting with Jack Black—she remembered and liked us. In *Garbage Castle* Dynasty Handbag lives in one room SRO on top of a pile of trash. She has a roomate, Alfred, a possum who lives in a trash can at the foot of the couch, played by the brilliant Cole Escola.

28 *Garbage Castle*, Video, 2019. See appendix.

Alfred is a puppet—and was operated by an actual *Muppet Show* puppeteer. Her landlord is a burnout hippie billionaire, Yoyo, played by Maria Bamford.

Kate at FX gave us feedback, starting with our pilot script. At first we were resistant, but soon surrendered, thinking, well, she has actually made TV before, maybe we should listen to her? We had to scale back on some of the more niche jokes and lean into stuff that was more general; we had one joke about bougie LA people having minimalist succulent gardens and "desert triangle art"—she was like, what the hell are you talking about?

Kate wanted to lean into the feminist/woman part of the story. So, we punched up the jokes about DH being old and ugly with no sexual currency. Much of the content and humor had become ingrained in the persona of Dynasty Handbag over years, so it felt very uncomfortable spelling it out. We had to remember we were trying to reach other audiences and introduce the idea of this failed woman and make sense of her. The plot of our pilot is that Yoyo is raising her rent at the SRO, and Alfred teaches DH to HairPNPee her apartment, which is utterly filthy. She must learn to clean for the first time and make it attractive to the bourgeoisie.

We got our pilot meagerly funded by FX for their alternative programming block called Cake—their version of Adult Swim. Cake had animation and weirdo web shorts; much of it was interesting and good. We built an apartment in Starburns's enormous stop-motion animation studio in Burbank. Peggy Noland was the set designer. It was a sitcom-style setup, with a couch front-and-center, across from a TV. Since it was a one-room SRO, it was one room; the "kitchen" was exposed and consisted of a sink with a hose coming through the window and one rusty hotplate with crumbs and crust all over it. We got the furniture from the Salvation Army in Lincoln Heights. Peggy covered the couch and TV with this mysterious foam substance that squirted out from a can and then hardened. Then she painted it. Everything looked lumpy. Like the right general shape, but with lumps. She sprinkled cheerios all over the couch, which you couldn't see on camera but definitely helped us feel gross. There was also a fish tank that had no fish, filled with brown water, cigarette butts, and other trash. Our prize item score was a small statue of *The Thinker* with its face ALREADY smashed in. We are smart, but I don't think even we could have come up with that.

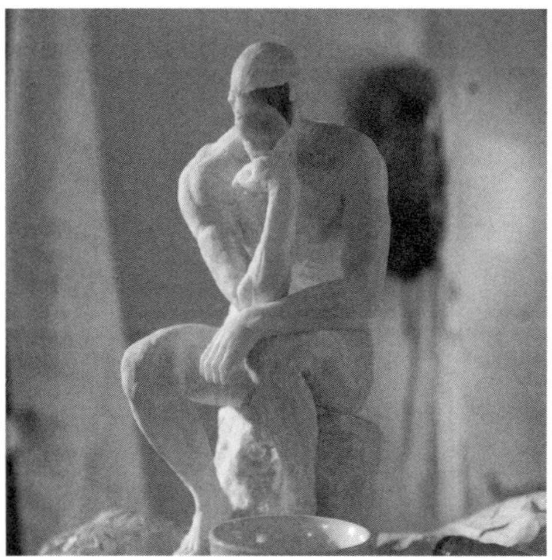

The walls were painted to look like they were rotting, and there were random boots on shelves and piles of garbage everywhere. We had put a call out to the Starburns staff for them to save all of their clean trash. We spent hours crumpling it up and hot gluing it delicately to the bottom of Alfred's garbage can condo.

Another genius set item was our shit pile. At one point, when Alfred tells DH she must clean her apartment, DH has an existential crisis narrated by Werner Herzog (me) about what and why cleaning "is." How it only exists to prevent death.

Clean. What is clean. Why is clean?
We clean only to escape death
Filth collects
Bodies corrode
Something something
Until it atrophies, withers and dies

When she finally starts trying to clean, her solution is to rinse out a potato chip bag and then place it delicately on top of another pile of trash. As she does this, she notices a coily, dark brown turd on the floor! Could it be Alfred's? Or . . . hers!? She pauses in horror and confusion. Oh, I KNOW! She gets a pumpkin spice candle—which I created a label for in Photoshop, "Jankee Candle Company"—from the shelf, lights it, and firmly places it atop the turd, squishing it down flat with the satisfaction of a job well done.

We knew this was going to be a money shot, so we made a cache of backup turds. Amanda spent a lot of time perfecting them.[29] We used Duncan Hines chocolate frosting, which she piped out onto a cookie sheet covered in parchment paper. At first, they were just blobs, readable as turds, surely, but lacking the definition that implies . . . what? . . . good gut health? Which somehow implies purpose—as in, were the turd diarrhea style, maybe it was an accident. But if it were, shall we say, properly executed, well, that turd was intentional. Yes, that's it. Then she would put the tray in the refrigerator until it was time for the turd and candle scene. At any rate, one of Amanda's and my most favorite moments, the moment we looked into each other's eyes and knew we had actually created a miracle for ourselves, was the first time we heard the AD yell, "Turd flyin in," when we had to do another take. I will never ever forget that feeling.

29 Amanda, Michaelangelo-ing a shit pile, Photo. See appendix.

FX loved the pilot and ordered four episodes, which we wrote in the Starburns headquarters in Burblank. It was a crummy 70s office complex, and they had an empty room for us to work in with a brown couch saggy from healthy use and the 1,000,000 farts stored in there, a big, ugly 80s desk, a lamp, and a whiteboard upon which I drew dirty cartoons. It had a classic perforated ceiling with a giant brown water (or something) stain. We loved it.

We were so happy to have a place to go, a purposeful destination that felt professional and fun. The rest of the floor was peppered with animation desks. The animators were not unfriendly, but certainly not socially comfortable, to say the least. And about 98% were men. We stuck out a bit, and no one really talked to us except this older gay guy with pink hair who brought his cute dog to work every day. No one bothered us or checked in. It was great. The crafty room had the lowest-common-denominator snack supply. Stale Fig Newton bars, M&Ms in a dingy turn-the-dial-and-four-will-come-out-in-your-hand dispenser, spotty bananas, cereal (!). From time to time some kind soul would bring in doughnuts for all to share.

We wrote in our little room for a couple months. Amanda sat at the desk and typed up our scripts in Final Draft as I lay on the couch, dramatically ideating, occasionally sitting up with a flash of inspiration. With our "nothing's too stupid" motto, we forged on. Developing five-page sitcoms was challenging. We needed to create an arc. We would write it all out and then have to slash and burn to fit the time slot. One episode was about Dynasty Handbag creating a Ponzi scheme. She quickly learns that Ponzi schemes are for men, and pyramid schemes are for women. She invites all her friends (Alfred, Yoyo, and a witch who lives next door) to hear her exciting pitch. She describes her product, which turns out to be nothing. Just words about something you can't live without. There was also an episode that guest-starred Paul Reubens as Dynasty Handbag's greaser ex-con ex-boyfriend who had escaped prison on a motorcycle. DH tries to resist him but when he talks with an Australian accent, she can't help herself.

By February of 2020 we had finished four scripts. We turned them in on March 3rd. That week there was a company meeting about this new virus that was going round, and the protocols they were going to enlist around safety. This was the first time we had been with everyone in the company, seeing everyone together as well as the collective "who gives a shit" vibes. It was as though these dudes had been living in their own low-rent imagineering cubicles for so long that they didn't take the outside world into consideration. In my community of hypervigilant care-queers, people were already masking up and hand sanitizing, washing their vegetables and advocating for immunocompromised people. In this universe, everyone was bored and confused and seemed to just want to slink back to their animation consoles and lose themselves in whatever they were intensely laboring over.

We sat in rows of chairs listening to the head of the company try to give some direction about what we were supposed to do.

Ok, um, so yeah, just like, wash your hands and well we are still open until they shut us down so yeah, just . . . carry on!

You can guess how this turned out. We kept working for another week before shutdown came upon us. The show was cancelled. In fact, the whole programming block was cancelled. We tried to get it back in circulation, but our producer had quit the company and we couldn't figure out how to get it into the right hands.

I still think it is one of the best things I have ever made. That it was cancelled was just part of everything that was happening. Everyone I knew was having heartbreaking professional disappointments on every level, and of course much much worse. I did not have one of those "residency pandemics" that people talk about—where they write a new album or start growing artichokes. I was so depressed and terrified that my arm stopped working?! I honestly believed that it was over and that I would never perform again. I had been performing at least once a month for the past 20 years. My body was shutting down. I eventually got a witch to fix it. You can't throw a crystal in LA without hitting someone who can cure a mystery illness with vibes.

In fall of 2020 me and Mariah made a *Weirdo Night*[30] film, which brought me and my arm back to life. Sundance programmer and lesbian person Shari Frilot happened to be on my mailing list and got wind of *Weirdo Night* the movie and asked us to submit it formally, and it got in, which was incredible because we hadn't planned on submitting it anywhere. That year the festival was online, so I didn't get to go to Utah or wherever the fuck Sundance is and hobnob with execs and stars, but it was still a big deal. We are very proud of it even though it didn't sweep the nation or get picked up for a series. We even hired a publicist, for SIX THOUSAND DOLLARS, to try and get meetings and sell it. That's not what publicists do, as it turns out. We didn't get a single meeting.

Wikipedia states bluntly that, "All of Cameron's attempts at television have failed." Not not true. Why doesn't TV want me . . . or do I not want it? I'm still trying to understand this relationship. The mad queer hiring spree of the late 2010s has all but dried up. What's selling now seems to be shows about 90s white lady actresses in wigs with vacation homes somewhere WASPY with a nefarious secret and a dog that you are worried will be murdered in the process of figuring out the mystery. Which I will watch, of course.

---

30 *Weirdo Night*, Film, 2020. See appendix.

TWENTY: WEIRDO NIGHT

I started the variety show Weirdo Night in 2016, around the time that the TV show stuff was starting to feel like a disease. In fact, I developed an ulcer. I needed something going on in LA that had nothing to do with success. I wanted to create something celebrating un-success, that is so failure-forward it erases failure.

Weirdo Night emerged from the marvelous congealing of a few different elements. First, beyond the desire to get back to art for art's sake, I wanted a performance outlet in Los Angeles. I wanted a place that had good sound and a decent stage for me to perform regularly so I would be forced to write new work every month. I distinctly remember Cole Escola in the late 2000s telling me this was why they were doing a monthly show at Club Deluxe in the West Village, so that they'd be forced to write, because people were gonna come whether they liked it or not! At the time, it seemed like my choices for performing live in LA were either art world galleries or comedy clubs. While I enjoy a comedy club every now and again, I don't quite fit into the stand-up world, and I didn't want to dive that deep there. I'd already tried my hand at this at UCB and had decided I didn't like that world. I do get booked on a few "alternative comedy scene shows," that kinda world. I have this small, bizarre fan base of semi harsh dude comedy fans who are also weirdos. I get it, I am crass and make fun of lesbians, and what man doesn't like that? Sometimes I see myself as a mélange combo meal of stupid man comedy and raging feminist belligerence. I was performing on John Early's variety show once. The first comedian to come out was a white woman who was pissed as hell and immediately launched into angry jokes about Hillary Clinton and abortion (anti-Hillary/pro-abortion). I sort of hated her. The next comedian was a giant sloppy jokester man who opened with, "Hey you guys like my pants??!!" I sorta hated him too but also acknowledge I may be a combo meal of these two people.

Weirdo Night also came out of my desire to be in community with people. I felt the creative worlds in LA were disconnected from each other—in part due to the geography of the city, and in part, I believe, because the film and TV industry is enormous, powerful, and largely commercial here. In New York, not to be all "New York's like this, LA's like this," but truly, the art, music, film, performance, drag, and comedy worlds feel a lot more interdepartmental or interdependent, (and San Francisco, too, come to think of it). I didn't feel that happening as much in LA.

Many incredible artists from New York and other cities would ask me, *Where do you perform in LA?* Great question. In fact, the first Weirdo Night was launched because Joseph Keckler, a goth, operatic, singer/songwriter/ghost-fucker—and, I would argue, bone dry comedian—was coming to LA for something, and asked me, *Where do people like us go?* There was always the ride-or-die weirdo palace, Human Resources, which actually started as a venue for performance—but they've since moved, and the current space is too echoey. I've performed there many times, and no one could understand anything I said. There were comedy clubs, but they were not always amenable for music, there were music clubs, but they were not always amenable for performance.

I told Joseph that I would set up a show in LA for us, get one more act, and make a variety evening of it. I cold-emailed this ridiculous venue, El Cid, in Silver Lake, and told them my idea. I said I had following and could bring in a crowd on a Sunday evening. The manager was a burly LA rocker chick who wore skin-tight, pegged jeans and low-top converse, had stick-straight hair (each strand with a split end), a Danzig tattoo, and chain-smoked. She loved the idea! She wanted "more weird shit" at the club.

El Cid is an old flamenco dinner theater club. It has a beautiful stage that has been steadily flamenco'ed on for the past 50 years. At that point, they still had flamenco shows on the weekends, but the rest of the week was booked with bands and comedy shows and whatever else they could get in there. The dining room was where people sat to watch the show. It had high ceilings and no windows. The walls were painted to make it look like you were outside in a plaza, in the middle of a bunch of breezy Spanish apartments—windows with ladies in silhouette watering dangling plants as colorful laundry items dried on clotheslines. It's not exactly a trompe-l'oeil, or whatever—the painting is really bad, the lighting is all wrong—but you get the sentiment. It's the thought that counts. The chairs were shiny, wood monstrosities that took up a lot of visual space, surrounding behemoth, white-table-clothed dining tables. You could order "food" if you wanted, mozzarella sticks or shrimp cocktail or a slider, or just cheap wine. There is something medieval about that room.

My intros to the show were often something like:

Welcome to my creepy mansion! One of you will not make it out of here alive, Will it be the Professor? The Baker? The Candlestick Maker with the candlestick? Will it be me? Who's going to murder me and if you are going to do it will you do it soon?

Joseph didn't end up coming out, but he has been in many Weirdo Nights since. I had the show booked anyway, so I did it with Kate Berlant—I think she was the only guest. I hosted, meaning I treated it like a variety show, but it was really just me and her. I probably did an opening monologue, and then I did fake movie reviews. I vaguely recall a joke about queers seeing themselves reflected more in popular culture now that *Mrs. Doubtfire* was going to be on Broadway. I sang a little song, then Kate did a killer set, and I closed the show with another number. It was a hit. It was evident I was scratching a big itch in Los Angeles. They came out in droves of at least 60 people! The place was packed. We came back the following month and had to turn people away at the door. Soon enough we had gone from charging zero dollars to five whole dollars.

El Cid suddenly changed ownership. The rocker chick quit, and the new management decidedly did not want our show. Just when we were about to blow up, we were without a home. I was still new to LA and didn't know how to find a good spot—when a freakish miracle took place. A Brooklyn club that was a beloved music venue and late-night hang for music nerds around the globe, Zebulon, opened a space in LA, in Frogtown. The Brooklyn Zebulon was minuscule—one tiny room with a bar and a small stage for bands. Or, did it even have a stage? Bizarrely, back in 2009 I had a friend from San Francisco who wanted to perform in NYC, and I set up a show for her there, with me opening. The lineup also had some video-art videos, including one by her that I had always loved. I had called the show Weirdo Night. And now, in 2016, Zebulon LA became Weirdo Night's forever home.

Around this time, I was asked to do a performance at a big alt-comedy festival in Palm Springs put on by Sarah

Silverman, Reggie Watts, and that other guy who's name I can't ever remember. Amanda and I were walking around the giant backstage green room area and feeling like lesbians. Thankfully, Maria Bamford was there, and we are friends so we got to hang out with her a little and hear her new set, which she performed for us at a table at a tiny French bistro in town. Besides that, we generally felt out of place. We spotted a tall, charming looking dude playing a saxophone in the corner. Amanda noticed he was wearing special shoes. They are called Nike blah blah blah and apparently were very rare. She knew because she used to work in vintage clothing.

This guy has a story, let's go talk to him.

He was an utter gentleman, a polite, look you in the eye, shake your hand sincerely kind of fellow. *It's a pleasure to meet you. I'm Taylor.* He was a jazz musician and at the show improvising with Tim Heidecker's band. I asked him if he had any interest in hopping on stage with me. Something about him just really made me want to try it out. *Absolutely, I would be delighted.* I figured if he was working with Tim, he knew how to be in a freaky comedy zone and riff around. Besides, what is improv if it's not jazz, am I right? Or what is jazz if it's not improv?

That evening he joined me on stage for the first time. Did he play along with me as I mimed breaking into a house to throw up in a toilet? I can't remember exactly, but it was hilarious and so much fun. He followed along with me easily, throwing in little honks that would throw me off at times, which made it even funnier.

After that Taylor began to play with me at Weirdo Night every month. He's been a solid Weirdo Night feature for almost nine years now. We never rehearse. I usually just bring in whatever pops into my mind and he is down to clown. We go ham on stage. Sometimes he plays along with a backing track, sometimes we act out a whole story and he does sound effects using a saxophone, a flute or an EWI (electronic wind instrument!). His nickname is Taylor the Sax Bottom because Dynasty Handbag is, if you haven't guessed it already, a top, but a top that tops from the bottom.

Structurally, the show is set up like this: when doors open the audience comes into the room to a playlist of old music videos. Curated by me, they range from all kinds of music, but mostly it's stuff that was made before the internet so hasn't been seen ever or in a really long ass time. This is one of my most beloved parts of producing the show, watching video after video on YouTube of all the amazing musicians and performers I love.

After everyone is seated, the lights go down and I appear crazy-style on stage, guns blazing to an entrance song. Usually something with big drums, loud, energetic. For a long time, I entered to Miles Davis's jazz/funk epic "On the Corner," but in recent years I've been going with whatever is moving me that month. A couple nights ago I came on stage to "Jump Around," which got me in the mood immediately because it's so infectious and so incredibly stupid. I also learned recently that the loud, high-pitched noise is actually a horse whinnying that they pitched up. When I'm mad, I'll come on to Bad Brains, Danzig, Black Sabbath. "Crazy on You" by Heart is also a wonderful entrance song because I'm truly about to go crazy on the audience so it's sort of a preparatory warning. I dance around and get the crowd hyped for the night.

After my entrance number, I do a sort of monologue/current events moment much like a Late Night show where the host comes out and says stuff like, *Hey man, pretty crazy out there huh, taxes, the president blah blah*, usually I'll just make some stuff up cause things are so bad that there's no reason to talk about it and everyone knows. I like to make jokes about nothing happening at all. Or make a joke about what astrological season it is. *It's Leo season, everyone! I can't fit through the door because my hair is so big and wonderful! I am sorry, are you dying from lack of oxygen cuz I just sucked most of it out of the room?... It's Pisces season everyone, Knock Knock, who's there, it's a Pisces! I'm so sad, can I borrow a cup of antique poison to kill myself with?* Sometimes I'll do some kind of slideshow—the last Weirdo Night I did a current events slideshow, which was basically what I've been watching on TV and what I've been googling. Taylor played along with that too, accompanied by Musak downloaded from YouTube.

Then I introduce the first act. There are usually three performers on the show. Between each one I come out and do a little number, make a comment or two about what has just been seen. Sometimes if the performer is someone I know I'll roast the shit out of them, and if it's not someone I am friendly with, I will either compare myself to them, "I could do that," or make fun of the audience for not doing something well. For example, if it's an electronic musician and they have one million pedals, or a classical violinist, I will lay into the audience like a disappointed dad for being lazy and never learning how to do anything. If it's awards season here in LA I make sure to tell everyone I know they have failed cuz they're not at the Emmys or Cannes. *You have a phone! Why haven't you made your feature film yet!?* To wrap up the show I usually do a big finale number where I move a lot or I'll do a group karaoke. Recently, along with a nine-piece goth choir, I led a sing along to "I Wanna Know What Love Is".

The combination of all of these scenes and artistic practices I have been involved in or dipped in and out of is the reason why I am able to collect so many weirdos for Weirdo Night. I have touched the worlds of improvisation, punk bands, traditional theater, being gay, drag, dance, experimental music, film, video, performance art, comedy, academia, and "other" categories. I also know what would go over well with an audience because I have developed excellent timing and can gauge what will hold people's attention, as well as what type of flow will keep people interested. Acts get ten minutes max. If it's great—leave 'em wanting more; if it's a stinker, it will be genuine variety and over quickly. I usually have a comedian on but not always, and if I do it's got to be a total freak. There are plenty of comedy clubs around, but not many stages for, say, a goth opera or a group of people dressed like monsters singing "Tale as Old as Time."

I am adept at this curation and the audience has grown to trust me. At this point I can bring whoever I want, and the performer will receive attention, warmth, and a solid space to do their work that has good sound and decent lighting. I feel grateful to have been able to cultivate this—the rewards by far outweigh the work and the stress of putting it together. People tell me that Weirdo Night is "gay church," it has been called "cathartic, soothing, hilarious, and brilliant." Every single show, someone comes up to me and says, "I needed that so bad." A couple weeks ago on the Marc Maron podcast, Sarah Sherman said it was the best show in LA.

I had to learn the art of hosting for Weirdo Night, which was a new skill for me. Dynasty Handbag rarely broke the fourth wall before I started MCing as her. I thought back to all the variety shows I had been on. Drag performers taught me how to host; Murray Hill showed me the art of razzing people to death with love. I can't tell you how many times Murray said something to the effect of, *Sorry guys, I had no idea*, after I finished a set on their show. My hero Vaginal Davis taught me to gas people up in a perverted way and to always be generous. *What a gorgeous and sexually arousing young stud, I am ready for the marital chambers.* Vaginal also sends a handwritten thank-you letter to everyone who performs with them. What a master. My improv skills have been sharpened to a deadly point by having to be quick-witted and roll with whatever is happening on stage and beyond. I am the go between—a belligerent traffic cop, a stewardess on your direct flight to the afterparty in hell!

Another aspect of the show I love is that the status, for lack of a better word, of performers ranges from famous and fancy to "might have been found on craigslist." And they perform side by side. The evening that Jack Black and his wife Tanya Haden performed, they were alongside Holland Andrews, an experimental vocalist with a bonkers range and a million pedals and loopy machines, and SKYNSUIT, two creepy drag queens dressed like bugs who did a slimy sexual dance number. John C. Reilly came on and did his old-timey jangles music alongside a UCLA performance art major who did a frantic monologue about butt fucking or something. Carrie Brownstein and Kathleen Hanna have both been on the show and come as audience members regularly. Carrie read from her book, and Kathleen did a Le Tigre song, and everyone lost their minds. I guess in some ways Weirdo Night has failed at being a failure, because it has had many people who are now heavy hitter stars—Ayo Edebiri, Sarah Sherman, Cole Escola, Kate Berlant, Maria Bamford, John Early. Those people have all done a zillion comedy shows but I think it's special they were on Weirdo Night because it's NOT a comedy show. It's a show for weirdos. But I have always invited unsuccessful people, too. And if the heavy hitters ever have a fall from grace, are cancelled for being a commie, dry up, have crippling depression and drug issues, they are always welcome back on my stage.

Recently I was at Weirdo Night, crouched amid little piles of costumes from my tiny quick-change area in the DJ booth while watching Sally Spitz do a set. Sally Spitz is a musician who sings along to whimsical and melodic tracks she's written. She was performing in cute long red braids and a snazzy Gen Z outfit, and she danced along with the instrumental parts in this unselfconscious, mellow, slightly lazy style that was so fun to watch. Her music was polished and melodic enough to hold a very loose stage presence, and I loved the contrast. But I couldn't pay close attention because my mind was starting to attack. It was saying I wasn't being funny enough during my interval moments on stage. As Sally wrapped up, I scrambled for something to say about their piece that would:

sum up it up but
be poignant and hilarious
and also tender and respectful
to show that I cared
and that I was in control
and maybe you didn't like it, but you still like Weirdo Night, and more importantly, me.

I took a deep breath and said to myself:

Just go up there and thank them and get one more round of applause for Sally, talk about Sally! But also . . . go inside.

When I feel the desperation of wanting affirmation from the audience, "go inside" is my solution. I extract my brain from the room I am in and go into the place that I have created in my imagination. I picture my make-believe so strongly that I am not even capable of noticing the audience anymore. Actors do this all the time—the trick with DH is that I break the fourth wall often and interact with the audience—"crowd work" is what they call it. If I'm not feeling confident, I act like a child who's being ignored because they are annoying, who's just getting more annoying and therefore being ignored more. I need to calm down and stop shooting lassos out into the void trying to catch some attention. Sometimes I have to close my eyes to go inside, which makes it look like I am feeling something deeply on stage—and that's actually what I'm trying to do. In the case of Sally, I needed to be somewhat in reality to acknowledge her performance. And then I turn to just telling the truth.

I got onstage and said:

Sally Spitz everyone! Excellent job, what a talented, adorable person with great hair. Did anyone happen to notice what a freaky freaky dancer she is? Then shut my eyes and imagined her dancing and sincerely tried to dance like her. I'm sure it looked slightly mocking (that is the DH brand, after all), but I was also trying to honor her lazy, millennial, 90s moves. They were very specific, and when you imitate someone to their face, the person who is being imitated becomes more visible, and it's a surprise, and funny, because it shows us how different we all are. It turned out to be such a lovely and goofy moment for the crowd and for me and Sally. We all relaxed and enjoyed being idiotic and talented.

Weirdo Night is queer, but it isn't a "queer night" or "LGBTQ night;" there's no theme, really, except what it's called. Weirdo Night. And therein lies its beauty: my opinion of what a weirdo is. Drag performers, clowns, comedians, violinists, dancers—these people are not inherently weird. They may be artistic, even funny or talented, but to be considered weird is a specific thing. When I get down to the essence of what a weirdo is to me, I actually think it's someone who does things that are, in essence, not weird on purpose; what makes them weird is their commitment to them. Everyone is a weirdo, but it can be beaten out of us to varying degrees by our circumstances. Weirdness in art is really not actual weirdness at all—it's more realness, if I may be so bold, than it is weird. As in, this is the reality I want to exist in, and it digresses from the reality that is the cultural norm being sold to me. I guess the essence for me is "truth." But how to know if someone is trying to be weird, or truly is weird? Or, how to know if art is good? Again, I go back to the sincerity of it. The dedication to one's own creative interest. Which sounds gaggy, but I think that might be it.

Let's take a recent performance by singer, songwriter, sorceress, and wig stylist Isaac Prado. Issac came onto the Weirdo Night stage in drapey witch gear. They are roughly 6'2", gorgeous, with long brown curls and shimmering brown eyes. Their first number was a song they wrote called "Divine." They began gently plucking the ukulele and singing, *You are Divine, I am Divine, we are Divine*. They have, for lack of me looking for better words, the voice of an angel. This combo sounds like a nightmare to me. Someone diddling on a ukulele, affirming the divinity of themselves and others? Ouch. However, Isaac's portal was wide open. Isaac's truth was showing—they meant it, they meant every word of it, in fact they clearly knew it, and then you believed it. Their skill level matched their grandiose statement making, so that helped as well. If the medium is the message, and the medium is a truly god-given singing voice, and the message is saying you are Divine, well, I guess it must be true. And that is weird.

There is a fine balance with talent, as well. Sometimes the talent is really polished, and the weird needs more space, or vice versa. Or, sometimes a weirdo just perfects their weirdness, and it's perfection—but there isn't really a home for it. It doesn't exist in any container, really, except "performance art"—which is how I ended up where I am, incidentally.

If I was newer on the scene these days, I would probably be considered a clown. I have always recoiled from that word, perhaps because I was trained by one of the world's most famous clowns—but, still. When I was at camp, there was Improv, and there was Clowning. They were very different. I did take a clowning class, and I learned how to fall down and do a few hat gags. Place a hat on the ground in front of your feet . . . you bend down to pick it up . . . while bending down you kick it lightly, making it look like it moved on its own before you could pick it up. I guess it's just semantics, but it's annoying to me that the funny performance artists I see are now called clowns. Am I a clown? Wrong answers only.

At any rate, the people and the clowns of LA loved Weirdo Night. By the end of 2016, I had a solid following. The shows were selling out. In Orlando on June 12th of that year, a man took a gun into Pulse nightclub and shot 49 people, the biggest mass shooting in the U.S. to date, and it was in a gay Latinx club. I was supposed to do a Weirdo Night the next night. I was very stressed out about it. I had so much anxiety I remember wanting to drink, which rarely happens to me. I considered cancelling and made many frantic phone calls about this decision. But in the end, I decided to put on the show.

I know it doesn't matter, in the grand scheme of the hell we are in, whether or not I did my avant-garde variety show that night. But the moment has become significant to me because it was the first of countless national and international tragedies that have taken place on or around the day of a Weirdo Night and that demanded I contend with how to move forward and show up for the show.

How does one navigate this weird job amid mass shootings, fascist takeovers, devastating natural disasters, genocides, and the worst of it all, Pride month? I think it depends on the event in some ways, of course, but fundamentally I have learned to keep the focus on the show—and to remember that people need to be together in times of shit. And these are some shit times. My job is to give people a place to live-larff-love without making it an escape from what is happening, but rather to have a both/and experience. I usually offer an acknowledgement of the horrors of some kind, either by making a joke that there is "not much happening," and then framing the joke around another news item that is not important at all. Like:

You guys the news has been really insane. Like too much. I can't believe that the New York Yankees have dropped their no beard policy. How disgusting. Now all those ugly men will have ugly beards.

If there is news that is piercing in a different way—say, a mass shooting—I usually do not try and make any kind of joke references at all, and I avoid pieces that have super activating visceral stuff them such as *One Man*, where I imitate a man shooting people, duh, or my piece *Remote Penetration*,[31] where I embody a drone blasting rockets, or my song "Suicide," about suicide. Such a situation calls for more uplifting works, or at least otherworldly in some way. This is usually when I call upon José Muñoz's *Cruising Utopia* premise that we, as queers, create new worlds for ourselves. When we create a new world together, in that moment, we acknowledge our need for it. Therefore, we are not necessarily escaping, but we are also not activating the wound. When we (I guess me?) are really raw, I try to use the space of performance-making to move the feeling along in some capacity. My work is always funny, so that helps, but it's got layers of harshness to it.

For the 2016 December post-election show, I remember feeling afraid of physical violence in public. This wasn't exactly paranoia, as there were instances of people getting hate-crimed all over the place. I had terror in my body that I was going to be harmed. I was living near Echo Park Lake, where people blithely walk their dogs and drink $8 matchas, but I was thinking, I can't go down there! I could picture it taken over by a bunch of hicks in gigantic trucks with confederate flags who'd hog-tie me and run me up a flagpole. A FAGPOLE!

---

31 *Remote Penetration*, Video, 2012. See appendix.

Or, when Mariah and I went to the movies for the first time since Trump was first elected, at the Americana Mall, I was worried people were going to throw Junior Mints or Milk Duds at us in the theater, because we were filthy queers. It was a strange, fragile moment for me. So, for that first post-election show, I did a version of "Baby, It's Cold Outside" but changed the lyrics to "Baby, There's Nazis Outside."

January 2025's vibe was tense and angry because it was right before Trump's second inauguration. I chose Rage Against the Machine's "Killing in the Name" for my entrance music. An incredible song, IMHO, one that harkens back to the idiotic time of early 90s Lollapalooza hypermasculine rage, but I still love it. I watch the music video on the regular for inspi-rage-tion (sorry). The bassist's stance alone can make me crack up. Spreading his legs so far apart he looks like he's about to split in half, he headbangs and slaps that bass into the grave, motherfucker! The lyrics are perfect—boiling down to, cops are all in the KKK and *fuck you!* I knew I had anger to get out, and this worked but didn't set me up to take myself too seriously (which may be the key to all my performance work—take the feeling seriously, but don't take myself too seriously).

February 2nd, 2025's show was right after the inauguration and the LA fires. Vibes were as raw as they come. I decided to go sincere with my opening number, and chose the club remix of Whitney's "I Didn't Know My Own Strength." When Whitney hit her interminable highway notes, I stuck my tongue out and wagged it around crazy. The performance was drag queen lip-sync for your life, but I'm Dynasty Handbag, after all; I look insane, and move my mouth outside the lyrics—I clearly know the song, but I don't hit it exactly right. That way I can stay true to my idiocy and still honor the music.

There have only been three incidents that have thrown me onstage at Weirdo Night, and only one so badly I let it show. A drag queen wanted to do a finale moment for her set, in which audience members were invited on stage to dump cans of ravioli on her. That was a hard no. I had had to institute a no food, liquids, or glitter rule at Weirdo Night due to some performers balking at the word Weirdo and overcompensating. She told me her piece would be tidy because she'd be in a kiddie pool, and she had just performed it and it brought the house down boots. She promised it would be *ahhhhmaaaazzzzziinnnnng*. I said ok, fine, but if it's at all messy you have to clean it up immediately. She sang a number that was about how she liked really awful idiot guys—it was a rap, actually and she's white, though it was in 90s talky-style, so not as offensive as it could have been, I guess? It was also funny. Her assistant came out and set up the kiddie pool and placed roughly six open Chef Boyardee ravioli cans around it. Then she instructed the audience to come on stage and throw raviolis on her when she got in the kiddie pool and posed dramatically for her final moment. When this moment came, people rushed the stage, picked up the cans, and started chucking raviolis all over the place. What she had failed to say was that they needed to not throw the raviolis but *pour* the raviolis *on* her—*dump* them on her. Chef Boyardee raviolis are basically made of petroleum. They plopped and slid across the stage, leaving a thousand glossy trails in their wake. There were splatters of tomato sauce and fat little pasta pillows all over the place. Like a battle had been fought and the raviolis lost.

I let the scene play out till there was no more ammunition. The queen sort of yelped and ran off. There was a moment of silence, then I tottered carefully onto the stage. I was mad. I looked around and asked, *Do you want me to die? I could die here!* I had a number prepared with Taylor the Sax Bottom that involved dancing, which would surely be the end of me if I attempted it on this stage. *Also, PS! Is anyone going to clean this up? Hello? Will someone help me?* No one did. Every time I cried out in despair the audience laughed. As though it were all a gag, all a set up. I can only blame myself. I still somehow appeared to have been steering the ship. Suddenly, a dumpy queer crawled onto the stage and started to slowly pick the raviolis up, putting them in their pockets. Then they started eating them. The crowd roared in disgust. This motherfucker was trying to get some stage time! Then they threw raviolis at the audience. Mayhem. Everyone yelled. Then I yelled. *Get off my stage! Go away! You are not helping! This is not your 15 minutes you troll!* Still, no one came to my rescue. I begged, *Will someone please bring a towel up here? Can anyone, anyone help me? What the fuck is happening?* My pleas hung in the air like a sad fart. The person who came to my rescue was Mariah. Of course. She had gone and fetched a mop and dragged it onstage. I sincerely commend the Zebulon employees for not helping—I wouldn't either if I worked there. But it was sad that it had to be Mariah. Everyone in the audience went *AWWWWW* when I acknowledged that she was my lesbian lover, and forever my knxght in shining denim. *This is not right. Not right and not ok,* I cried! FINALLY, the queen came back on stage with her assistant, apologizing profusely and scrambling to finish the clean-up. Why did it take them so long? Did they go all the way downstairs to the green room while this was happening, maybe took a few sucks on their vape and had a couple nachos? Were they watching from the sidelines? We shall never know. I ended the show early that night, foregoing my "What Have I Done To Deserve This" sing along, because the stage was so oily. Safety First!

One of my all-time favorite Weirdo Night performances was by Will Schwartz, of the band Imperial Teen. He is a singer and a songwriter and a very talented guitar player. He also went to high school with Monica Lewinsky. He had video footage of them in a production of *The Music Man*. I asked him if he would show the footage from it and talk about his friendship with Monica, and also do whatever else he wanted.

Will came up with a set for the show. He first showed a video of his bar mitzvah in 1980s New Jersey. In it, he's wearing a tuxedo and a top hat and belting out "New York, New York." He is taking the multipurpose room by storm—flying all around, leaping in the air, spinning and waving his tiny cane to the music. There is no doubt he will make it there and make it anywhere. This is a showbiz kid. This is a tiny, triple-threat homosexual. The aunties fawn over him. Then he showed video footage of him and Monica Lewinsky performing "He's My Shipoopi" from *The Music Man* at Beverly High School. Once again, Will steals the show, practically levitating with musical theater virility. Meanwhile, Monica, his Shipoopi, slumps in the corner, wearing bloomers and timidly singing along. She had a crush on Will, and they were pals. She hung out at his house and was even friends with his mom.

When she became The Monica we all know and love a mere few years later, Will's mom pronounced in her thick New Jersey accent, "Well, she couldn't get Will, so she went for Bill!" As Will is telling this story on stage, we feel he is leading somewhere—maybe the story is going to be about his career in entertainment, or more about Monica and his relationship—but what it arrives at is his queerness and subsequent disillusionment. The world of musical theater and magic starts to crumble under the reality of bigotry. His story continues. He's troubled. He has pain. He discovers heroin. He becomes a junkie. His dreams of the stage are crushed. Not even crushed—made to seem silly, unimportant, corny, whatever. But then, as we do, we join our own bands, with other junkies who were in musicals once upon a time. We still have our gifts. We still have our passion for music and for singing. Then Will sang a heart-splitting rendition of PJ Harvey's "Rid of Me" accompanied with acoustic guitar. I related deeply. All I wanted as a kid was to be sent away to the Fame school so I could break into song and dance on top of yellow taxi cabs in Times Square, or sing with all my classmates about lunch around a piano in my leg warmers. But whatever happens to us, we can't shake who we are from birth. Born this way. Born to sing and tap dance. Born to be a homo. Born to go a different way.[32]

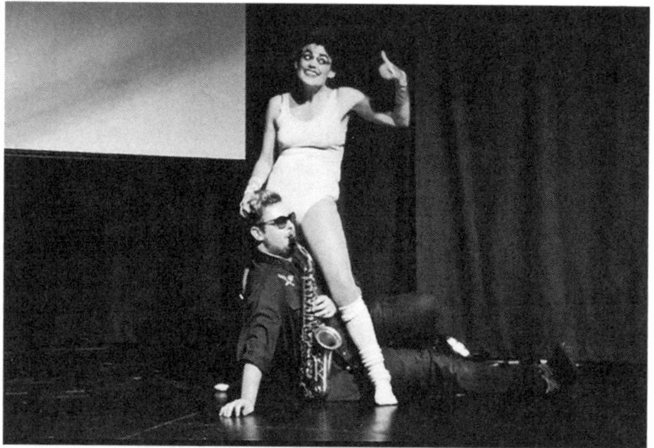

Dynasty Handbag facefucking Taylor "The Sax Bottom" Plenn, Weirdo Night, 2018, Zebulon.

32 See appendix for a Weirdo Night Video Library and other footage from the show.

TWENTY-ONE: TAKE A LIFE

In the fall of 2024, my dog died. Or, shall I say, I took his life. This was not the first time I have had to make arrangements to take out a loved one as you know. Both of my parents died this way, with us having to tell the doctors it was time to end life support. But with them, the choice was clear, at least to me. Clyde, on the other hand, was still present. He was still conscious. Still walking and talking. Eating and drinking. He was peeing and pooping (all over). But he had late-stage, severe dementia. He was 17 years old. Most dogs don't live long enough to get drain bramage, so it's pretty confusing when it comes, because they are not physically sick, really. He was dealing with a collapsing trachea and had a bad cough, but we were managing with supplies from the opioid crisis. With dementia, he would walk into rooms and clearly not remember where he was, and at the same time, his balance began to go—sometimes he would just be standing around and he would all of a sudden tip over. He cried when he was left alone because he was confused spatially, not knowing where he was a lot of the time. It was heartbreaking. We started calling him Joe Biden.

Clyde was a gray, five-pound Chihuahua from Staten Island. I got him in 2007, he cost $800. At the time I was living with my partner Sophie, and she bought him for me. She had her own Chihuahua named Pirate, who I adored. I had a habit of talking a lot about other people's dogs, and Sophie was convinced I needed one of my own. I was certain I was incapable of that responsibility. Just over a year sober, I was still learning how to go to the grocery store. Sophie was very good with animals and said she would teach me all there was to know. First, we looked into adopting, but New York did not have the bounty of Chihuahuas there is in Los Angeles, where I live now. So, we went to a breeder she had heard of through other animal people, and whose website offered an exciting visual smorgasbord of HTML pizzazz and early sparkling GIFs. The Chihuahuas were displayed individually, sometimes on a miniature chaise, on lace fabric or a doily. Chris, the breeder, had provided lengthy explanations for every aspect of the process and thorough descriptions of each dog for sale. Some of the photos featured a rhesus monkey wearing a diaper and posing with the puppies. Her name was Emily.

We drove out to Staten Island to look at the doggies. Chris lived in a gigantic old house with a huge backyard (that we were not allowed to see) where she raised Chihuahuas, Rottweilers, and miniature horses. After trying and failing to get a peek at the miniature horses, we were led into a parlor room where we sat on a big pleather couch. Her son came in with an armful of squirming Chihuahua puppies and placed them carefully on the floor. They wobbled and sniffed and were insanely cute. We met a lot of puppies. At some point we got brave enough to timidly ask,

Is Emily here?

Oh yeah, she should be coming in soon.

We figured that meant one of the sons would bring Emily in to meet us. Suddenly the door opened, and Emily was hanging off the doorknob wearing a polka-dotted diaper. She had let herself in. She hopped down and walked around the room. She inspected the puppies, checking in on them, sniffing around to make sure they were ok, like a factory floor manager doing quality control. Then she bounced onto the couch and maneuvered behind me and Sophie to sniff our hair and pick at our sweaters. I guess she approved of our dandruff and lint levels because then she made her way back to the door, opened it, and left.

This tiny, grey Chihuahua who looked like a Husky that got left in the dryer too long crawled onto my lap. He proceeded to growl at all the other dogs.

I want this one! He likes me!

That's not what that means. How about this one? She's so cute and docile, look!

She looks boring! This is the guy for me.

Naturally, I wanted the asshole. On the way to the truck to get the cash for the dog, his name popped into my head. Clyde. I knew one human named Clyde, he was an AA old-timer with a cane, who was always at 12th Street Workshop in the East Village. He always said the same thing:

Hello family my name is Clyde I'm an alcoholic and I'd like to thank you and god for my sobriety.

He died shortly after I got Clyde the dog.

Like all dogs, Clyde was magnificent. He was feisty. He was tiny. He was my best friend. Hearing about people's dogs is a bit like hearing about people's dreams, or children—very important to the narrator but a certain kind of hell for the listener—but I don't give a shit, because he was the love of my life!

He didn't like when people put their face in his face. He bit many noses. He didn't have many teeth, though, so if he bit you, it was mild, it felt like a nip from two wet erasers. He bit me only once in our lifetime together. It hurt me deeply, but only emotionally. I had found him deep inside of a potato chip bag; his chunky gray butt was sticking out and he was in a licking frenzy. I pulled him out and he was pissed.

Like his mother, he did not like loud men. While dog-sitting him on Fire Island, my friend Allison took him to a birthday party. Clyde was sitting on Allison's lap when a tall fag with a screechy gay voice came out carrying a giant cake with a million candles on it, singing "Happy Birthday" at the top of his lungs. Clyde launched himself off of Allison's lap and began biting this horrible intruder's ankles, causing the guy to hop around screaming while still trying to balance the giant sheet cake.

He was spicy for sure but could be quite docile. You could put him in a basket. You could put him in a pot on the stove. You could put him in a dress. You could put him in a backpack and ride your bike all over Brooklyn. You could put him in a tote bag and sneak him into a museum or a restaurant or anywhere dogs were not allowed. You could put him on top of the Roomba and set it to go and he would just sit there.

Mariah knew of a dog psychic many of her friends had been using to talk to their pets. When Clyde was about ten, we made an appointment with Brenda at Communication Is Key dot Biz, to converse with both Clyde and Tammy—Mariah's Chihuahua, my beloved step-daughter. They were both having mild behavioral issues: Tammy was anxious and barky, and Clyde had stopped wanting to go for walks. We also just really wanted to experience this. We didn't care if it was real or not. It's worth the money to hear someone pretend to think like a dog.

Upon our first phone meeting with Brenda, the first thing Clyde shared with us was (as channeled through Brenda):

He was wondering when he might get some more scrambled eggs.

He had only had them once or twice, and it had been a few years. Absolutely, sir, coming right up.

We asked him, through Brenda, why he no longer liked to go for walks. Whenever she was telling us what the dogs said,

Brenda would go silent for a bit before responding. Then her voice would get a bit higher and quicker and more breathy.

Brenda: *Well, he says he doesn't know what's coming around the corner, there could be a big dog or a car. And he can't run fast anymore.*

Mariah: *Can you tell him that we will protect him if anything happens? We will pick him up.*

Brenda: *He says you can't run fast either.*

Not not true.

Most decisions don't really matter in the long run, even when they are big. Deciding to put Clyde down was perhaps the hardest decision I have ever made. How does one choose to end another life—even when it's the most merciful thing to do? It seemed impossible. When the vet told us it was time to consider letting him go, and that we'd need to make a decision within the next couple weeks, I couldn't stand it for too long. I agonized for a couple of days, then woke up and knew I had to do it right away or I never would. I called Hearts and Halos, professional pet assassins, and made the appointment. They came that afternoon.

On his last day, Mariah laid out a buffet of his favorite foods: a pile of scrambled eggs, mushy bananas, shredded chicken, and a lump of cheese. A bunch of my friends came over to say goodbye. My sister J'nai came, too. At 4:00 PM it was time. The angel of death arrived at our door. She had a beautiful face and shiny black hair, a gauzy robe outfit, and a kind, otherworldly demeanor, like she'd flown in on a swan. Probably a failed actress. The queers were all instantly in love. She was gentle and patient, as a reaper should be.

I won't go through the heinous details of how she murdered him, but I will say that I sobbed harder than I ever have in my life. It was tremendous. I shocked myself. As I was heaving and wailing, I was also thinking, *Dang I'm really upset! Dang I really love this dog! Dang this is really hard!* I was dissociating to think about how proud of myself I was for not dissociating. I was a real boy now.

After he was gone, the reaper glided out to her Honda Element to fetch his casket—a tiny basket bed with purple satin sheets and a bedspread that had the words *I Love You* all over it in a curly font. We placed him in the bed, and she laid a perfect white orchid atop his body. I set a blueberry on his pillow next to his little round head, so that he could play his favorite game, chase the blueberry, for all eternity. And he was gone.

His ashes came back a couple weeks later, with a certificate of aquamation in a little box. While I enjoy all manner of ghoulish death details, I never looked up aquamation and don't know what it is and never will. Did you know ashes are not usually ashes? They're often the remnants of whatever they burned the body in because there's usually very little of the actual body left. The fire is just too damn hot. My mom's cremains had little tiny pebbles in them, which were bone. We found a vintage Japanese ceramic sugar bowl in the shape of a mushroom on Etsy for Clyde's final resting place. I keep it nice and shiny. He had also told Brenda where he wanted to be placed in the house when he died:

Across from the couch so he can see what you are eating.

It's true we have no dining table and eat most of our meals there.

I've never wanted my ghosts to visit me. I don't want my mom coming around, and my dad—for some reason I feel like I can evoke his memory, but I don't feel he is really ghost material. "When you're dead, you're dead!" he used to say. Clyde, on the other hand, is a spirit I welcome and can truly feel. And the grief is pure. It's not complicated—it's not unfair, and there is nothing unresolved. It's not a tragedy. The love and the sting of it all is unadulterated and potent. It feels like I am alive, like I am experiencing a new level of living. It's a change, but not . . . bad. I *feel* bad, as in sad. I miss him every day. But it's not a bad feeling. I am not spooked out or trying to fight off this sadness. I *want* to think about him, I *want* him to haunt me. I sleep with the fuzzy blue blanket he died in every night and ask him to visit me in my dreams. *Come see me! I'm here!* I saw a rabbit the other day that looked like him, and why wouldn't it be him? What do I know of where souls go? I got into it with a flickering lightbulb one morning, pretty sure it was Clyde telling me he was hungry. I mimed making him scrambled eggs and put the invisible plate on the floor. The light stopped flickering. Then it twinkled again. Mariah eventually changed the bulb. I think she was a tad worried about me.

People always talk about how it's "unconditional love" with a pet. This is only possible because the animal is unconditioned. Unless at some point they have had their loyalty and gentleness beaten out of them. We of course impose all kinds of human bullshit on our animals—overpriced vets, stupid clothes, ridiculous farm-to-dog food bowls—and that is us, it's not them. If it weren't for us, they would exist outside of our social constructions. And to the best of their ability, they do.

Clyde, first of all, was genderfluid, as all animals are, including humans. We have biological stuff of course, but animals know nothing of gender roles inherently. They don't naturally use separate bathrooms, nor do they police your toilet choice. And Clyde was definitely experimental with his gender, labels be damned. Sometimes he would be a plump church lady wearing a big hat and carrying a little purse. He was also an older gay man from Pasadena who loved 90s food and Sur la Table. Who said things like:

Oooh sage ricotta ravioli, yum!

I love my ex-wife, we have three beautiful children.

Those are fun! (when looking at potholders with chickens on them or something)

He was also a short, English prince in silken pantaloons:

Mummy, I don't want to go shooting with papp-ah, I want to stay here with you!

Mummy, what's for pudding?

Mummy, must we walk? Can't we take the motorcar?

Clyde was also a nurse. He was a pig, a mouse, a hedgehog, a linebacker (broad shoulders), a ballerina, a Borscht Belt comedian. He had charisma, uniqueness, nerve, and talent. He was many things; he contained multitudes, and it was easy to see that. This is what we people are all trying to say to each other all the time: *Look! I contain levels. I have so much going on. I'm this, I'm that. See me!*

My relationship with Clyde felt queer. I don't know exactly why but there are some reasons why that might be. I prefer the company of people who know that this world is not the way they would set up a world, and do their best to get out of it, to "queer" it, as it were. I don't believe animals would set up the world this way either. They didn't—they adapt and mostly manage to maintain their selfhood. They embody "I am what I am."

In relating to animals, you are very much taking things at face value, you are in the moment with them, it's improvisational, it's whatever is next is next! They don't manipulate or control . . . who am I kidding, my dog can get me to do anything he wants, but that's a me problem.

My dog taught me how to pay attention to a being's needs, and in turn my own needs, which are actually pretty simple.

On a basic level, he needed food, shelter, warmth (or AC). He needed to hang out, be touched, cuddled, and played with. He needed his walnut-sized brain to be stimulated and creative. And he needed rest. These are things I didn't get regularly myself when I was a kid, and I was able to give them to him. I also gave him a big family to care for him when I wasn't able to be around. He had a lot of friends and was very popular. Which was also a gift because having him forced me to ask people for help. Not something that comes naturally to me. He forced me to go outside, to be in the world and therefore in community with people. To talk to strangers, even if it was to say, "Don't come near him, he will bite you!" The queerness of it all is that these relationships with animals exist in a space of exploratory intimacy, where you are present and feeling it out, and it can be many different things at once.

Sometimes, when I am on vacation, I feel like the world is closing in on me (what a sentence, bitch get a life). I feel like I don't know who I am, I can't see any reflection of myself. Then I realize I just haven't seen any queers in a few days. Last summer Mariah and I were in the Hudson Valley visiting some friends. All straight. Nice. Lovely. Kind. Smart. Not dicks. But in crept the fog of heterosexuality, a subtle noxious gas that slowly but surely makes you feel like something is wrong with you. We found ourselves drifting away from each other and away from ourselves. We were about to go visit another set of friends, a straight couple with a four-year-old in Maine. We knew we needed a queer reset, so we made an emergency booking at a B&B in Ogunquit on the way up. Ogunquit is definitely not a radical queer revolutionary utopia—it's an old theater town on the beach, excruciatingly quaint and overrun with tourists, but still there are gays everywhere. There's a famous gay piano bar called The Front Porch that Mariah's grandma had taken her to when she was in her late 20s. The B&B was exactly what we needed.

When we arrived, the innkeeper, Danny, greeted us warmly and showed us around.

Annnnnd we have the breakfast room, which has fresh coffee and cookies any time of day or night. For breakfast we have eggs, sausage, bacon, and downright evil chocolate chip pancakes! They are in-cred-i-ble. Not so good for the waistline but ya only live once girls amirite!?

A couple of lesbians doing a cat puzzle gave us the butch nod. Danny walked us through to the wrap-around porch.

In the evenings you can take in the view with a glass of sangria. On the house of course!

There was nothing remarkable about this stopover per se. We went for a walk on the shore where everyone walks. Lots of gay men couples with fancy little dogs. Lesbians with less fancy dogs. It was chilly, so I bought a Maine sweatshirt, like everyone buys. I think I saw at least ten of these sweatshirts on other people's bodies on our walk. We ate overpriced, mediocre pasta; Mariah ate a lobster roll. We got ice cream. I bought souvenir magnets to add to my beloved collection. We stopped by The Front Porch, but it was Friday night and too crowded. There were many old queens but lots of straight people there, too. After all, we know how to have the best fun. The vibe was cheerful, but the piano man was playing my least favorite kind of music—like, the Carpenters, Carole King, music that reminds me of puffy blonde hair and sandals and heterosexuals. So, we went back to our quaint hotel room and watched *Shark Tank* and talked about how much my gay dog Clyde would have loved this hotel.

In the morning, we packed up and said our goodbyes to Danny. I bought a hideous pewter medallion-shaped Christmas ornament which featured the hotel in relief with its name in big cursive letters. It cost $25. At home I display it not on the Christmas tree, it's too ugly for that, but on the bulletin board above my desk—a reminder of queer joy. It reminds me of Clyde and of my weird little family I made, and my big weird family I belong to.

The faggy B&B in Ogunquit is a weird spot to end my book, but it's got to happen somewhere. Toughen up, Mary.[33]

33 "Toughen up, Mary," is a quote made famous by Kirk Read.

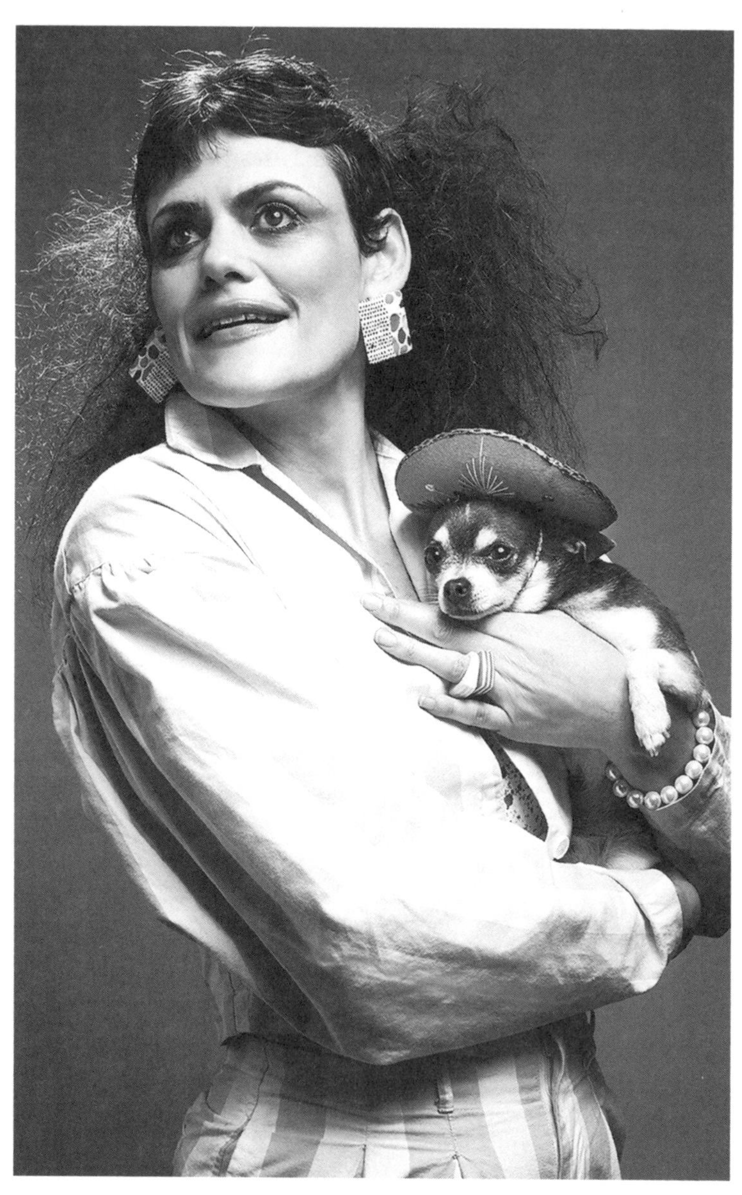

Dynasty Handbag and Clyde by Alison Michael Orenstein.

APPENDIX

To see more performance, video, and photos
from the Life and Times of
Jibz Cameron and Dynasty Handbag, please visit
https://www.dynastyhandbag.com/hellinahandbag
or use this QR code.

ACKNOWLEDGMENTS

Like all creations this book is a collaborative effort.

Thank you Michelle Tea and Beth Pickens of DOPAMINE press for asking me to write a book, believing I could, for editing, and for encouragement. Thank you Megan Milks for being a rock solid support, champion, and brilliant side piece editor. Thank you to the PARAKEET workshop for accountability and support. Thank you to all my writing group comrades of ShriNp Group, SWG, and Writing Groupé—Emilia Richeson, Paris Hurley, Rachel Yoder, Jess Arndt, Carolyn Pennypacker Riggs, Seth Bogart, Amanda Verwey, Gabby Levine. Thank you Sarah Greenburger Rafferty for steady commitment and all our co-work hours. Thank you Chris Vargas, Svetlana Kitto, Beth Lisick, Sacha Yanow, Jaquita Ta'le, Katie Brewer Ball for reads, encouragement, and retreat support. Thank you Craig Willse and Rumaan Alam for your guidance and wisdom. Thank you Jack Black, Tanya Haden, Andros Zins-Browne, Ali Liebegott, KC Perry, Jamie Cadwell, Ash Jones, Brooke Palmieri, Hedia Maron, Stephanie Markowitz, Lisaida Marrero, and Simone Sant Laurent for being my friends and helping me make space to write. Thank you Sarah and Mark Rodriguez for generously opening your home to me. Thank you Lila Garnett for the cottage time and care. Thank you Marie Condron and Allison Michael Orenstein for our meetings and your clarity and love. Thank you Tony Tulathimute for all your belligerent wisdom and support and all the spring Critters of 2025—Elise Liu, Andrew Ricketts, Torrey Paquette, Matt Tyler Zborg, Jenna Krumminga, Michael Goldsmith, JP Infante, Molly Lynch. Thank you Clyde and Tammy for loving me and letting me love you. Thank you to my sisters J'nai Cameron and Jyoti Cameron and to my brother David Kalish for love, hilarity, and consistency. Thank you to the moon and back to my partner Mariah Jennings Garnett for being my steady champion, my reader, for helping me tell the truth always and for being my true love. Merry Christmas.

ABOUT THE AUTHOR

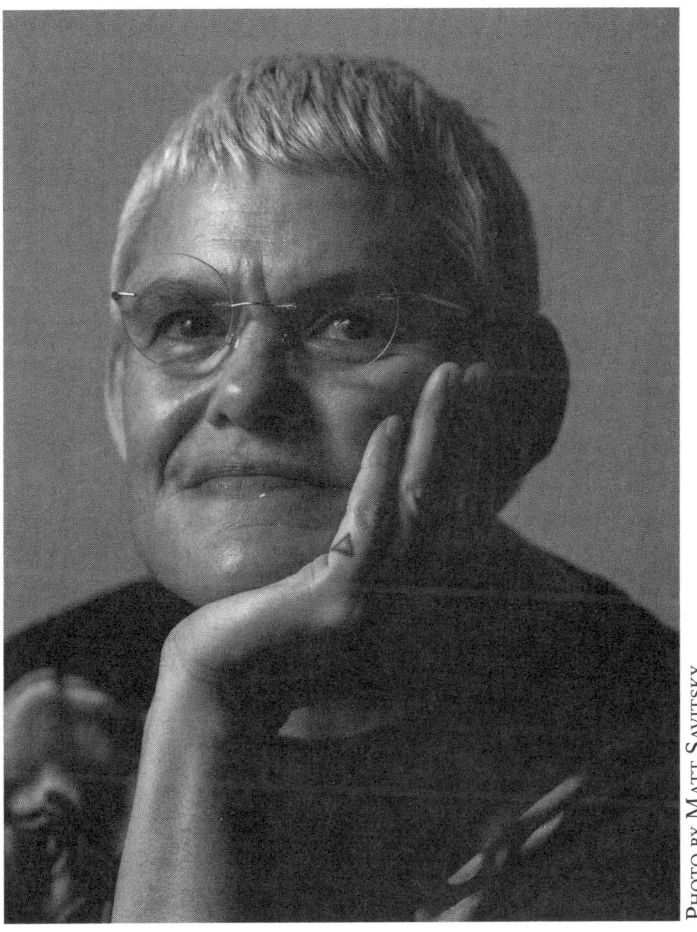

PHOTO BY MATT SAVITSKY

Jibz Cameron is a writer, performer, visual artist, and actor. She is most well known for her multimedia performance work as alter ego Dynasty Handbag, which has spanned over 20 years. Jibz is a 2022 Guggenheim fellow, a 2021 United States Artist Award recipient, and a 2020 Creative Capital Grant awardee. She lives in Los Angeles.

ALSO BY DOPAMINE BOOKS

SLUTS Anthology, edited by Michelle Tea.

NEW MISTAKES, by Clement Goldberg.

HOW TO FUCK LIKE A GIRL, by Vera Blossom.

DAYS RUNNING, by Shawn Stewart Ruff.

WITCH Anthology, edited by Michelle Tea.

SELF-ROMANCING, by L. Scully.

BARGAIN WITCH: ESSAYS IN SELF-INITIATION, by Brooke Palmieri.

SOULMATE AS A VERB, by Kelsey L. Smoot.

HELL IN A HANDBAG, by Jibz Cameron.

CLOWNS Anthology, edited by Michelle Tea.

For more information and news, go to DOPAMINEBOOKS.ORG